LEE COUNTY LIBRARY SYSTEM

The Complete HOME INSPECTION KIT

William L. Ventolo, Jr.

 D1202490

Longman Financial Services Publishing
a division of Longman Financial Services Institute, Inc.

DUNBAR JUPITER HAMMON LIBRARY

While a great deal of care has been taken to provide accurate and current information, the ideas, suggestions, general principles and conclusions presented in this book are subject to local, state, and federal laws and regulations, court cases and any revisions of same. The reader is thus urged to consult legal counsel regarding any points of law—this publication should not be used as a substitute for competent legal advice.

Publisher: Kathleen A. Welton
Acquisitions Editor: Wendy Lochner
Cover Design: Sam Concialdi

©1990 by Longman Group USA Inc.

Published by Longman Financial Services Publishing
a division of Longman Financial Services Institute, Inc.

All rights reserved. The text of this publication, or any part thereof, may not be reproduced in any manner whatsoever without written permission from the publisher.

Printed in the United States of America

90 91 92   10 9 8 7 6 5 4 3 2 1

Library of Congress Cataloging-in-Publication Data

Ventolo, William L.
    The complete home inspection kit / by William L. Ventolo.
        p.   cm.
    ISBN 0-88462-988-0
    1. Dwellings—Inspection. 2. House buying. I. Title.
TH4817.5.V46 1990
643'. 12—dc20   89–14543
                                                              CIP

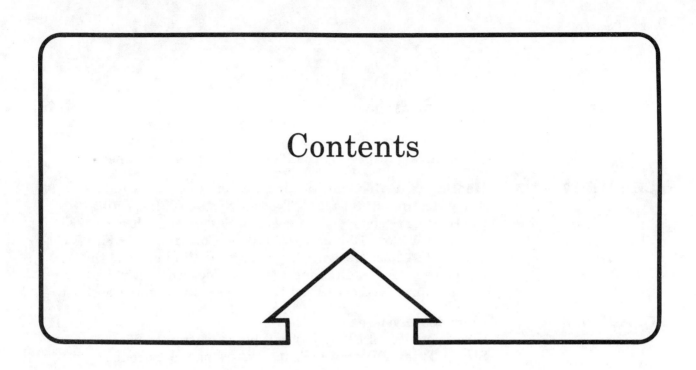

Contents

PREFACE   v

CHAPTER 1   **Locating the House on the Site**   1
Subdivision Planning • Restrictions on Land Use • Soil
Composition and Topography • House Location and
Orientation on the Lot • Inspecting the Neighborhood
and the Site • Inspection Checklist

CHAPTER 2   **House Styles and Types**   13
House Styles • House Types • Adding on to a House
• Return on Investment • Inspection Checklist

CHAPTER 3   **Interior Design**   25
Circulation Areas • Zones within a House • How to Read
a Floor Plan • Inspection Checklist

CHAPTER 4   **Foundations and Framing**   37
Foundations • Floor Framing • Wall Framing • Stairways
• Ceiling and Roof Framing • Types of Roofs • Termite
Damage and Wood Rot • Radon Gas • Inspection Checklist

CHAPTER 5   **Exterior Finish**   57
Roof Sheathing • Roof Coverings • Inspecting the Roof
and Gutters • Wall Sheathing • Exterior Wall Coverings
• Inspecting the Siding • Windows and Doors • Window
Functions • Types of Windows • Location of Exterior Doors
• Parts of a Door • Types of Doors • Inspecting Windows
and Doors • The Garage • Inspection Checklist

CHAPTER 6   **Plumbing Systems**   **79**
Early Bathrooms in America • Plumbing Systems
• Plumbing Drawings • Installation • Plumbing Fixtures
• Materials • Inspecting the Plumbing • Inspection Checklist

CHAPTER 7   **Heating and Air-Conditioning Systems**   **95**
Early Heating in America • Types of Systems • Inspecting
the Heating System • Chimneys and Fireplaces • How a
Chimney Works • Chimney Design and Construction • Fire-
places • Fireplace Design • Inspecting the Chimney and the
Fireplace • Air-Conditioning • Cooling Methods • Air-
Conditioning Systems • Duct Insulation • Inspection Checklist

CHAPTER 8   **Electrical Systems**   **115**
Characteristics of Electricity • Types of Current • Wire
Sizes • Types of Wiring • Wiring Diagrams • Service to
the Panel • Inspecting the Electrical System
• Inspection Checklist

CHAPTER 9   **Insulation, Interior Walls and Ceilings**   **127**
Insulation and R-Values • Walls • Gypsum Wallboard
• Plaster • Wood Paneling • Decorative Finishes
• Inspecting the Insulation, Interior Walls and Ceilings
• Inspection Checklist

CHAPTER 10   **Finish Flooring and Interior Trim**   **141**
Hard Floors • Resilient Tile • Resilient Sheet Flooring
• Carpeting • Interior Trim • Inspection Checklist

CHAPTER 11   **Site Finishing**   **149**
The Site Plan • Finish Grading • Driveways and Walks
• The Landscaping Plan • Inspection Checklist

CHAPTER 12   **The Energy-Efficient House**   **159**
Air-Infiltration Controls • Orientation of the House
• Proper Equipment Sizing • Energy-Efficient Water
Heating • Other Ways to Make a House More Energy
Efficient • Inspection Checklist

APPENDIX A   **House Diagram**   **169**

APPENDIX B   **Measurement and Metric Conversion Tables**   **170**

APPENDIX C   **Radon**   **171**

APPENDIX D   **The Value of Home Improvements**   **173**

APPENDIX E   **Special Building Requirements**   **174**

APPENDIX F   **Master Inspection Checklist**   **184**

GLOSSARY   **205**

INDEX   **215**

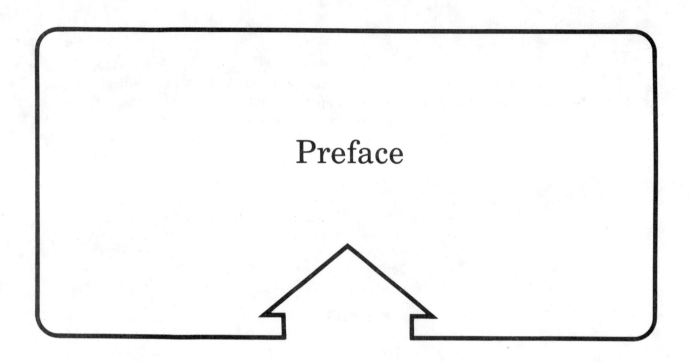

Preface

The Complete Home Inspection Kit is intended to help the potential homeowner and the real estate salesperson or broker recognize and evaluate the construction details of residential properties. Since many structural components of a finished house are hidden, it is important to be able to judge the condition and quality of the building on the basis of visible clues only. *The Complete Home Inspection Kit* was written to provide the reader with enough background information to make sound judgments on building merits and defects.

Property owners and real estate professionals (salespeople, brokers, property managers or appraisers) should know the construction features that determine quality, show good craftsmanship and indicate upkeep or neglect, especially visible flaws that could indicate significant structural damage. At the very least, the homeowner and the real estate professional should know how to describe a property and how to recognize property differences.

The Complete Home Inspection Kit is heavily illustrated with drawings and photographs to help the reader visualize the many concepts presented. The book begins with a look at the site. Subdivision planning, restrictions on land use, soil composition, topography, house location and orientation on the lot are among the topics covered. The book then discusses house styles and the details of interior design. How a typical residential house is built is the next area explored. The chapter-by-chapter presentation follows the normal sequence of constructing a house—from foundation to finish work. Finally, the energy-efficient house is treated. The chapter focuses on measures that can be taken to save energy, make a house more comfortable and at the same time reduce heating and cooling costs.

Detailed checklists at the end of each chapter will help you evaluate the true condition of your present home or any home you're thinking of buying. The "no" responses indicate possible weaknesses in the property. Your ability to spot flaws and strengths in a house will allow you to determine whether an asking price is justified or whether your offer should be contingent on the owner making necessary repairs.

The appendixes are valuable tools for both the homeowner and the real estate professional. Appendix A illustrates the structural parts of a house, appendix B presents land measurement and metric conversion tables, appendix C illustrates how radon gas enters the home and the different ways to test for it, appendix D takes a look at how some kinds of home improvements increase house value, appendix E discusses special building requirements for different regions of the country, including earthquake-prone areas, and appendix F is a master checklist to help you inspect and evaluate a house in a rational, organized manner. A comprehensive glossary and topic index complete the contents of *The Complete Home Inspection Kit.*

Locating the House on the Site

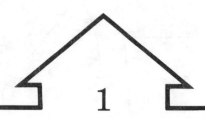

American cities were unprepared for the thousands of immigrants who sought housing there in the nineteenth century. While overcrowded, substandard housing remains a problem, community planning and land-use controls have done much to help the situation. Planned unit developments and subdivision zoning restrictions ensure that the residential, commercial and industrial sectors of a community are not randomly and incompatibly located. Deed restrictions and municipal building codes regulate the size, design and placement of individual houses. Builders today must take into account these considerations plus taxes, assessments, easements and other restrictions that might affect building decisions.

SUBDIVISION PLANNING

Most single-family residences are built as part of a subdivision; that is, on a piece of land that has been sectioned into two or more building lots.

As seen in Figure 1–1, acreage may be subdivided into 1,000 or more individual building lots, which may be built on immediately by the subdivider-builder or only when a purchaser decides to build on his or her lot. The Levittown communities in Pennsylvania and New York consist of houses built by the subdivider for efficiency and economy. Because of their simple yet well-planned and expandable design, these houses have remained popular since they were first constructed in the 1930s and 1940s. Not all postwar subdivisions were as well designed, however.

Currently, subdividers are more likely to begin actual construction of a house only after it is purchased. High interest rates on construction loans and skyrocketing costs for lumber and concrete will not allow builders to let homes lie idle until buyers can be found. An exception to this is the growing market for townhouses. It would be impractical to add on at a later date a house that shares a wall with another house.

Where the market for townhouses (usually priced substantially lower than separate houses of comparable footage) is strong, prebuilding is still feasible.

FIGURE 1–1.   Subdivision plat.

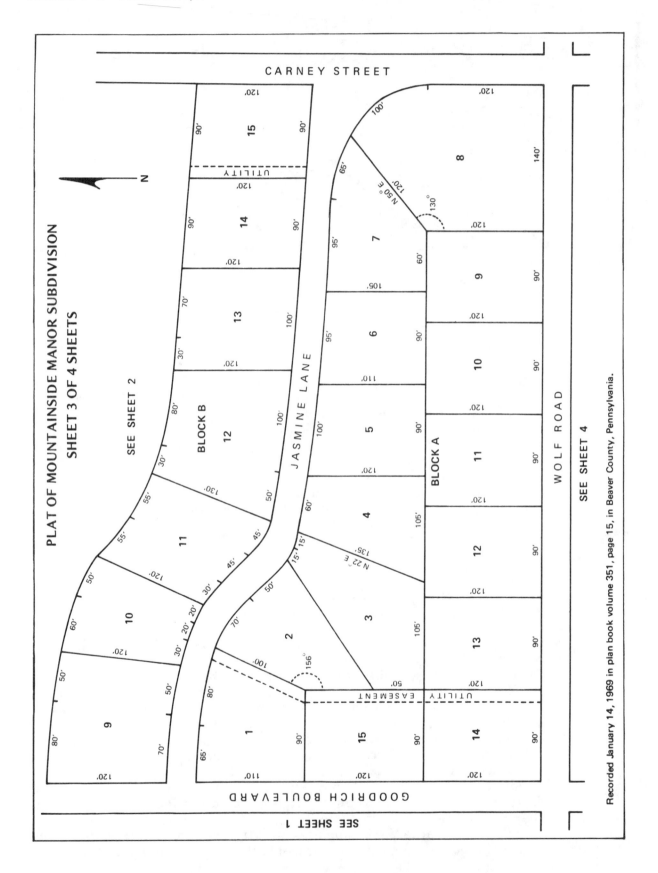

Even townhouses, though, may be sold from models before actual construction of the homes has begun.

Condominiums, introduced in the 1960s, spawned the construction of apartment-like complexes in areas that had previously resisted any but single-family residential buildings.

Apartments, too, can now be part of a well-designed subdivision in a planned unit development (PUD). In many ways superior to the worst of the tract housing in some subdivisions, the PUD provides the ultimate in community planning: residential, commercial, and industrial sectors can be juxtaposed for both economic and aesthetic reasons. Columbia, Maryland, and Reston, Virginia, are two successfully planned communities that incorporate all of these elements.

Even before the PUD, communities were undertaking the task of preventing the haphazard combination of residential and other land uses.

RESTRICTIONS ON LAND USE

Zoning

Not until this century did cities try to legislate land use. Although multistory tenements and row houses (which we now refer to as townhouses) had crowded city lots for almost a century, population density became critical only with the wave of immigration that began in the late nineteenth century. Their settlement pattern is still evident today. The propertyless and generally penniless newcomers gravitated to the poorest section of a city, crowding many more families into that area than had been there before. As these groups prospered and were able to afford better and more spacious accommodations elsewhere in the city, or even in the suburbs, other groups, equally poor, took their places in what became a new ghetto. Of course, buildings undergo steady deterioration, and the general condition of the neighborhoods worsens with each succeeding group.

Since it would be impossible to enforce legislation limiting the number of occupants in a building, the first zoning legislation, in New York City, sought to limit building density in terms of the size of each building and its placement on the lot, with minimum requirements for front, rear and side yards. By 1930, cities were also regulating land use. Although some separation of residential, commercial and industrial properties had already taken place naturally, as in the case of industries that flourished in areas offering good, cheap transportation and proximity to natural resources, zoning finally enabled specific areas to be designated for only one use, even when other uses would also be suitable.

Today, zoning laws may be so specific in residential areas as to limit house size, placement and even design. Zoning information can be obtained from the local building department.

Zoning Variances.   If a financial burden will be placed on a property owner unless he or she is allowed to violate a zoning law, the local zoning board may grant a variance that exempts the property owner from that law. Sometimes a variance benefits the community as a whole. For example, a nonpolluting, well-designed, low-profile and highly taxable office building might be an asset to an area zoned for strictly residential use. If too many variances are allowed, though, an area's primary use could change.

Building Codes

Zoning laws are not the only means by which building limitations are imposed. Building codes, with minimum requirements for building size and construction, are another means of controlling land use. Most building codes also require permits for any additional changes to a property after a home is erected, such as remodeling, building an addition or installing a swimming pool. The local building department also provides information on building code requirements.

Deed Restrictions

In some cities, deed restrictions, which the buyer agrees to by his or her purchase of the property, perform the same function as zoning and building codes. These restrictions are usually placed in the deed by the original subdivider, although it is not uncommon for the members of a subdivision to vote on the inclusion of a new provision in the deeds for their properties.

Easements

An easement is a right of ingress, egress, or use of property that an owner grants to others. The owner of a lake lot may grant an easement so that the owner of an adjacent lot can have lake access.

An owner may be prohibited by law from building on any part of the property that provides access to utility installations. In Figure 1–2, for example, a space extending 10 feet from either side of an electrical line, running parallel to it, is an easement to the power line. When the line runs between two properties, each property has a 10-foot easement running the length of that lot line. The easement also extends from the power line to the street. Again, the line runs between two properties, and each has a 10-foot easement running parallel to the power line from the back to the front of the lot.

Any easements will be included in a property's legal description.

Taxes and Special Assessments

Although they are not actually restrictions, taxes and special assessments on property can block its future use if the property is confiscated by the government for nonpayment of lawfully levied fees. Taxes usually pay for schools, road maintenance and police and fire departments. Special assessments include payments for such items as sewer installation, curbs and sidewalks. Information on taxes and other assessments can be obtained from the county assessor's office.

Availability of Utilities

Information on availability and cost of utility installations can be obtained from local utility companies. Responsibility for utilities yet to be installed should be determined at the time of a real estate sale. If the buyer has not made sure that the lot will include electrical and telephone lines, water and gas, he or she may have to make an expensive installation before building can proceed. Advertisements for the questionable desert land schemes that peaked in the late 1960s showed homes that could be expected to have all utilities installed, as they probably did. Yet, when the buyer of a lot in the "development" contemplated building on it, he or she usually found that the cost of having utility installations extended to the lot was prohibitive, possibly many times over its purchase price. Many of these buyers did not even visit the property before making their purchase to ensure that there was a road to it.

SOIL COMPOSITION AND TOPOGRAPHY

With the plat lines defined, availability of utilities assured, and an architect's design that takes into account any easements, zoning or deed restrictions, and building code requirements, the builder must analyze the composition of the soil. Soil tests will indicate the bearing capacity of the soil, the kind of footings and foundation that are best suited to the site and the feasibility of on-site sewage.

FIGURE 1–2. Easement.

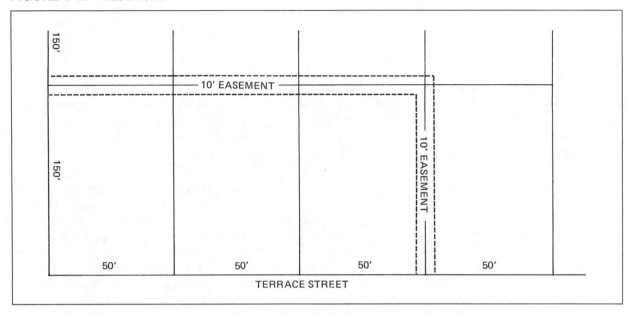

In the most general sense, soil is simply the covering of the earth. Bedrock is close enough to the surface to build on in some places and provides the firmest support for a building foundation. Hardpan, a mixture of clay with sand and gravel, has the next highest bearing capacity. In decreasing load-bearing capabilities are gravel soils, sand soils, clay soils and silt soils. Gravel consists of ¼- to 3-inch particles of rock. Both gravel and boulders, larger rock particles, are worn off bedrock by the action of the elements, such as the movement of water or the friction of freezing and thawing.

The essential difference between sand and clay, both of which are composed of very fine particles of rock, is their degree of cohesiveness. Boulders, gravel and sand are granular—they are composed of relatively large particles—while clay particles, sometimes not even visible with a low-powered microscope, are cohesive. Granular soil particles tend to be rounded, with very little space between particles. Clay, on the other hand, has sharp-edged, scaly, and more widely spaced particles. These differences are magnified in Figure 1–3.

Ideally, soil tests would be made of every building lot to determine the optimum foundation requirements. Practically, however, builders generally study the success of foundations in the immediate vicinity.

The load-bearing capacity of the soil will determine the type of footings used to support the foundation of the house. Topographical features can be dealt with in one of two ways. The house may be designed to suit the peculiarities of the lot, by building part of the ground floor into the side of a slope, for example, with entryways on both the higher and lower levels of the slope. Another alternative is to allow the design of the house to dictate alterations in the natural topography of the lot. This latter alternative is seldom pursued, since the most harmonious and economical use of a property is one that incorporates its natural features.

At some point below the surface of the earth the soil is saturated with water. The *water table* is the depth below the surface that this *ground water* begins. The water table will affect the type of foundation built and may necessitate special waterproofing measures. In some localities, such as the Gulf coast and lower eastern seaboard, the water table is high enough to preclude basements or other below-ground construction common in areas with lower water tables.

FIGURE 1–3. Soil types.

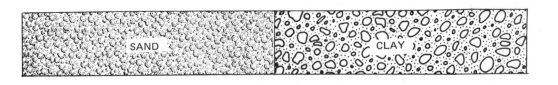

HOUSE LOCATION AND ORIENTATION ON THE LOT

Many good sites have been spoiled to some extent because of improper positioning of a house on its lot. A house that is correctly oriented and intelligently landscaped, that has windows and glass doors in the right places and adequate roof overhang, can save its owner thousands of dollars in heating and air-conditioning bills over the years. The location of a house on the lot can also make the difference between being able to enjoy a house and grounds at all times or having to adjust to the unpleasant fact that some areas are uncomfortable during certain hours of the day—or even for entire seasons. Improper positioning is probably the most common and costly mistake made in house planning today.

Most lots are rectangular, with less street frontage than depth (a 1:3 ratio is recommended). This shape gives the greatest area of lot space with a minimum of expensive street paving. Irregularly shaped lots often have trouble meeting setback requirements.

Theoretically, the architect's design should always take into account the specific lot that the house will be built on. It also should acknowledge the need for privacy by allocating most of the lot for private living areas as opposed to public areas visible from the street. In practice, however, the vast majority of houses are still located on their lots the way buyers have come to expect them—with much of the lot open to public view by a large front yard, and with an interior that lacks privacy because of large, front-facing windows.

There is a trend now toward more home privacy. Cul-de-sacs and non-through streets have discouraged traffic in some areas. Floor plans based on a center atrium have turned the focus of the house away from the street and into the private living area. Large front yards do make a neighborhood appear spacious, but the house itself will feel more spacious if most of the unused part of the lot is retained for a large, private backyard.

Facing South

A house that is properly oriented in relation to the sun has nature working for it all year. Ideally, a house should face *south* and be positioned on the lot so that the main living areas have the best view. It has been scientifically established that the south side of a house receives five times as much heat in winter as in summer; the east and west sides receive six times as much sun heat in summer as in winter; and the north side receives no sun heat at all during winter months. Figure 1–4 shows why a southern exposure is usually the best. During the summer, the sun will rise almost due east, travel a high arc, and set almost due west. In winter, however, the sun will rise in the southeast, travel a lower arc, and set in the southwest.

These weather facts are important because they have a bearing on the best orientation for rooms. The secret of good orientation is to take advantage of the sun's angle. Since the south side of a house will receive the most direct sunshine in winter and the least in summer, it is usually desirable to place the main living area and the largest windows facing directly south. With sufficient sun heat entering through large glass areas, rooms on the south side can be kept warm, even on

FIGURE 1–4. The sun's arc.

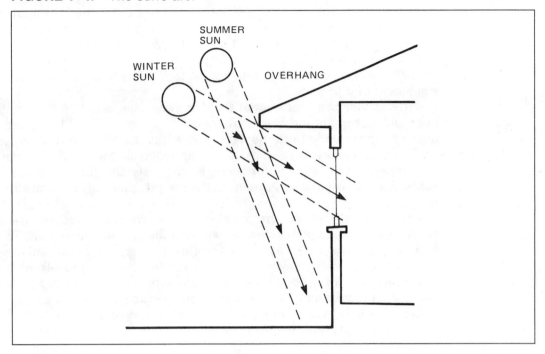

cold days, without an additional source of heat. According to a study published by the Smithsonian Institution, a house with a southern orientation will be more comfortable in winter and summer and require one-third less heating and cooling energy each year than a comparable house facing east, west, or north.

Most people prefer to have their living room and family room facing south. However, if these rooms are used more in the evening than in the daytime, it may be more pleasant and economical to allocate space on the south side to the daytime work areas. If rooms that are the center of daytime activity are placed where they receive the most natural light, the electric bill can be reduced.

In cold climates, a house that has large glass areas facing north or west will have large heating bills. Even double-layer glass, with dead airspace between, is insufficient insulation against cold northern winds, and the furnace must work harder to make up for the heat that is lost. Large windows that face east will admit sunshine during the early morning hours but will allow heat to escape during the balance of the day when the sun has moved away.

Unless some measures of control are used, the same sunshine that helps heat a house during the winter will make it uncomfortable during the summer. This dilemma can be solved very easily: because the summer sun rides high in the sky, a wide roof overhang will shade the windows by deflecting the direct heat rays. A roof overhang will not interfere with the sunshine in winter months because the winter sun travels a much lower arc and shines in at a much lower angle than the summer sun.

View

There are other important points to think about besides having the main living areas face south. There is, for example, a question of view. Naturally, the best view isn't always to the south. If the site has an interesting long view to the east or west, it might be well to take advantage of it despite the sun. A view of a lake, mountain or woods is an attractive contribution to a living place and can even help to sell a house. Everyone likes to look out the window and see beauty. If a site does not have a good long view, a short view of a garden or patio can be just as interesting if planned carefully.

Outdoor Space

Another important step in good site planning is to divide the lot into three different zones: *public, service* and *private*. The public zone is the area visible from the street—usually the land in front of the house. Zoning regulations specify how far back a house must be placed on a lot; ordinarily, there is no reason to want a large public area. The front lawn has yielded to the larger backyard designed for family enjoyment and privacy.

The service zone consists of the driveway, the walks and the area for garbage cans and storage of outdoor equipment. This area should be designed so that deliveries can be made to the service door without intrusion into the private area.

The private zone is the outdoor living space for the family. Unlike the backyard of years ago, it is planned for recreational activities for the entire family. An expanse of lawn, a patio, a garden, barbecue pit, and play area are included in this zone.

It is obvious that the minimum amount of valuable land be allocated for public and service use and the maximum amount for private enjoyment. The usual procedure is to set the house as far forward on the lot as local zoning regulations will allow. By positioning the house as close to the street as possible, only a short driveway and walk are needed—a substantial construction savings and a good way to cut down on maintenance jobs and snow clearance. In many cases, the fullest use of the lot is obtained by orienting the house toward the rear with the house itself screening the private zone from the street.

Drainage

What happens to rainwater or melted snow that falls on the site? Ideally, the house should be situated on an elevated part of the lot for good drainage. The best spot is a knoll from which land slopes away in all directions, as in Figure 1–5a. Also good is a gentle slope toward the road or street. Drainage problems will occur when water runs off across the site or down a slope toward the house, as in Figure 1–5b and c. Equally bad, and perhaps worse, is the site in Figure 1–5d, where water doesn't run off at all. Snow and ice can trap roof drainage around the perimeter of the house.

INSPECTING THE NEIGHBORHOOD AND THE SITE

The many unknowns of a new home and community can be intimidating. However, if you take a close look at your needs, life-style and priorities, you can pinpoint the kind of home and community that's right for you and your family. Before you buy, examine your expectations for a home. Consider the amount of space you need and the style of home you prefer. What are your family's interests? In what kind of community would you be most comfortable? How far are you willing to travel to work, school and community services? Consider all these important factors in assessing your needs. Also examine your priorities. What can you do without? What do you absolutely require?

As a potential buyer, you need to methodically inspect a house and give an opinion about its condition. This is best done by looking for specific problems rather than just checking the house in a random manner. You also need to examine the condition of the lot and its surroundings: the topography of the land for drainage, landscaping and privacy; the condition of contiguous lots; view; and street lighting and traffic.

When checking the site, note the condition of neighboring houses. Are the houses large or small? How well is the property landscaped? Are the lawns well kept? Answers to questions like these tell much about the quality of life in the

FIGURE 1–5. Land slopes and drainage.

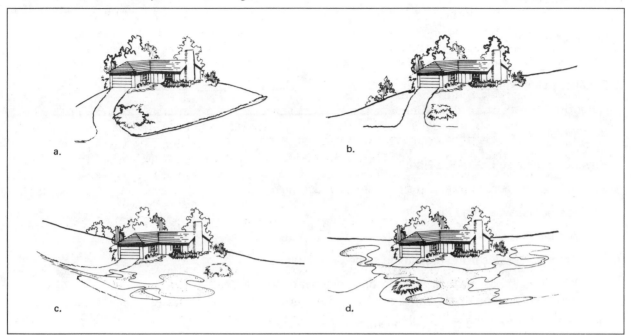

neighborhood. In most cases, visual inspection should disclose whether the house is located in a neighborhood that will retain its character and value or one that is headed for a gradual decline. A declining neighborhood might seem to offer some good bargains now, but what will happen to resale values in a few years?

Do the surrounding houses conform architecturally? Many houses suffer a loss in value because they do not conform to the neighborhood in which they are located. Too much conformity, on the other hand, where all the houses look the same, will also diminish value. Houses within a neighborhood should have enough variations in style and design to make the overall effect pleasing to the eye.

The direction the house faces can contribute to its marketability. Some buyers want the kitchen to be the sunniest room of the house and to have an unusually pretty view because they spend a lot of time there; other buyers look for a house with a screened-in porch that is shaded part of the day. A windowless wall or a fireplace in the wall facing winter winds can also be a selling point.

The poor location and orientation of a house on its lot detracts from its livability substantially. Unfortunately, the vast majority of existing houses are not advantageously located or oriented. A house oriented to topography, view, sun and trees will not conform to the neighborhood if the other houses are lined up in a row facing the street.

No other single element is more important in the selection of a house than its *location*. If you're new to an area, you can collect information from sources such as the chamber of commerce, real estate agents, and banks and other local businesses, as well as through personal inspection. Checking out a location for livability and investment potential may take some legwork, but it's worth it. In the long run you'll be glad you asked a lot of questions early.

The following *checklist* will help you research and evaluate a potential neighborhood and site to be sure that it offers the right living environment for your family's life-style.

After checking out all these points carefully, you'll be ready to start thinking about the house itself, with the assurance that you're buying in a neighborhood where you'll be happy.

INSPECTION CHECKLIST

Lot Information

Orientation of House: N   S   E   W

Distance to Lot Boundaries: Front _____   Sides _____   Back _____

Other Structures: _____

Best/Worst Views: _____

How Does the Neighborhood Rate?	**Yes**	**No**
1. Is the neighborhood stable, as opposed to in decline?	_____	_____
2. Are homes well cared for?	_____	_____
3. Are the lawns well kept?	_____	_____
4. Are most houses in the area in the same price range?	_____	_____
5. Who lives there—are their ages, income, number of children, interests same as yours?	_____	_____
6. Is the neighborhood quiet (i.e., no irritating noise levels from automobiles, trucks, airplanes, trains, buses, etc.)?	_____	_____
7. Is the neighborhood convenient to your place of employment?	_____	_____
8. Is public transportation available?	_____	_____
9. Is the neighborhood close to shopping, schools, churches, parks, and recreation centers?	_____	_____
10. Is the neighborhood in a low-crime area?	_____	_____
11. Are property values rising?	_____	_____
12. Have property taxes been steady in the past year or two?	_____	_____
13. Are taxes in line with those in other areas?	_____	_____
14. Is there adequate police and fire protection?	_____	_____
15. Is there convenient emergency medical service?	_____	_____
16. Does the area have plans for expansion and development?	_____	_____
17. Does the area have any zoning restrictions?	_____	_____
18. Have you checked whether any special assessments are anticipated?	_____	_____
19. Are the schools of good quality?	_____	_____
20. Do traffic patterns allow for pedestrian and vehicle safety?	_____	_____
21. Is there adequate street lighting?	_____	_____
22. Do the surrounding houses conform architecturally?	_____	_____

Site and House Location	**Yes**	**No**
1. Does the site have all the necessary utilities?	_____	_____
2. Does the topography of the lot allow for good drainage?	_____	_____
3. Is the property well landscaped?	_____	_____
4. Does the landscaping afford privacy?	_____	_____
5. Have you checked on any easements or deed restrictions?	_____	_____
6. Are you satisfied with the location of the site in terms of position in the block?	_____	_____
7. Is the size of the lot satisfactory?	_____	_____
8. Does the house take good advantage of natural conditions (sun, breeze, view)?	_____	_____
9. Are the public, service and private zones of the lot well defined?	_____	_____

Overall Rating	**Good**	**Fair**	**Poor**
Neighborhood	_____	_____	_____
Site	_____	_____	_____
House location	_____	_____	_____
Size of lot: _____ sq. ft.	_____	_____	_____

Major Problems: _____

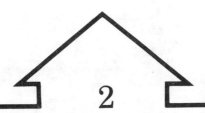

House Styles and Types

Driving through a single-family neighborhood, you may see a house that invites you to stop for a longer look. Usually it is no one thing that catches your eye, but a combination of features: an attractive entrance, balanced building proportions, color coordination or the feeling that the house looks right in its setting. Such effects are no accident—they are the result of careful thought and planning.

HOUSE STYLES

The homeowner's first decision is whether his or her life-style is suited to a dignified older residence or a new house with an open, airy atmosphere. The architect or builder will want to construct a house that meets the homeowner's requirements. House styles can be grouped under two broad categories: *traditional* and *contemporary.*

Traditional Styles

The charm of past architectural styles has a special delight for many prospective homeowners. Within this nostalgic design category, traditionalists have a wide range of individual styles to choose from: English Tudor, Spanish Colonial and Colonial American, to name a few. The traditional house derives its unique flavor from the handling of architectural details. Fortunately, good reproductions of the detailing found in many traditional houses are now being mass-produced. Ready-made entrance doors, mantels, moldings and parquet floors bear a close resemblance to their handcrafted prototypes.

Interior planning in traditional houses is another matter. Today's families, while they may prefer the look of another era, want a house that functions in a contemporary fashion. Most floor plans incorporate contemporary features. Most, for example, have a family room in addition to the living room; many have an open arrangement of kitchen and family room or of living and dining areas; and many have a master bedroom with its own full bath.

English Tudor. Its feeling of strength and longevity have made the traditional Tudor house more popular than ever. The one in Figure 2–1 has all the standard distinguishing features such as bay window, truncated roofs, massive chimney, diamond-pane windows, timber in the stucco and roofs of various heights.

FIGURE 2–1. Traditional Tudor.

Spanish Colonial. There has been a strong revival of interest in Spanish Colonial architecture. The Mexican or southwestern hacienda was designed for casual living, and its walled enclosure afforded great privacy—sought-after qualities in today's hectic, crowded world. The design, shown here in adobe (Figure 2–2), would be equally effective in stucco or painted concrete block. Other distinguishing characteristics include the red tile roof, oval top windows and doors and the wrought-iron exterior decorations.

FIGURE 2–2. Spanish Colonial.

Colonial American. Few styles of residential architecture anywhere in the world have the comfortable warmth of the houses built in America in the 17th and early 18th centuries. The secret lay in their simplicity, for these homes provided basic shelter without frills. The design in Figure 2–3, for example, has many early earmarks: the big chimney, narrow clapboard siding, small-paned windows, saltbox roof line and the paneled entrance door.

FIGURE 2–3. Colonial American.

Contemporary Styles

Contemporary architecture is for those who prefer to live fully in the present—without disguises, clutter or burdensome maintenance—and for those who want, above all, to connect a house with its surroundings. Although contemporary houses appear uncomplicated, many are clever examples of how to make the best use of materials and space. A distinctive contemporary look relies on the straight-forward expression of the structural system itself for design impact.

One great benefit of contemporary residential architecture is its responsiveness to indoor-outdoor living. Sliding glass doors, large windows, skylights, decks, terraces and atriums all contribute to this relationship. The large expanses of glass take maximum advantage of natural or urban views. Sliding windows join rooms to their outdoor counterparts, making these decks, patios and terraces an integral part of the overall house complex.

In Figure 2–4a, three pitched-roof elements cluster to form a contemporary house with ample light and outdoor living space. A raised portion of the roof, in Figure 2–4b, creates a vaulted ceiling in the living room.

HOUSE TYPES

Today's new materials and modern techniques can make a notable difference in the way houses are designed and built. The modern house, whether its style is contemporary or traditional, can exhibit the latest conveniences and building innovations. Thus, a new house can be traditional in design without being impractical and outdated. Large areas of double-paned glass open houses to sun, light and view without letting in cold and drafts. There is no longer a need for a fireplace in every room. A good modern house has central heating and lets us comfortably enjoy big rooms with large windows. Without coal bins, the basement is not essential to a house, although it can be great for recreation, storage and utility purposes. Air-conditioning and a change from traditional patterns of room arrangement have lessened the need for cross ventilation from two exposures in every room.

The One-Story House

The one-story house (Figure 2–5), often referred to as a *ranch*, has all the habitable rooms on one level. Its great advantage is the absence of steps to climb or descend, except to a basement. The one-story house is best adapted to the contemporary

FIGURE 2–4. Two contemporary designs.

desire for easy indoor-outdoor living. Porches, patios or terraces can be designed adjacent to any room.

Since no headroom is required above the ceiling, the roof of a one-story house is usually pitched low. This of course simplifies screen and storm window installation, painting, roof repair and gutter work. The low height simplifies construction too, but this does not necessarily mean a lower cost, since foundation and roof areas are generally larger than in other types of housing. The low, ground-hugging look of the one-story design is particularly pleasing, and resale value for this type of house is, therefore, excellent. The extra length of the ranch calls for a larger plot, but it also provides a liberal basement area for a heating plant, recreation room, laundry, workshop and storage space.

Zoning is especially important in a one-story design to ensure sufficient privacy and quiet. Good planning will separate bedrooms from the living and service space; storage areas can act as a sound buffer between active and quiet zones.

The One-and-a-Half-Story House

The one-and-a-half-story, or *Cape Cod* (Figure 2–6), is actually a two-story house in which the second-floor attic space has sufficient headroom to permit up to half the

FIGURE 2–5. One-story ranch.

FIGURE 2–6. Cape Cod.

area to be used as livable floor space. It has two distinct advantages: economy in cost per cubic foot of habitable space and built-in expandability.

Extremely versatile, the one-and-a-half-story can start out as a two-bedroom, one-bath house with an unfinished upper level as an expansion attic. This works well as a first home for people who want minimum living area at minimum cost but may want to add a bedroom or a second bath later. It's equally good as a retirement home: Upstairs rooms may be closed to lighten housework, opened to welcome visiting friends and family.

Because the story-and-a-half can grow, it must be carefully designed to include the amenities necessary to service the number of people it might ultimately house. Special attention should be given to living and service room sizes and to heating, air-conditioning, water, electrical and sewage ststems.

The Two-Story House

Gracious living in early America was almost always provided by two-story houses like the one in Figure 2–7. Living and service areas were located on the first floor, and sleeping areas were on the second floor. For many, this is still the ideal way to live.

Certain economies are inherent in the two-story plan. Because plumbing can be lined up, winter heating works to its best advantage–heat rises to the second floor after permeating the ground floor. The two-story house also offers the most living space within an established perimeter; the living area is doubled on the same foundation, which is economical when a good deal of space is required. More house can be built on a smaller piece of property with a two-story plan. The roof and foundation are smaller relative to the overall floor areas.

FIGURE 2–7.   Two-story design.

The Split-Level House

The split-level in Figure 2–8, is one of the most versatile designs, both in its allotment of space and in its placement on a particular piece of property.

Split-levels have four separate levels of space. Beginning with the lowest level, there is what would be called the normal basement. Situated below the outside finished grade, it usually contains the heating and air-conditioning system, storage space and a workshop. The next area—the one raised a half-flight from the basement level—is extra space found only in a split-level house. It usually includes the garage and recreation room, or a large foyer and a family room. Living and sleeping levels are above, taking up the total room area in a typical one-story ranch house of equivalent size. But the half-level difference between them affords greater privacy for the bedrooms and their baths.

Split-levels break down into three basic types, as illustrated in Figure 2–9. In Figure 2–9a, the side-to-side design places the living area on one side and the bedroom area on the other. Both face the street in a combination one-story, two-story

FIGURE 2–8. Split-level.

elevation. In Figure 2–9b, a back-to-front design, bedrooms (over the lifted basement) face the street and the living area is in the rear. This resembles the saltbox design, with a two-story front and one-story elevation at the rear. In Figure 2–9c, the living area in a front-to-back design faces the street and the bedroom area faces the rear. Because the bedrooms are over the lifted basement area, the house would look from the front like a single-story ranch.

FIGURE 2–9. Three split-level designs.

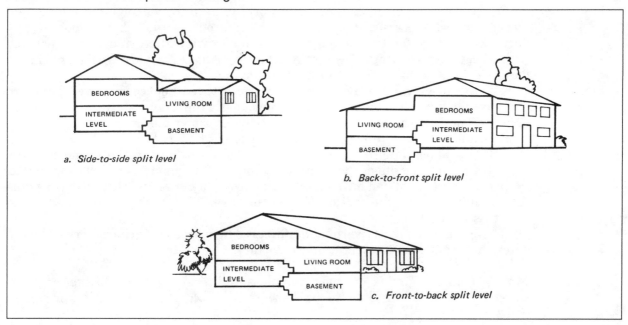

The Split-Entry House

A fairly recent architectural approach to residential housing is the split-entry design, sometimes called a *raised ranch* or *bi-level*. As seen in Figure 2–10, this is basically a one-story house raised out of the ground about halfway. The greater window depth admits more light to the basement area, making it more usable for recreation rooms, baths or bedrooms. In effect, the square footage of the house is doubled at a modest cost increase—merely that of finishing the rooms on the lower level.

The entrance Foyer in Figure 2–10 is located at grade level about midway between the upper and lower levels, with direct access to both. This arrangement reduces traffic in the main living area. The raised effect gives the exterior a more imposing look—larger than a one-story house, yet with a ground-hugging quality that can't be achieved with a two-story.

FIGURE 2–10.   Split-entry.

Manufactured Houses

Mention manufactured housing, and most people have visions of prefab buildings and flimsy trailers of the 1960s. That image nags at the manufactured-housing industry, which accounts for nearly 10 percent of the nation's entire housing stock.

In recent years, builders have been working hard to overcome those long-held biases against factory-built housing by turning out sturdier, better-looking products. Some manufactured home models are downright luxurious, with features such as cathedral ceilings, garages and family rooms. They are trucked to the lot for on-site anchoring to a cement foundation.

There are several disadvantages to manufactured houses, however. They are not necessarily less expensive than conventionally built homes, they are not available in all parts of the country, transportation can sometimes make the cost uncompetitive and there is a range in quality that forces buyers to be prudent.

While it is possible to buy a manufactured house "off the shelf," most buyers modify the models. One of the significant recent developments in house manufacturing is that a client can have an architect design a house and then give the plans to a manufacturer for fabrication. This option strengthens the prefabricated industry at its weakest point—design.

There are four basic types of manufactured houses; each is characterized by the extent of assemblage completed in the factory.

Mobile Home.   This is the most complete and least expensive of the manufactured houses, needing only to be anchored to a foundation and connected to utilities.

Modular House.   This comes from the factory in single-room or multiple-room sections, which are then fitted together at the construction site.

Panelized House.   At the factory, entire wall units, complete with electrical and plumbing installations, are constructed and transported to the site where final assembly begins. With the foundation laid, the house can be enclosed within a week.

Precut House.   As the name implies, materials are delivered to the construction site ready to assemble. Each piece should fit perfectly in its place, saving carpenters the costly amount of time needed to measure and cut materials.

ADDING ON TO A HOUSE

Let's assume that you are in love with a house and it's in a great neighborhood—but it only has three bedrooms and you've got four kids. In other words, if you buy the house, you'll need to add on.

Depending on how well it's designed, an addition to your home can dramatically increase or decrease its value. A well-planned addition should fit in with its physical surroundings as well as your family life. Although exterior materials need not match the original, the new space should complement both the existing house and the landscape. However, matching the addition's windows, exterior surfaces and other features with the originals can help prevent a tacked-on look. The slope, or pitch, of the roof on the addition should match that on the original house to provide continuity.

If you're shopping for a house with add-on potential, do some homework first. Contact the local building department for information about setback requirements and other zoning restrictions that might limit the kind of changes you could make. For example, zoning requirements often specify that no more than a certain percentage of the lot can be covered by structures. Local governments also decide what building codes apply in your area. The purpose of the codes is to ensure that you and others follow minimum standards for construction.

Before you begin any serious planning for an addition, keep in mind that adding to a house can put extra stress and strain on its structure and systems. To evaluate the effects of adding on, you need to know the exact condition, capacity and expected life of the home's structural and mechanical components. In later chapters, you'll learn to judge the condition and quality of a building that can help you eliminate those houses that are not suitable for adding on.

Here are the five basic house types and a capsule summary of the kinds of additions that work well with each of them.

One-Story House

A basic rectangular ranch can easily become an L (see Figure 2–11a). You can expand an L-shaped ranch into a U or something more complex by building a second wing in front or back—or both (see Figure 2–11b).

On a small lot where there's no room for outward expansion, consider building a full second story for maximum additional space.

One-and-a-Half Story House

Add a one- or two-story structure at the rear of a story-and-a-half. Or, add space with a smaller one-story addition at the rear, side or front.

A second-floor addition over a garage gives this type of house a dramatically different look and works especially well for a bedroom or den (see Figure 2–11c).

Two-Story House

An addition over the garage will bring more space to a two-story home. You might consider this kind of addition to create a large master bedroom suite.

Build on in front or back of a two-story, adding one or two stories as space needs dictate. For even more space and a symmetrical look, consider additions at both ends of the original house (see Figure 2–11d) or an addition that runs the length of the house. For maximum space, add on at the side, wrapping around to front or back.

FIGURE 2–11.   Common types of additions.
      a. L-shaped addition
      b. U-shaped addition
      c. Partial second-story addition
      d. Symmetrical additions at both sides

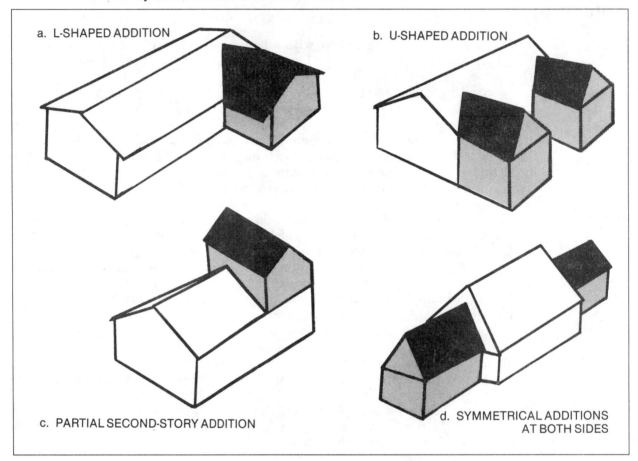

a. L-SHAPED ADDITION
b. U-SHAPED ADDITION
c. PARTIAL SECOND-STORY ADDITION
d. SYMMETRICAL ADDITIONS AT BOTH SIDES

Split-Level House

One way to expand a split-level is to add at mid-level, if the lot is large enough. This kind of addition often extends out from one side of the house.

A likely alternative is a one-story or two-story addition at the back. This is especially good for a family room because it gives access to the backyard.

Split-Entry House

Adding a single story to the entry level of a split-entry house provides more living space and a new look outside.

You can add a garage and a second floor to a split-entry for more space without altering existing floor levels. Again, the exterior view will be drastically changed.

Add a one-level or two-level addition at the back. This affects the street-side exterior view the least and provides privacy as well as space.

RETURN ON INVESTMENT

The home addition and remodeling industry has more than doubled since the early 1980s and continued growth seems assured. If you plan to add on or remodel, keep in mind what portion of your costs you'll get back if and when you sell your home.

Before making any major home improvements, look at the house the way a real estate appraiser would. That will help you judge the value of the changes you have in mind.

The first question you should ask yourself is, "How long do I plan to stay in this house?" If you plan to move in a few years, think about the resale value of your improvements. Many of your "wants" may end up hampering a sale; that is, it may be worth more to you than it would be to a buyer.

Refer to appendix D of this book. Notice that a swimming pool may add only 50 to 60 percent of its cost to the value of the home. The reason: A potential buyer may view this luxury as dangerous for young children or too expensive to maintain.

A finished basement commands 25 percent or less because buyers still consider it simply a basement no matter how fancy it may be.

On the other hand, remodeling a kitchen should normally bring 100 percent recovery of costs. A brand-new bathroom means you'll probably recover 100 percent of money invested, while remodeling an existing bathroom should command somewhere between 75 and 100 percent.

Neighborhood

Consider your neighborhood before undertaking drastic remodeling or room additions. If you were to add a room or two, would the value of the house become too high for the type of neighborhood you are in? Here's a rule of thumb: Do not make any improvements that will raise the value of your house more than 30 percent. You may price yourself right out of the resale market.

INSPECTION CHECKLIST

What kind of home are you looking for? Your home should be a very personal reflection of your interests, your preferences, your life-style. Some people love the openness of contemporary homes with living areas rather than traditionally walled rooms. Some people feel more comfortable in cozy spaces. Some want bold, architectural details; others want their home to be a "background" that doesn't intrude at all.

Your home should accommodate your style of entertaining. If you enjoy casual parties, how often would you use a formal dining room? If you'll only use it a few times a year, money for the dining room and furnishings might be better spent on a larger family room or country kitchen/dining area. If you like to entertain outdoors, look for homes with interesting patios, gardens or porches—preferably near the kitchen. If you have a strong preference, recognize it and try to find the home that fits.

There are no right or wrong architectural styles. There are no right or wrong house types. It's a question of personal preference. But there are certain principles of good design that will influence the livability of a house and its future market value. These will be discussed in the next chapter.

INSPECTION CHECKLIST

House Style and Type

House Style: traditional/contemporary

House Type: one-story/one-and-a-half story/
                                two-story/split-level/split-entry/manufactured/other

Age of House: _____

		Yes	No
1.	Is the house style and type suitable for your life-style?	_____	_____
2.	Has the house been built by a reliable contractor?	_____	_____
3.	Is it covered by a warranty?	_____	_____
4.	Is the style consistent throughout, and the lines and detail in pleasing balance?	_____	_____
5.	Are materials, scale and proportion consistent with the architectural style?	_____	_____
6.	Does the house blend with surrounding homes?	_____	_____
7.	Does the house have expansion potential?	_____	_____
8.	Are the other houses in the neighborhood expensive enough so that you can recover the cost of improvements?	_____	_____
9.	Does the house have good resale potential? (Ask the real estate agent. He or she has up-to-date information on what's happening in the neighborhood.)	_____	_____

Overall Rating	Good	Fair	Poor
House type and style meet your needs	_____	_____	_____
Expansion potential	_____	_____	_____
Resale value	_____	_____	_____

Major Problems: _____

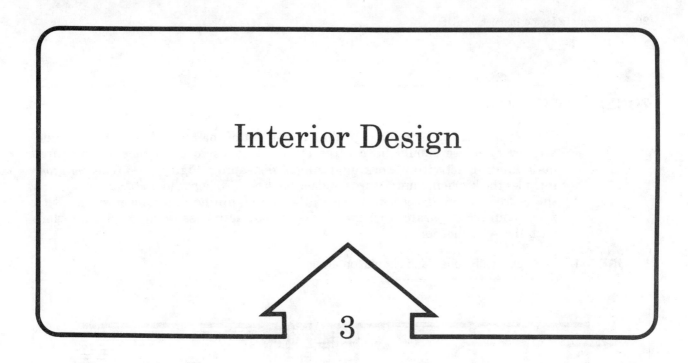

Interior Design

The interior design of a house is basic to a convenient and comfortable living arrangement. Within each house are zones that correspond to the daily functions of the occupants. These areas should be accessible to family members and yet afford them privacy. Unfortunately, many people recognize the good and poor qualities of an interior arrangement only after they have lived in a place.

Although it is not the intent of this chapter to train you to be an architect, you will want to know something about the dos and don'ts of planning individual rooms in a house. Size and location have a bearing on livability. The traffic, or circulation, areas are not rooms per se, but they play a major role in the organization of a house. An examination of the rooms of a house, their purpose, position, and relationship to the overall plan, will give you a clearer picture of interior zoning.

If you can read and evaluate a floor plan, you will know if a particular arrangement is suited to your needs. There are many questions about the interior of a house that must be answered before construction begins or before you consider buying an existing home. Features discussed in earlier chapters—site, orientation, type and style of a house—also affect interior design.

CIRCULATION AREAS

Circulation areas consist of halls, stairways and entries. Floor space used only to go from one room to another may seem like wasted space, but it often makes the difference between a good floor plan and a poor one. When you study a floor plan, take a long, careful look at traffic patterns. Can people get directly from one room to another without crossing other rooms? Is there direct access to a bathroom from any room? Is the stairway between levels located off a hallway or foyer rather than a room? You don't want to waste space on halls, especially if it can be put to better use. Properly planned, however, halls and entries permit good traffic patterns, help control sound, and create privacy.

ZONES WITHIN A HOUSE

Interior zoning refers to the logical arrangement of the rooms inside a house. Ideally, every house should have three clear-cut zones to accommodate the three main kinds of activities: working, living and sleeping (Figure 3–1). The *work zone* includes the kitchen, laundry area and perhaps a workshop; the *sleeping zone* contains the bedrooms; the *living zone* contains the living, dining and family rooms. Each zone should be separate from the others so that activities in one do not interfere with those in another.

FIGURE 3–1. Floor plan with zones and circulation areas.

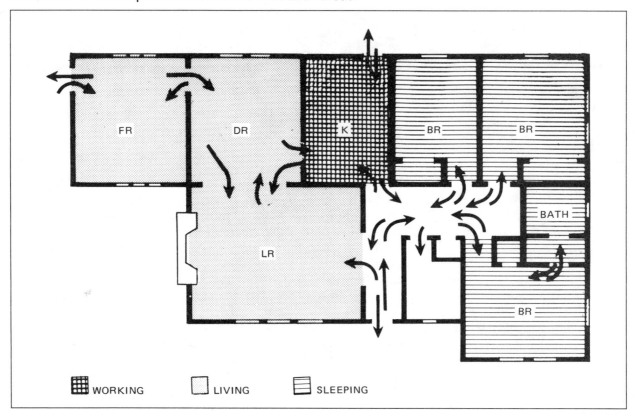

The Work Zone

Kitchen.   Since the kitchen is the control center of the house, it is crucial to any discussion of interior planning. In the old days the kitchen, with its fireplace in constant use, was the only regularly heated room in a house. It was the gathering place for the family. Families cooked, ate, talked, studied, played games and even bathed in the kitchen. As time passed, these activities moved one by one to other rooms, until the kitchen became a small room that was used only for the preparation of food. Now the pendulum has swung back. Kitchens are getting bigger and are becoming multipurpose rooms again. Today, the kitchen is the most used room in the house.

Because kitchen appliances emit heat into the room, the kitchen can be located on the cool side of the house. That means east or north. The kitchen should be centrally located so that it affords direct access to the dining area and the front entrance. It should be close to the garage so that heavy bags of groceries don't have to be carried very far. If there are small children in the family, the kitchen must have a good view of both the outside play area and the family room.

The nerve center of the kitchen is its *work triangle*, the arrangement of the refrigerator, sink and range in relation to each other. The location of these and other appliances is dependent on the plumbing and electrical currents. For maximum efficiency, the triangle should have a total perimeter of at least 12 feet but no more than 22 feet, with plenty of countertop space and cabinets. The room must be well-ventilated to keep it free of cooking odors.

FIGURE 3–2.   Work triangle in a U-shaped kitchen.

There are three basic kitchen layouts. The *U design*, with the sink at the bottom of the U and the range and refrigerator on opposite sides, is very efficient (Figure 3–2). The *L design*, with the sink and range on one leg and the refrigerator on the other, is sometimes used with a dining space in the opposite corner. The *parallel wall*, or *Pullman kitchen plan*, is one solution to a narrow kitchen (Figure 3–3). It can be quite efficient with proper arrangement of the sink, range and refrigerator.

FIGURE 3–3.   Kitchen types.

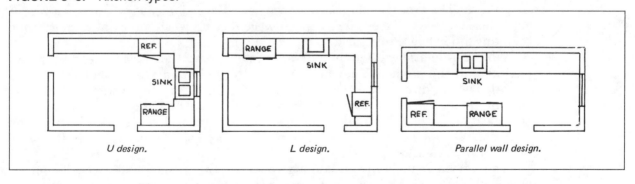

U design.   L design.   Parallel wall design.

Remodeling the Kitchen Can Be Expensive.   The kitchen is the most remodeled room in the house. More money is spent on redoing the kitchen than on any other type of home improvement.

The word *remodel* can mean a variety of things when you're discussing a kitchen. It can mean merely painting or wallpapering. Or it can mean such renovations as changing the locations of the appliances as well as replacing them, putting in new cabinets, installing a different floor covering, adding an exhaust fan, building a pantry, changing the electrical equipment or even removing a wall.

The more you look at kitchens, the better you will get at judging which types are for you. Get into the habit of taking a pencil and notebook with you so you can jot down any ideas you may pick up.

Because the expense of redoing the kitchen is likely to be substantial, you should have a fairly good idea of what you need and want before you buy.

Remember, a good kitchen plan keeps traffic out of the work area. A proven rule for layout involves a triangle, which separates refrigerator, sink and range from 4 to approximately 7 feet apart, measured center to center. In addition, a kitchen's work area and floor must be highly resistant to wear.

If you were designing the kitchen of your dreams, what would you put into it? To start with, the latest-model appliances would be essential, including a side-by-side refrigerator and freezer, conventional and microwave wall ovens, built-in dishwasher, dual rimless enamel sinks and more. And then, top-quality cabinets—and plenty of them to provide lots of storage. You'll want at least 10 linear feet along the base, plus 10 feet along the walls. More is highly desirable, and all should be accessible.

And counters should be convenient, 3 feet or more on both sides of the sink, 2 feet or more of heat-resistant surface next to the range and oven.

One of the more important reasons for remodeling a kitchen is to improve its lighting. Older kitchens tend to have too few light fixtures, and they're usually poorly placed. Often there's only one, centered in the ceiling, where it increases eye strain.

In addition to ambient illumination, a kitchen should have task lighting for the sink, range and counters. Usually, task lighting is installed under wall cabinets, though it may also be recessed into soffit or ceiling or come from track fixtures. Whatever the source, it should be in front of the cook so no shadow is cast on the work surface.

Natural daylight is another factor that can contribute much to the kitchen environment. A large window or a skylight would dramatically brighten and cheer the space.

While a kitchen necessarily must be somewhat altered to suit the preferences of the person who does most of the cooking, it should not be so individualistic that a future homeowner will find it unsuitable.

Laundry.   The average homemaker does more than 400 loads of laundry a year—eight loads a week. Except for preparing meals, the wash often takes more time than any other household task.

When automatic washers and dryers first came on the market, people usually put them in the kitchen. They don't belong there. Laundry equipment should be installed where dirty laundry accumulates and clean laundry is stored. That's the sleeping area, since clothes and bed linens make up the bulk of all laundry. The best location for laundry equipment is a utility room or a ventilated closet off the bedroom hall. As a compromise, it may be placed off the family room, in the basement, or in the garage.

The two basic tools in the laundry room are the washer and dryer. The other essential tool is a sink for soaking and pretreating small items and handwashing clothes.

The ideal laundry area should have plenty of shelves and cabinets for storing detergents, bleach, fabric softeners and other cleaning aids.

Every extra square foot of space should be given over to waist-high countertop surfaces for sorting and folding clothes as they come out of the dryer. Separating each family members' clothing right from the dryer cuts down the number of times it has to be handled.

The Living Zone

Living Room.   The living room is the next most important room. In small houses it is the center of family life and entertainment. In houses large enough to have both a living room and a family room, the living room is a quiet place for reading and conversation. It should be close to the front door, next to dining space, and away from sleeping areas. The view should be best from the living room. The room should have a south orientation to obtain maximum daylight in summer and maximum sunlight in winter (Figure 3–4).

Family Room.   The family room, the center of noisiest activity, should be as far from bedrooms and the living room as possible. However, it should be close to the kitchen so that food is only a few steps away. A family room that is near an outside entrance will allow children to come and go without having to walk through other rooms in the house. Since the family room is the "action center" of the house, view is not too important; nor does it matter which side of the house the room is on (Figure 3–5).

FIGURE 3–4.   Living room with floor-to-ceiling. window.

FIGURE 3–5.   Paneled family room.

Dining Room.   People spend only a few hours a day eating, so a separate room for that purpose alone is expensive space. Even so, many people don't want to eat all meals in the kitchen, where they spend so much of their time. And if they do much social or business entertaining, they don't want to serve dinner to guests in the family room. Besides privacy, a separate dining room offers an attractive setting for showing off silverware, glassware and china (Figure 3–6).

If a separate dining room is too expensive, people will compromise and use a dining space that is part of the living room, so long as there is some visual separation between the two. Dining space in the kitchen, either in an alcove or a large bright corner, is a feature of many new homes. Snack bars were popular in the kitchen for a short time, but people soon learned that eating side by side on stools didn't work well in the family routine. For large families and people who entertain informally, the family room makes good dining space. It is close to the kitchen and can be decorated with easy-to-clean surfaces.

The Sleeping Zone

Bedrooms.   Although they deserve as much thought as any other room in the house, bedrooms are frequently the forgotten parts of a house. They get whatever space is left over after living space is planned. Bedrooms don't need a view or a lot of sunlight, but they should be on the cool side of the house—north or east—and on the quiet side, away from such noisy rooms as the family room and kitchen. They should be out of sight from the entrance door and living area so that they don't have to be kept meticulously clean.

Every bedroom is home to someone—a space where one can feel secure and have privacy. This is especially important to a child, even though he or she may have to share the room for a while with a brother or sister (Figure 3–7). When you

FIGURE 3–6. Formal dining room.

FIGURE 3–7. Bedroom for teenagers or guests.

look at bedrooms, keep in mind the family's needs. Does the parents' bedroom have sufficient closet space for two? Does it have direct access to a bathroom? Does the teenager have shelf space for collections, desk space for studying and wall space for posters and clippings? Does the younger child have a place to store toys as well as floor space to play? Can a child look out the window without climbing on a chair?

How many bedrooms should a house have? From the mid 1940s through the 1960s the number of bedrooms in most new homes grew to three and then to four. Families today are smaller, so the trend is reverting to the three-bedroom house. The market for two-bedroom houses is generally limited to older couples and young couples without children. Even families of this size, however, can use a third bedroom occasionally. Keep an eye on popular trends. Few experts predicted that family size would shrink as it did, and the trend could reverse itself in the next few years.

Unzoned Space

Bathrooms.   As a general rule, allow one bathroom for every two adults and one for every three children. For convenience, there should be a toilet and lavatory on every level. A private bathroom for the master bedroom is a good selling feature in many new houses.

You can put a complete bathroom in a space 5 feet by 7 feet, but the trend is toward much larger bathrooms. A double lavatory is very popular, although there are times when two toilets would be more practical. The bathroom closest to the master bedroom should have a tub-shower combination. A shower stall instead of a bathtub in a second bathroom is usually adequate. Another tub-shower combination is even better, however, since it takes up only slightly more space than a shower stall and costs about the same.

A good floor plan locates bathrooms close to bedrooms, in an area where children can reach them easily from outdoors, and in a private, convenient spot for guest use. For years, builders preferred to build from plans that had bathrooms back to back or, in multistory houses, one above the other. This does save plumbing costs, but it usually means changing a good floor plan. The buyer won't see the savings in plumbing costs, but he or she will see the resulting flaw in the plan.

Storage Space.   Few houses ever have enough storage space. A sound floor plan will include a closet at least 4 feet wide by 2 feet deep for every family member, a linen closet big enough to hold blankets, a guest closet near the front door and, in colder climates, one near the rear door. Also look for a place to put books, toys, games, tools and out-of-season clothing. Larger areas for building and repairing things, storing garden tools, bicycles and other outdoor equipment, as well as bulk storage for "junk," are invaluable. Kitchens should have lots of storage space, all of it within reach of a small person.

Garage. A garage doesn't need sunlight, nor does it need to stay cool in summer and warm in winter. It can have any orientation, but the best place for the garage is on the west or north, where it can protect living space in the house from the hot afternoon sun in summer and from howling winds in winter. More important than orientation is convenience. A garage should be close to the kitchen, and it should not obscure light from other rooms. It should never be placed so that drifting snow will block the door. If the lot is big enough, the garage should be turned so that the door does not face the street. There is nothing attractive about the inside of a garage. Besides, a street view of an open empty garage tells burglars that nobody is home.

The garage should always be big enough for two cars. Even with small cars, you will want inside dimensions of at least 23 feet by 23 feet. And since a garage costs less per square foot to build than the main house, it would be sensible to make it large enough to accommodate extra storage and work space needs.

Basement. A basement has many uses. Since you have to go below the frost line with the foundation anyhow, a basement adds little to the building cost in cold climates (but more as you go south). A basement is always economical space if you can also make it convenient. It provides low-cost space for heating and cooling equipment, bulk storage and so forth.

If the building site slopes so that a ground-level entrance can be provided, a basement is good for workshops and family rooms. It stays cool in summer and warm in winter. A basement is not a good living space, however, unless it is bright and cheerful with adequate light and air (Figure 3–8).

HOW TO READ A FLOOR PLAN

Floor plans and an architect's rendering of the exterior of the house are visual aids to help you see what the house will look like when construction is completed. Because architects must work with a reduced scale and with two dimensions rather than three, symbols and abbreviations are used to indicate many of the important elements of the house. They are a form of shorthand, intended to save space and avoid cluttering up the plan with extensive detail. If you want to understand what a plan says, you must learn to recognize these symbols and abbreviations. The most frequently encountered standard symbols are explained in Figure 3–9.

One of the best ways to understand what a floor plan means is to imagine yourself walking through the house. As you read this section, follow the floor plan in Figure 3–9. Look first for an always-present and rather dominant symbol—the heavy black arrow that points to the primary entrance from the outside of the house.

Imagine yourself opening the front door and stepping into the foyer or vestibule. Chances are at this point you will see a small enclosure with a letter *C* in it; that is a closet, and in a well-designed house it is rare not to find one near the primary entrance, where it is needed for guests' coats and hats.

Now move mentally from the foyer into the main living area. If you encounter a series of close-spaced lines running perpendicular to the line of your walk, you have reached a stairway. The number of lines indicates the number of treads (steps) in the stairway, and you will find an arrow pointing either up or down. If the house is a split-level, you will see that up and down stairs are often placed side by side. In standard floor plans of split-level houses, two separate levels are generally shown in one drawing and additional levels in another. You can go through both

FIGURE 3–8.   A finished basement is a good substitute for a family room.

the living area and the bedrooms on one drawing; then you have to go back to the foyer on another drawing to start a trip into the recreation area on a lower level.

In many living rooms you will find an obvious symbol for a fireplace—a heavy black mass with a small white square in it to indicate the flue in the chimney. You are also likely to see a notation for some special type of window, such as a bow, a bay or a sliding glass door. To get a more graphic idea of what this means you must examine the sketch of the exterior of the home (which is called a *rendering*). There you will see more precisely how the window looks.

Room dimensions are generally stated in feet and inches. For example, 20′ 6″ × 15′ means that the room is 20 feet 6 inches long and 15 feet wide. These figures are not very meaningful unless you have something to compare them with. As you study a plan, you might find it helpful to measure some of the rooms in your present house; this will give you a better idea of what the dimensions in the plan will mean when the house is built. The dimensions, incidentally, are *inside* dimensions—distances from one interior wall surface to another. For irregular, L-shaped rooms, two sets of dimensions are given, as if the two sections were separate rooms.

Continuing your tour into the bedroom area, you will find symbols for closets, usually with the largest storage space in the master bedroom and correspondingly smaller spaces in the second and third bedrooms. Look for the bathroom facilities, easy to recognize from the distinctive symbols for tubs, toilets and lavatories. Note the access routes. Most up-to-date designs allow for at least one full bath that can be reached from the central hall in the bedroom area and another that can be reached only from the master bedroom.

Once you have toured all areas of the house to check its facilities and the adequacy of its dimensions, there is another easy way to test the quality of the plan in one of its most important aspects—traffic circulation. Go back to the front entrance and see if it is possible to go directly to each of the three major zones without having to go through another. Try the same thing at the rear entry or the service entry. A house is much more livable when it's possible to go to the bedroom without hav-

FIGURE 3–9. Floor plan with architect's symbols.

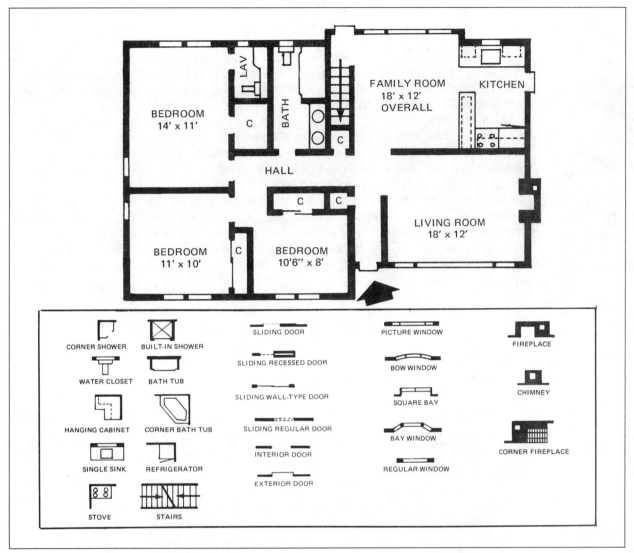

ing to go through the living room, or directly to the basement from the rear entrance without having to walk the full length of the kitchen.

INSPECTION CHECKLIST

The personality of a house is revealed in its door and window designs, roof lines, siding materials, use of color and other exterior features that give it a distinctive and handsome appearance. A house's interior is just as important as its exterior. You should be conscious of features relating to spaciousness, window placement, floor coverings, available wall space, openness of rooms, privacy, decorative details and luxurious appointments such as fireplaces, built-ins, hardware and millwork that contribute to a house's quality.

The traffic patterns within a house affect living patterns, yet many people are unaware of this relationship. A good traffic pattern or floor plan can be a great selling point—of which even the owner may not be aware. Rooms should not be corridors. People should not have to walk through living and dining rooms to get to other parts of the house. The family room, especially, should have a separate entrance to save wear and tear on the carpets. See if the rooms for quiet activities are situated near each other. It is a plus having the master bedroom located over the living room in a house where the place for noisy activity is the family room.

Be aware of centers of interest within a room, such as a fireplace or bay window. If an owner has decorated a room attractively, use this to learn what can be done with wall or floor space. Note the advantages of certain features, such as the way louvered doors help maintain an even circulation of air.

A house should be safe, durable, comfortable, economical to operate, easy to maintain and lasting in dollar value. Good construction and design impart these attributes. Houses differ widely, and good and bad construction methods, workmanship and materials are found in all price ranges. In some houses you get your money's worth, while in others you don't.

You won't learn all you need to know about good construction and design in the following chapters of this book. Even a construction expert can't give a totally accurate report on the condition of a house, simply because there are many things hidden from view. But if you know the facts on the different parts of the house, you will have the solid fundamentals that it takes to judge any house, new or old.

INSPECTION CHECKLIST

Room Sizes

Living Room: _____

Dining Room: _____

Kitchen: _____

Family Room: _____

Bedrooms: 1 _____   2 _____   3 _____   4 _____   5 _____

Bathrooms: 1 _____   2 _____   3 _____

Basement: _____

Garage: _____

Floor Plan	**Yes**	**No**
1. Are main interior zones—living, working, sleeping—clearly separated?	_____	_____
2. Does the front door not enter directly into the living room?	_____	_____
3. Is there a front hall closet?	_____	_____
4. Is there direct access from the front door to the kitchen, bathroom and bedrooms without passing through other rooms?	_____	_____
5. Is the rear door convenient to the kitchen and easy to reach from street, driveway and garage?	_____	_____
6. Is there a comfortable eating space for the family in or near the kitchen?	_____	_____
7. Is a separate dining area or dining room convenient to the kitchen?	_____	_____
8. Is a stairway located in a hallway or foyer instead of between levels of a room?	_____	_____
9. Are bedrooms concealed from the living room or foyer?	_____	_____
10. Are walls between bedrooms soundproof? (They should be separated by a bathroom or closet.)	_____	_____
11. Is the recreation room or family room well located?	_____	_____
12. Is the basement accessible from outside?	_____	_____
13. Are outdoor living areas accessible from the kitchen?	_____	_____
14. Are walls uninterrupted by doors and windows that could complicate furniture arrangement?	_____	_____

Kitchen	**Yes**	**No**
1. Is base cabinet storage space sufficient?	_____	_____
2. Is wall cabinet storage sufficient?	_____	_____
3. Is counter space sufficient?	_____	_____
4. Is lighting sufficient?	_____	_____

		Yes	No
5.	Is there a counter beside the refrigerator?	_____	_____
6.	Is there enough window area?	_____	_____
7.	Is the kitchen free of poorly placed doors that waste wall space?	_____	_____
8.	Are work areas separate from heavy traffic areas?	_____	_____
9.	Is there enough counter space on either side of the sink?	_____	_____
10.	Is there a counter beside the range?	_____	_____
11.	Are the sink, range and refrigerator close enough together?	_____	_____
12.	Is the kitchen modern enough?	_____	_____
13.	Are there lights over work centers?	_____	_____

Miscellaneous Things To Look For

		Yes	No
1.	Does the house have a full bathroom on each floor?	_____	_____
2.	Is there at least one bathroom for every two people?	_____	_____
3.	Is there adequate closet space throughout the house?	_____	_____
4.	Is the laundry area in a satisfactory location?	_____	_____
5.	Is the garage wide and long enough?	_____	_____
6.	Does the garage have direct access to the kitchen?	_____	_____

Overall Rating

	Good	Fair	Poor
Floor plan	_____	_____	_____
Room sizes	_____	_____	_____
Kitchen	_____	_____	_____
Bathrooms	_____	_____	_____
Living room	_____	_____	_____
Dining room	_____	_____	_____
Family room	_____	_____	_____
Bedroom	_____	_____	_____
Closets	_____	_____	_____
Storage	_____	_____	_____
Laundry area	_____	_____	_____
Basement	_____	_____	_____
Garage	_____	_____	_____

Major Problems: _____

Foundations and Framing

Throughout this chapter many construction terms and concepts will be presented and discussed. As you read, refer to the house diagram (appendix A), which provides an overall picture of how housing components fit together into the end product.

FOUNDATIONS

The foundation is the main support of a house. It is the substructure on which the superstructure rests. The foundation includes the footings, foundation walls, columns, pilasters, slab and all other parts that provide support for the house and transmit the load of the superstructure to the underlying earth (Figure 4–1).

Foundations are constructed of cut stone, stone and brick, concrete block or poured concrete. Poured concrete is the most common foundation material because of its strength and resistance to moisture.

Footings

A footing is a base for a wall (Figure 4–2) and is almost always made of reinforced concrete. Footings should be placed below the frost line so that the contractions caused by freezing will not heave them out of place. In warmer climates they may be placed only slightly below the surface of the soil. Sharp trenches may be cut into the soil to provide a form for the concrete footings, but if the soil does not permit this, wooden forms must be built for the concrete. A *key slot groove* in the top of a wall footing will act as a water barrier when the foundation wall is poured.

The size of the footings is based on the load-bearing capacity of the soil and on the thickness of the walls they will support. One rule of thumb is to make the footings twice as thick as the walls, with the walls centered on the footings. If the exterior of the house is wood—that is, wood stud construction and an exterior material such as siding or shingles—the foundation walls should be 8 inches thick and the footings must be at least 16 inches wide. If the exterior of the house is brick or stone veneer, the foundation walls should be 10 inches thick

FIGURE 4–1. Foundation.

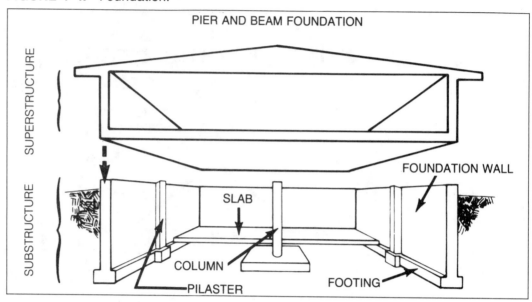

and the footings should be 20 inches wide. Steel reinforcing rods should be used in the footings wherever they cross pipe trenches. Wall footings on slopes may be stepped, with the vertical part of the step poured at the same time as the rest of the footing.

FIGURE 4–2. Wall footing.

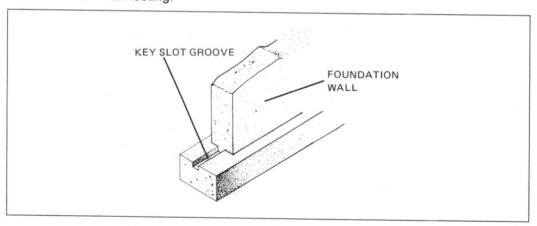

A footing for a pier, post or column should be square. Notice that in Figure 4–3 the footing is built up with a pedestal in which a steel pin is partially embedded. The pier, post or column is anchored to this pin. Piers are often used to support joists in the middle of a house with a crawl space or in vacation houses near lakes and rivers.

Foundation Walls

Foundation walls form an enclosure for basements or crawl spaces. They also carry wall, floor, roof and other building loads.

Most foundation walls are made of poured concrete or concrete block. For a poured concrete wall (Figure 4–4) wooden or lightweight metal formwork is constructed, and anchor bolts for the sill plate are placed partway into the top of the wall before the concrete sets. Concrete block walls can be placed without formwork (Figure 4–5), but if the blocks are arranged in a stack bond pattern they should be

FIGURE 4–3. Pier, post or column footing.

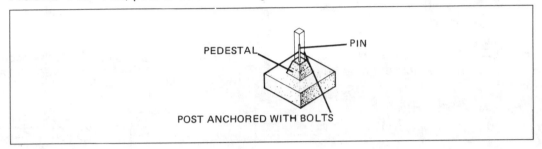

FIGURE 4–4. Poured concrete foundation wall.

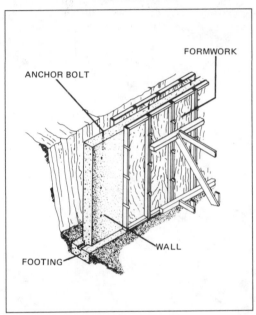

FIGURE 4–5. Concrete block foundation wall.

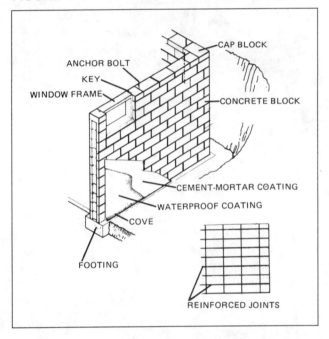

reinforced with steel rods. Some building codes also required *pilasters*, column-like supports, at interior corners.

Adequate waterproofing, provided by cement plastering and coating the outer foundation walls with tar or asphalt and installing a clay drainpipe and crushed stone around the outer perimeter of the foundation walls, is essential for any type of basement construction. Crawl spaces, much cheaper to construct than basements, are a must in areas with a high water table (ground water level). No excavation is necessary within crawl space walls, nor does a crawl space demand the outer foundation wall waterproofing and drainpipes required in a full basement.

The construction of a foundation wall is almost the same for houses with basements as for houses with crawl spaces. The only difference is the basement floor, which rests on one side of the footing.

Concrete Slab Foundations

A house built on a concrete slab usually has a foundation wall, as shown in Figure 4–6. The slab has a gravel base and rests on top of the foundation wall. It has to have insulation at the edge and waterproofing material called a *vapor barrier* under the slab.

Figures 4–6 through 4–8 dissect typical slab foundations—the *monolithic* slab, which is poured as a unit with the foundation wall, and the *floating* slab, which is poured after the foundation wall, with a layer of insulation in between. Insulated slabs, poured separately from the foundation walls, are usually used in cold climates.

FIGURE 4–6. Floating slab with reinforced grade beam.

FIGURE 4–7. Floating slab with concrete block wall.

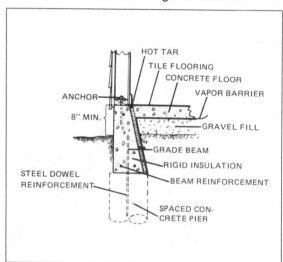

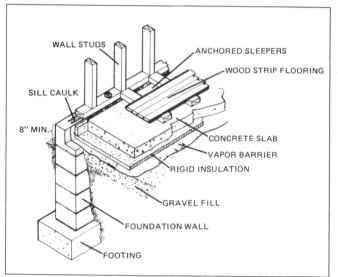

FIGURE 4–8. Monolithic thickened edge slab.

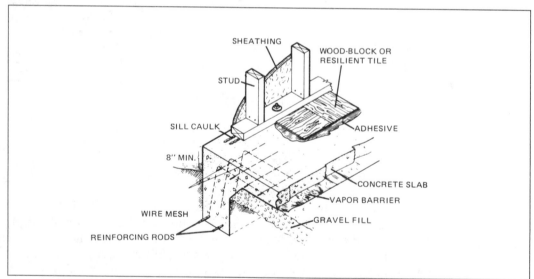

A concrete floor for such spaces as a garage or porch often doesn't rest on a foundation wall. Instead, the slab is poured with a thickened edge, as in Figure 4–8, which serves as a footing and provides the needed bearing surface. This type of slab floor is not used for basements.

Combination Foundations

Figure 4–9 illustrates a situation where several types of foundations are used in a single house. Part of the house has a full basement with a foundation wall. Another part has a crawl space with a shallow foundation wall and center piers. The attached garage has a concrete slab floor. A stepped footing is used when you want to combine a partial basement with crawl space or build a foundation wall on a sloping site.

FIGURE 4–9. Single house with several different foundations.

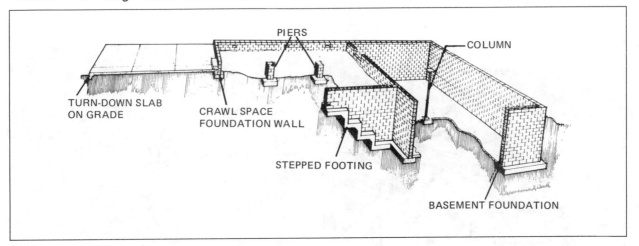

Inspecting the Basement

A basement is always the lowest level of a house and is usually left unfinished by the builder. As you have seen, the exterior walls of a basement are also the foundation walls of the house. If the basement of the house you are inspecting has not been finished, the exposed foundation walls can tell you a lot about the structural soundness of the house. For example, look for curves or bows in the foundation walls. They might indicate excessive weight being applied to that area.

Wet basements can cause extensive damage. Cement flaking from walls and dark stains on the ceiling and walls are common signs of leaks and seepage. Look also for mildew and wood rot in the basement ceiling beams and structure. Check the condition of the exterior foundation walls around the house. Are there cracks and signs of water penetration? Correcting a wet basement condition is often expensive and sometimes impossible if the house was not built properly.

A vapor barrier, one of the best features of today's well-built houses, protects basements from water damage. It is usually a thick polyethylene sheet laid on the earth underneath the house. In slab construction, the barrier is between the concrete floor and the layer of gravel spread over the ground. Although the barrier is completely hidden in slab or basement houses, it should be visible in crawl spaces. Clay drain tiles laid along the outer base of the foundation wall leading away from the house are another protection against basement water.

FLOOR FRAMING

Figures 4–6 through 4–11 also expose the flooring construction over a slab foundation. Tile can be laid over an adhesive that is applied directly to the concrete, or wood sleepers can be laid over the concrete to accept wood strip flooring. In cold climates, a heat duct may be run through the perimeter of the slab to help combat one of the slab foundation's major drawbacks.

Floor framing for houses with basements or crawl spaces consists of the same basic elements: wood or steel posts that support beams, sill plates anchored to the top of the foundation walls, joists supported by the beams, and a subfloor, usually plywood, laid over the joists. The plywood subflooring can run at right angles to the joists, but diagonal placement is most common. In any event, plywood subflooring should always end directly over a joist. The subflooring stabilizes the joists and keeps them from twisting or buckling. If the subflooring is at right angles to the joists, the finish flooring should run at right angles to it. If the subflooring is

FIGURE 4–10. Basement construction.

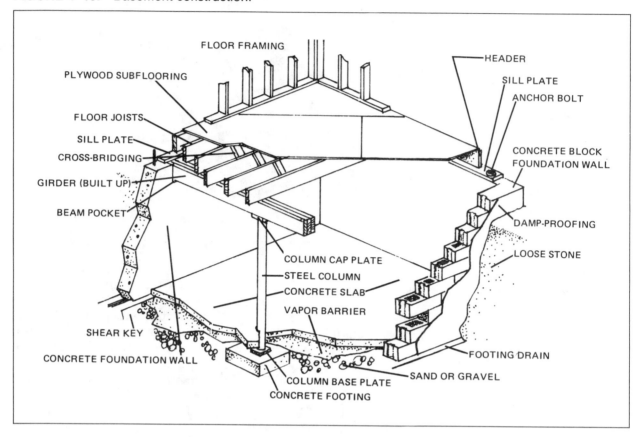

diagonal to the joists, however, the finish flooring can be laid either parallel or at right angles to the joists.

Plank-and-beam floor construction (Figure 4–11) makes use of 2-inch by 6-inch or 2-inch by 8-inch tongue-and-groove or splined boards nailed directly to beams. Boards should always end over a beam.

Defective Floors

Vibrations over a period of time may loosen the subflooring, causing houses to develop floor squeaks. High traffic areas in the house tend to develop squeaks first. However, keep in mind that the better the floor system has been constructed to carry the weight load, the less likely the floor will squeak when you walk over it.

There probably is no reason to be concerned with minor squeaks, but when other symptoms are evident, such as sagging and sloping floors, you need to find out if the problem is a basic structural one. Perhaps the floor joists are too small or lack support from adequate bridging, thereby causing the sagging or sloping. Excessive settlement of the house or defective framing can also cause floors to slope or sag—creating an even more difficult problem to deal with.

Floors that have been exposed to water may warp and bulge upward. Wide cracks between the floorboards are a sign of poor workmanship or shrinkage caused by wood that was improperly dried or not stored correctly at the time of installation.

If the floor is level and sound, but the finish is in bad condition, it can be refinished by sanding, applying a protective stain and adding one or more coats of lacquer or varnish.

FIGURE 4–11. Plank-and-beam floor.

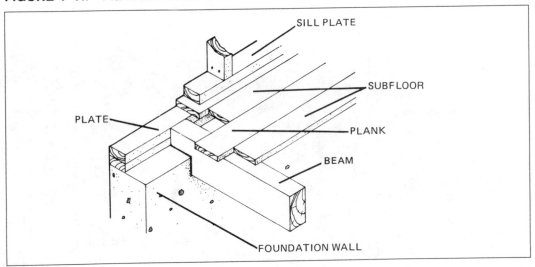

WALL FRAMING

Until about 1850, building construction was a rigorous, demanding task. Heavy wood beams had to be mortised and tenoned together or joined with wood dowels. Things changed, though, when the industrial revolution swept the construction industry. By 1850, machines were able to mass-produce nails for one-eighth of what they had been in 1800, and nails were a vital part of new building techniques. Relatively light wood beams, called joists, could now be nailed to supports, called studs, to form a framework for exterior and interior finishing.

Skeptics gave the new style the derisive term *balloon frame* because, they said, it would probably blow away with the first good wind. But they were wrong; the balloon frame proved both economical and practical. It was not difficult to build, and it required no special tools. The westward expansion of the United States probably owes as much to the balloon frame as it does to any other factor—including the gold rush. The incredible, almost overnight growth of cities like Chicago and San Francisco would not have been possible without a cheap, easily mastered building technique.

Other framing styles have evolved from the balloon frame, but all of them rely on the same kind of light structure. The true balloon frame, shown in Figure 4–12, has studs that run the full height of the building. The joists are nailed to the studs at the desired height of the next ceiling. Because of the openness of its construction, the balloon frame has poor fire resistance. The longer studs required for this type of construction cost more than the shorter studs used in other framing systems.

In *platform framing*, shorter studs, which are cheaper and easier to handle than those used in balloon framing, are assembled on the floor (platform) and lifted into place (Figure 4–13). This variation on the balloon frame is also called the western frame because of its popularity with the early settlers. Today it is the usual choice for both one-story and two-story residential structures, for it affords the best protection against the spread of fire.

The *plank-and-beam construction* is another light, easy-to-build frame. In this style, too, the studs extend only from floor to floor (Figure 4–14). Instead of joists, heavier beams support planks that form the subfloor. Plank-and-beam framing is used for contemporary designs where framing members are left exposed (as in exposed beam ceilings) to serve as part of the decor.

FIGURE 4–12.   Balloon frame construction.

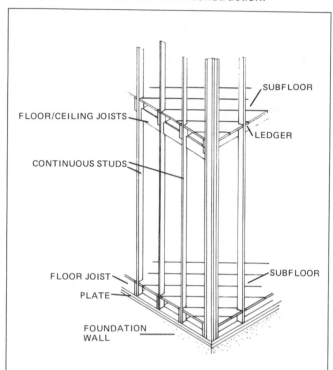

FIGURE 4–13.   Platform frame construction.

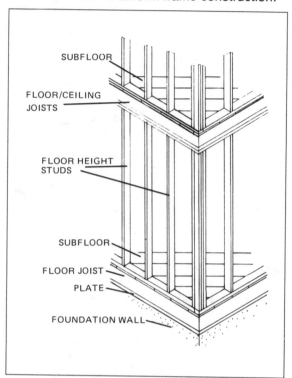

Figure 4–15 shows how window and door openings are made in the wall frame. The window may be higher, lower, wider or narrower than the example, as long as it retains all of the essential elements.

Defective House Framing

A defective house frame is difficult if not impossible to correct. You can often detect framing defects after a house is a few years old. If you encounter several signs of weakness, seek the advice of a competent builder as to what may be done to correct the problem.

Walls.   One sign of a structurally unsound house is bulging exterior walls, which you can see best by standing at each corner of the house and looking along the wall. A sure sign of frame trouble is a large crack developing on the outside of the house between the chimney and the exterior wall. Cracks running outward at an angle from the upper corners of windows and door frames are another tip-off to defective framing.

All cracks in the walls are a cause of concern, but they are not conclusive evidence of framing problems. Houses settle unless they are built on solid rock; rare is the house that does not develop some wall and ceiling cracks. These types of hairline cracks should be noted, but are of concern only when accompanied by other signs of defective framing. On the other hand, cracks that are wider at the top than the bottom, called V-cracks, should give cause for alarm. V-cracks are signs that point to a settlement problem.

Windows, Doors and Floors.   Jammed windows and window sills that are not level are signs of settling, defective framing or faulty carpentry. A careful house inspection includes the opening and closing of every window. Also, check all doors; a sagging frame could cause them to stick. Look at the bottom to see if they were resawed to allow free movement.

FIGURE 4–14. Plank-and-beam construction.

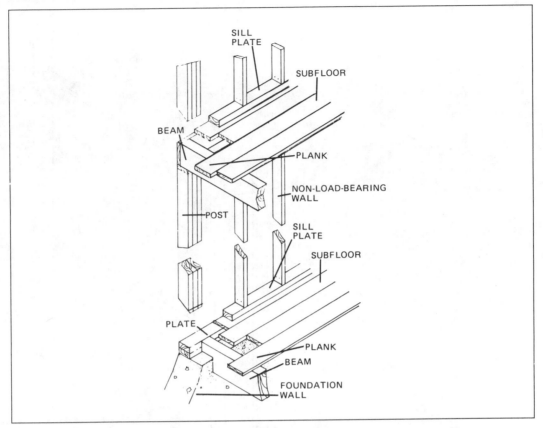

Sagging and sloping floors are usually easy to detect: an easy test is to place a marble on the floor and see if it rolls away. If it does, this may be a sign of a framing problem or it may be caused by defective floors only. If you suspect that a house is structurally unsound, get professional advice to confirm your opinion.

STAIRWAYS

Stairways are an integral part of the traffic pattern in a multistory house. A house may contain two types of stairways, both of which should regulate indoor traffic safely and conveniently. The main stairway must be wide and open, with enough headroom to allow for the passage of people and furniture. A well-designed and attractive main stairway can be a good selling point.

On the other hand, the service stairway leading to a basement or attic need not be visibly appealing, but should also be wide and convenient for the safe transport of bulky equipment. As with all other parts of the house, there are certain rules that must be followed in stairway construction, and special terms and parts that you need to know.

Terminology

Several of the terms that apply to stairways are given below. As you read, refer to Figure 4–16.

- The *run* is the total horizontal length of a stairway.
- The *rise* is the total vertical height from finished floor to finished floor.

FIGURE 4–15.   Window framing.

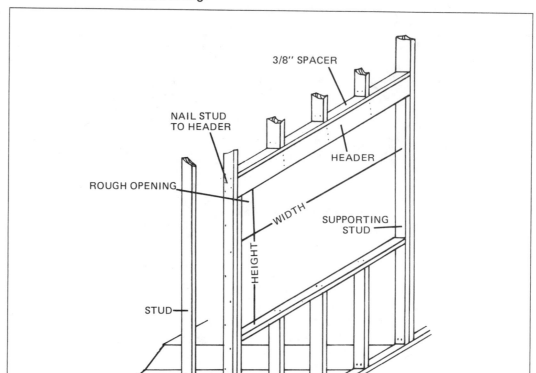

- A *tread* is the horizontal width of one step, measured from the face of one riser to the face of the next. Winders are wedge-shaped treads at turns.
- A *riser* is the vertical height of a step from tread to tread.
- A *stringer* is a long diagonal support that runs from one floor level to another on each side of the stairway. Stringers are cut to receive risers and treads.
- A *handrail* is the piece to grasp for support when ascending or descending a stairway.
- A *flight* is an unbroken series of steps.
- A *landing* is a platform that separates flights of steps.
- A *nosing line* is an imaginary diagonal line through the front edges of steps.

Stairway Design

Statistics show that nearly half of all accidents in the home are falls, many of which occur on steps. A steep stairway is dangerous, especially when going down, but a gradual stairway also can be dangerous if you have to take a longer-than-normal stride to step from tread to tread. Building codes based on HUD (Department of Housing and Urban Development) minimum property standards allow a maximum riser height of 8¼ inches and a minimum tread width of 9 inches.

Three other dimensions are relevant in stairway design: width, headroom and handrails.

FIGURE 4–16. Parts of a stairway.

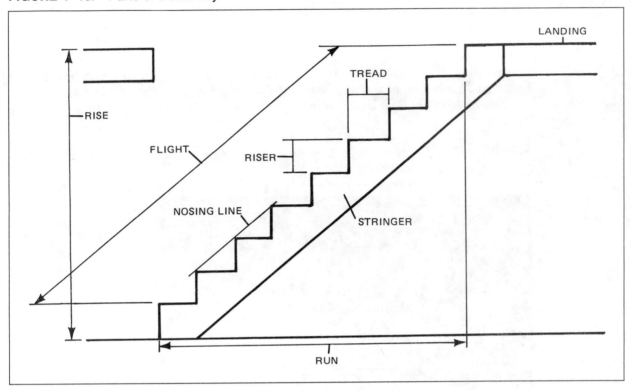

FIGURE 4–17. Standards for main stairs and basement stairs.

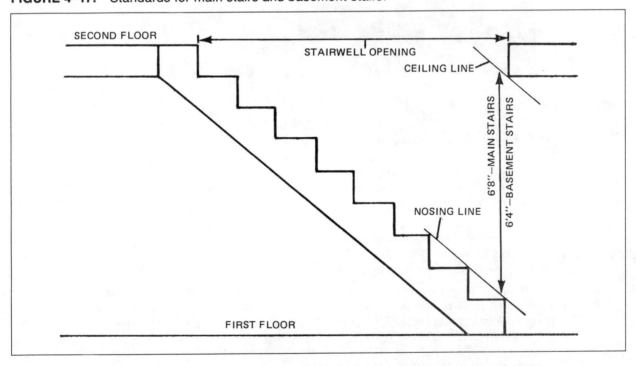

Width. A main stairway, the most heavily trafficked one, should be at least 36 inches wide from wall to wall; for basement stairs, 30 inches is sufficient. It would be difficult if not impossible to move furniture along a stairway any narrower than this.

Headroom.   The minimum vertical height between the nosing line and the ceiling of a main stairway should be 6 feet 8 inches; 6 feet 4 inches is adequate for a basement stairway (Figure 4–17). This is plenty of headroom despite the fact that clearance is less when descending the stairs than when going up.

Handrails.   These must be 30 to 34 inches above the nosing line. A handrail is required on one side of the stairway only, usually to the right as you descend.

Figure 4–18 shows a living room with an open stairway leading to the sleeping area.

FIGURE 4–18.   Open stairway with wall on one side. A closed stairway would have walls on both sides.

CEILING AND ROOF FRAMING

The basic requirement for ceiling construction is that the joists to which the gypsum or plasterboard is nailed be exactly 16 inches on center. Other than that, ceiling design depends on roof design.

TYPES OF ROOFS

Of the common roof designs in Figure 4–19, the easiest to build is the shed design, which rests on another wall. The flat roof appears the least complicated, but it requires extra waterproofing and extra wall support for heavy ceiling joists.

Conventional roof framing, seen in the gable design in Figure 4–20, relies on joists to which rafters are nailed. A *ridge board* runs along the peak of the gable to receive and align the rafters, and *collar beams* give rigidity to the rafters. Thanks to prefabricated *trusses*, most gable roofs can be assembled quickly and easily on site. Figure 4–21 shows two types of trussed rafters; both have upper and lower chords reinforced by *W* diagonals that take the place of the collar beams in the conventional roof. The wood used is usually 2 inches by 4 inches or 2 inches by 6

FIGURE 4–19. Roof types.

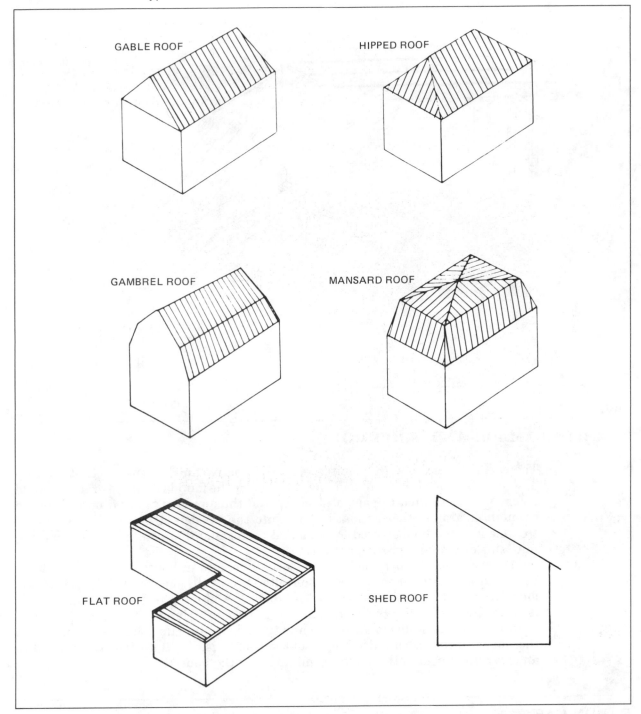

inches, with the lower chords either overlapping or abutting each other when they rest on a center wall. The framing members can be joined by ring and bolt or plywood gusset. The gusset plate is both glued and nailed.

Other popular styles of roof framing are illustrated in Figures 4–22, 4–23 and 4–24. By providing a clear expanse to the joists, which are the only ceiling and roofing members, they allow cathedral ceilings and large areas of glass on end walls.

FIGURE 4–20. Conventional roof framing.

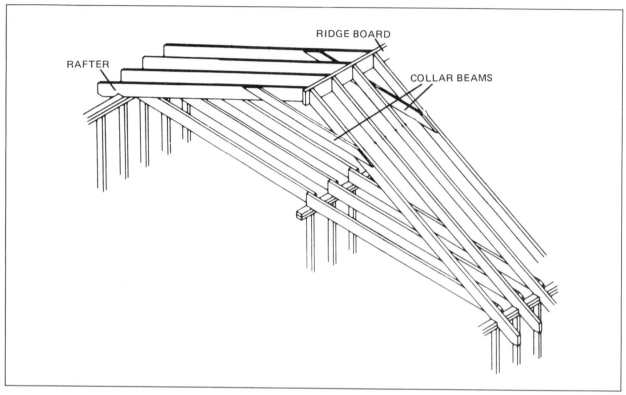

TERMITE DAMAGE AND WOOD ROT

The earth is infested with termites, extremely active ant-like insects that are very destructive to wood. Prior to pouring the slab for the foundation, the ground should be chemically treated to poison termites and thus prevent them from coming up through or around the foundation and into the wooden structure. The chemical treatment of the lumber used for sills and beams and the installation of metal termite shields will also provide protection.

Damage from termites or wood rot usually occurs in houses more than 5 to 10 years old and is hard to detect. A termite check calls for careful probing of the foundation and base wood structure of a house. A probing tool such as an ice pick is used. Normally, the pick will sink into a beam if it is eaten away inside. A telltale sign of termites is flattened mud tunnels leading up a foundation wall into the house. Termites can also be present without visible signs; it is best to call in an exterminator for a thorough examination of the house.

RADON GAS

Radon is a colorless, odorless, tasteless radioactive gas that comes from the natural breakdown of uranium. It can be found in most rocks and soils. Outdoors, it mixes with the air and is found in low concentrations that do not harm people. But indoors, it can accumulate and build up to levels that are dangerous.

High levels of radon in the home can increase your risk of developing lung cancer. Currently, this is the only known health effect. The Surgeon General recently drew attention to the dangers of radon by announcing that it is second only to smoking as a cause of lung cancer.

FIGURE 4–21.   Truss roof framing.

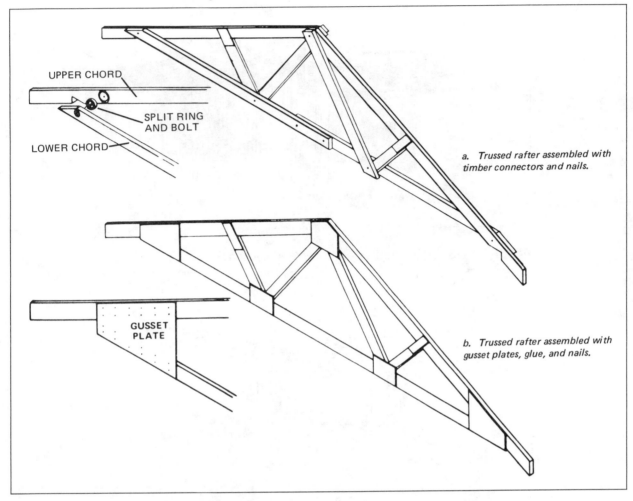

UPPER CHORD

SPLIT RING
AND BOLT

LOWER CHORD

*a. Trussed rafter assembled with
timber connectors and nails.*

GUSSET
PLATE

*b. Trussed rafter assembled with
gusset plates, glue, and nails.*

But how does radon get into a house? The amount of radon in your home depends on the home's construction and the concentration of radon in the soil underneath it.

Refer to the graphic in appendix C. Radon can enter a home through dirt floors, cracks in concrete foundations, floors and walls, floor drains, tiny cracks or pores in hollow-block walls, loose-fitting pipes, exhaust fans, sump pumps and many other unsuspected places, including even the water supply.

A lot of the variation in radon levels has to do with the airtightness of a house. The more energy-efficient a home, the more likely that it will have higher radon levels. In the average house, there is one complete air exchange every six to seven hours. That is, about four times a day all the air from inside the house is exchanged with outside air. The tighter your house, the more likely it is that the air exchange will come from beneath the house, from the air over the soil that may contain high levels of radon gas.

INSPECTION CHECKLIST

You can repair minor problems like leaky gutters and squeaky doors with a little time and money. But some parts of a home's foundation and framing are, for all practical purposes, invisible. Therefore, evaluation of them becomes difficult even

FIGURE 4–22.   Sloped joist roof framing.

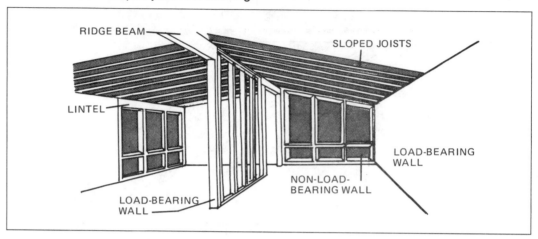

FIGURE 4–23.   Plank-and-beam roof framing—longitudinal beams.

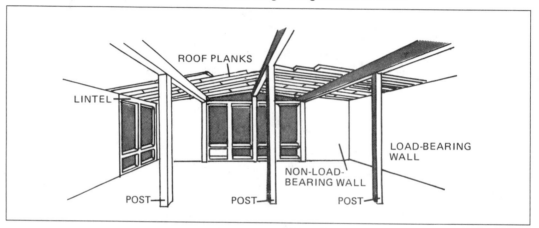

FIGURE 4–24.   Plank-and-beam roof framing—transverse beams.

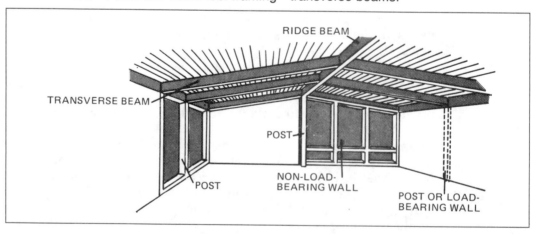

for the careful homebuyer. Because these things are hidden, they are often overlooked. And, in fact, there is no way to be positive that a small crack in the foundation, for example, won't enlarge, or that there is good drainage beneath the foundation.

Inspecting the structural aspects of a home can be a confusing, bewildering experience for some homebuyers, especially if they've never bought a house before.

The checklist on the next page will help you ask the right questions, be alert to features, and get the information you need to make an intelligent decision.

If, however, after going through the checklist, you still have doubts about the structural soundness of the house, you should hire a professional to make a complete inspection. A professional knows what to look for and what the various defects in the house will cost to correct.

INSPECTION CHECKLIST

Structural Information

Foundation: poured concrete/concrete block/stone/brick

Wall Framing: platform/balloon/plank-and-beam/other

Roof Types: gable/hipped/gambrel/mansard/flat/other

		Yes	No
1.	Is the house situated on an elevated part of the lot for good drainage?	_____	_____
2.	Does water flow away from the house (not settle into the foundation)?	_____	_____
3.	Are the foundation walls free of vertical cracks?	_____	_____
4.	If cracks exist, are they hairline cracks rather than V-cracks?	_____	_____
5.	From the crawl space, is the foundation free of large cracks?	_____	_____
6.	Are piers in the crawl space free of cracks?	_____	_____
7.	Does the crawl space have adequate ventilation?	_____	_____
8.	Are the foundation walls straight? (Make sure there are no obvious curves or bows.)	_____	_____
9.	Does the house (with a basement) have a foundation drain system; that is, gravel and pipe that lead water away from the house?	_____	_____
10.	Are there properly installed vapor barriers?	_____	_____
11.	Does the house smell clean (not musty)?	_____	_____
12.	Are the basement walls dry?	_____	_____
13.	Does the slab floor feel dry?	_____	_____
14.	Are the roof, windows, and walls free of leakage warning signs?	_____	_____
15.	Has there been a recent termite check by an exterminator?	_____	_____
16.	Are wood beams and surfaces free of termites or wood rot?	_____	_____
17.	Are the floors firm? (Squeaks might be part of a serious structural problem.)	_____	_____
18.	Are the floors level? (Make sure they don't sag or slope.)	_____	_____
19.	Has the house been tested for radon gas?	_____	_____
20.	Is the radon level within safe standards?	_____	_____
21.	Do all windows fit and operate easily?	_____	_____
22.	Do all doors open and close easily?	_____	_____

	Yes	No
23. Is the driveway free of severe cracks?	_____	_____
Is the patio?	_____	_____
Are the walks?	_____	_____
24. Are ceilings level? (Make sure they don't sag.)	_____	_____
25. Is the height of each step (the rise) in the stairway the same?	_____	_____
26. Is the width of each step (tread) the same size and deep enough to accommodate a large foot?	_____	_____
27. Are the stairs solid when you walk on them; that is, they do not squeak or bounce when weight is applied?	_____	_____
28. Is there a handrail on each stairway (particularly on steep ones)?	_____	_____

Overall Rating	Good	Fair	Poor
Foundation:	_____	_____	_____
Drainage:	_____	_____	_____
Framing:	_____	_____	_____
Radon gas level:	_____	_____	_____
Termites:	_____	_____	_____

Major Problems: _____

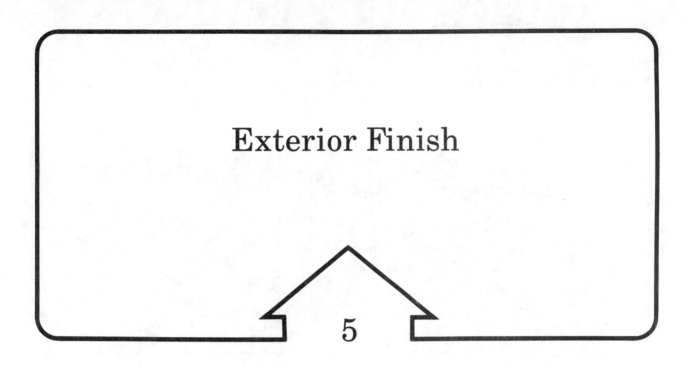

Exterior Finish

5

The roof and siding together form the protective exterior of the house. Applied layer by layer, they create a seamless series of overlapping materials that keep out rain, snow and winds. They also hold in heat during the cold winter months and cool air during the hot summer months.

The roof and siding also constitute most of the decorative elements of the home's exterior. Although the house may have shutters, trim on the eaves or architectural features such as a stone chimney, a circular glass bay or a skylight, the roof and siding are the main things a potential buyer will notice. That means they should be appropriate to the style of the house, they should harmonize with one another and they should be in good repair.

The previous chapter examined the major structural components of a house, including floor, wall and roof framing. This chapter focuses on nonstructural elements, referred to as *finish*. Exterior finish comprises such items as windows, doors and stairs as well as wall and roof covering.

ROOF SHEATHING

After the wall studs and roof rafters are in place, they are sheathed, or covered with 1-inch lumber or plywood. This covering braces the house frame, eliminating most of the stress from earthquakes, settling or other ground movement. Board sheathing may be laid either horizontally or vertically, and the boards may be closed or spaced. Spaced boards are used in damp climates to allow for expansion and closed boards are recommended for areas with wind-driven snows. For purposes of illustration, Figure 5–1 shows both on the same roof; in reality you would use one or the other.

Plywood offers flexibility in roof design, for it is equally effective under any type of shingles or built-up roofing. It is a durable material that can be installed with minimal waste. Unsanded (sheathing grade) plywood is ordinarily used, and it is laid with the grain perpendicular to the rafters, as illustrated in Figure 5–2.

FIGURE 5–1. Open and closed board roof sheathing.

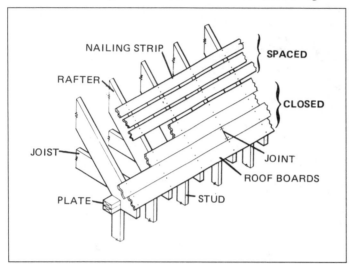

FIGURE 5–2. Plywood roof sheathing.

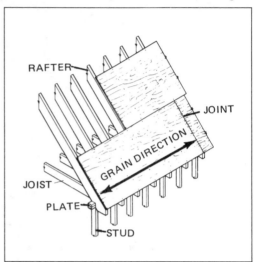

Sheathing Paper

Overlapping strips of waterproof sheathing paper are placed on the boards or plywood. The paper prepares the roof for the final exterior cover of wood or asphalt shingles, metal sheeting, tiles or slate. Figure 5–3 illustrates the application of wood shingles over plywood sheathing covered with sheathing paper, which is water-resistant but not vapor-resistant. Gable ends that extend beyond the exterior wall line can be closed off to form a cornice.

This area also allows for attic ventilation through a screened slot that extends the length of the soffit board. Smaller ventilators can be used in the narrow box cornice. The wide box cornice depicted in Figure 5–4 includes a horizontal board, the lookout, which lends additional support.

FIGURE 5–3. Roof covering and narrow box cornice.

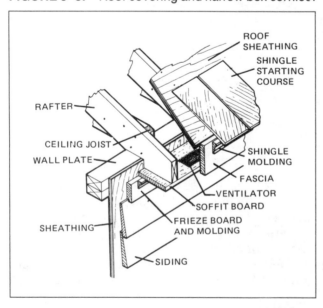

FIGURE 5–4. Wide box cornice.

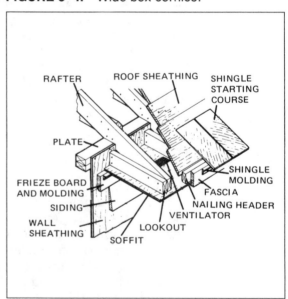

Roofing Felt

In cold areas, heavier roofing felt is used in place of paper sheathing to guard against ice dams that can form on gable ends when melting snow from the roof reaches the colder cornice.

The ice eventually backs up under the shingles, too. Roofing felt, available in 36-inch-wide rolls, is laid horizontally, with higher layers overlapping lower ones.

Figure 5–5 illustrates how ice accumulation can effectively dam a roof eave: melted snow and ice saturate the wood framing, setting the stage for deterioration and decay.

Good attic ventilation, like that provided by soffit ventilators, is also necessary to prevent ice dams from forming.

FIGURE 5–5.   Ice accumulation along roof eave.

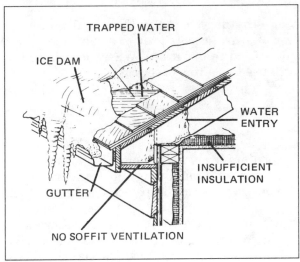

FIGURE 5–6.   Application of asphalt shingles.

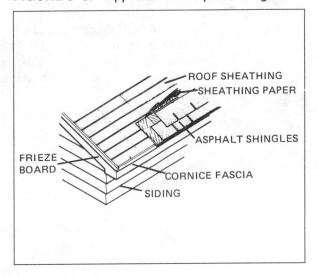

ROOF COVERINGS

The appearance of a roof is perhaps less important than its practicality. The main concern is whether it will provide adequate protection. However, you should consider looks as well as strength.

The usual roof coverings are asphalt shingles, wood shingles and shakes, tile and slate. Each of the various kinds of materials used in roofing has its own special qualities.

Asphalt Shingles

Reasonably priced, easy to install, and available in a wide variety of styles and colors, asphalt shingles cover more roofs in this country than any other roofing material. They have a center core made from cellulose fibers or fiberglass that is coated with asphalt on both sides and topped with a protective mineral aggregate. Asphalt shingles come in 12-inch by 36-inch strips that, when overlapped and nailed in place, give the appearance of individual shingles (Figure 5–6). They cost less in terms of labor and materials than individually nailed wood shingles or shakes, and they need replacement less frequently.

Underwriters Laboratories (UL) rate asphalt shingles A, B, or C, with A being the highest in fire resistance.

Wood Shakes and Shingles

Shakes are made from pieces of wood that have been machine- or hand-split; they are lapped when put in place on the roof. Wood shingles are the same as shakes, except they are smaller and lighter—and less expensive. Both shingles and shakes are mostly cut from red cedar, requiring no paint or stain.

Tile or Slate

Tile or slate roofs are expensive and heavy, requiring a stronger roof support structure than shingles. Many people find such roofs extremely attractive, especially if the house is of a Spanish-style design. However, tile and slate are brittle as well as hard and can break. But they are fireproof and will last a lifetime.

Roll Roofing

Roll roofing is composed of the same materials as asphalt shingles, but it comes in a roll rather than individual strips. The roll is applied like felt, with tar at the edges.

Built-Up Roof

Flat or low-pitched roofs may be *built-up*—that is, covered by three to five layers of tar-coated roofing felt and a final layer of gravel-covered tar or a cap sheet of roll roofing. Gravel-covered tar is frequently used in dry areas. Where local building codes allow, rolls of plastic film are also used as a roof covering.

INSPECTING THE ROOF AND GUTTERS

Stand back and look at the roof (use binoculars if you have them). Try to determine the type and age of the roof so you can estimate its remaining life. If the house has asphalt shingles, as do the majority of houses, they can be expected to last 15 to 20 years.

Dark patches on asphalt shingles indicate that the surface granules have worn away. These are weak spots in the roof. Are any shingles broken, cracked or curled, which could allow water to seep underneath? These are sure signs that the roof is comparatively old and has not been kept up. Are any shingles missing? Once one is missing, the wind will begin to pull others away.

Look at the flashing around vent pipes, chimneys or the conjunction of two walls. Cracks or gaps in caulking material are a possible source of leaks. Check to see that the flashing on the chimney is still firmly embedded in the mortar between the bricks. Loose mortar will allow water to get behind the flashing.

Carefully check the valleys on the roof to be sure they are undamaged and in good condition—and free of debris.

On flat roofs, a low spot where water collects is potential trouble. Look for bubbles in a tar and gravel roof, which often indicate moisture has worked its way under the roofing felt.

Now move closer to the house and look up at the eaves for obvious signs of rot or decay. This is a particularly common area for rot to set in because water can be driven up under the shingles through rain or freezing action. Push the tip of an ice pick or screwdriver into the wood on the edge of the eaves to check for wood rot.

Gutters are installed on eaves to collect rain or melting snow from the roof and channel it into downspouts that direct the water away from the house foundation. All gutters should be examined for leaks, cracks and weak spots. They should be clean, without sags, and firmly in place. Leaking gutters can cause damage to siding and trim and allow water to enter the basement.

Note the material from which the gutters are made. Galvanized metal gutters are the most common kind and must be kept painted inside and out. They require less frequent painting if they have a baked-on factory finish. Although seldom seen today, wood gutters were once the standard. Aluminum and vinyl gutters require virtually no maintenance and are a good investment.

The best time to check for roof and gutter leaks is during a heavy rain. Signs of trouble include water flowing over the top of the gutter, leaks at seams and other places, sagging gutters, damaged downspouts, corrosion and evidence of loose spikes and straps.

When the gutter-downspout system isn't functioning properly, the homeowner will pay for it sooner or later. Water that fails to drain away from the house will cause damage to the structure in the form of leaking and flooding, which are the very things gutters and downspouts are designed to prevent.

Now take a good flashlight and check inside the attic for leaks. If the house has an uninsulated attic, light may shine in through holes in the roof. Carefully look over each rafter. Even if you haven't seen a leak in the house, water could be leaking through the roof, running down a rafter and dropping between the siding and the inside wall, a situation you can spot by telltale water stains on the rafter. Use your screwdriver to poke any suspicious-looking spots for possible wood rot.

WALL SHEATHING

Wall sheathing serves the same important function as roof sheathing by bracing the house against ground movement. The best wall sheathing begins at the foundation wall and is nailed securely to the wall studs. The four most common wall sheathing materials are wood, plywood, fiberboard and gypsum. Sheathing may be applied horizontally or vertically, depending on the material selected.

Plywood sheathing adds considerably more strength to the frame than do diagonally spaced boards. Plywood is usually applied vertically to exterior walls, as in Figure 5–7; it can be applied horizontally, but only with diagonal bracing or horizontal blocking between studs.

FIGURE 5–7. Vertical plywood sheathing.

As with roof sheathing, sheathing paper should be applied next to provide a water barrier. It is not usually used over sheet materials such as plywood, for these are already water-resistant.

EXTERIOR WALL COVERINGS

Exterior wall coverings fall into four general categories: siding, which can be wood or a nonwood material such as aluminum or vinyl; shingles and shakes, which can be wood or a nonwood material such as asbestos-cement shingles; masonry veneer, which may be used in combination with siding; and stucco or other **cement-plaster** finish.

Wood Siding

Wood siding is the most widely used exterior wall covering. It is available in a variety of sizes, shapes and edge treatments and can be installed either horizontally or vertically, depending on the type selected. Bevel siding is suited to horizontal application (Figure 5–8). Drop siding may be arranged either horizontally or vertically; it is applied directly to the studs, so it serves as both sheathing and exterior wall covering. Board siding is suited to a vertical, board-and-batten type of application and to horizontal (clapboard) application. Plywood and similar sheet materials are usually applied vertically. Shingles and shakes are popular choices in siding, largely because they are easy to install. Shakes are a thicker, rougher type of shingle.

FIGURE 5–8.   Vertical and horizontal siding.

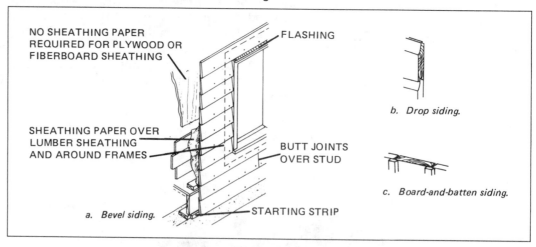

Wood is a good, durable insulator. It is easy to cut, fit and nail into place. With wood surfaces, walls can be easily altered or repaired. Most types of wood siding are furnished in paint-primed condition to protect them from moisture. Exceptions are cedar and redwood, which may be stained or left to weather to a neutral gray color.

Aluminum Siding

Aluminum siding has long been used to resurface older houses but is now a strong competitor with wood and other materials on the exterior of new houses in all price classes. Although it is thin, its backing of fiberboard or polystyrene foam improves the insulating characteristics of the siding and makes it more dent-resistant.

Aluminum siding is available in a variety of colors that do not fade. It can be bought with a baked-on enamel finish or with a vinyl coat that never needs paint. The surface can be smooth or embossed for a wood-grain effect, as in Figure 5–9.

Soffits.   The overhang is probably the most difficult and cumbersome part of any house to repaint. That's why so many homeowners today are installing aluminum or vinyl soffits (eave coverings) and fascias (roof trim) to protect the roof overhang from the effects of moisture condensation that can destroy paint and promote wood decay.

Soffit panels should provide some ventilation, however, to prevent excessive moisture buildup in the walls and ceilings. Soffits with lanced louver vents can be installed in combination with solid panels to provide proper ventilation. The soffit, gutter, downspout and trim in Figure 5–10 are all made of aluminum with a baked-on enamel finish that is virtually maintenance-free.

FIGURE 5–9. Wood-grain aluminum siding.

FIGURE 5–10. Aluminum soffit, gutter and downspout.

Window Frames. Peeled and cracked wood window frames can also be covered with aluminum window trim for long-lasting protection.

Vinyl Siding

Solid vinyl siding is impervious to common exterior problems, such as peeling and denting. Like aluminum siding, it can be bought with either a smooth or wood-grain surface. Vinyl is used for finishing new homes as well as for re-siding old ones.

Brick Veneer

Figure 5–11 dissects a brick-veneered wall, the most common type of masonry material used on houses. Standard 4-inch brick needs a 10-inch-wide foundation wall; the brick rests on the outside 4 inches and a stud wall on the inside 4 inches. The brick wall covers the structure but does not support it. The stud wall provides the support. The space between the two walls is dead airspace that has good insulating value and prevents condensation.

Refer to Figure 5–11 as you read. Starting with the inside of the wall, you will first encounter wallboard or plaster. Next is a vapor barrier made of paper, plastic or metal to keep moisture in the house from getting into the wall. Insulating material fills the space between the upright studs. Nailed to the outside of the studs is the sheathing—usually plywood sheets or insulating boards. Over the sheathing is sheathing paper to keep out wind and water. Flashing at the base of this paper carries off water from the wall, and weep holes between bricks allow water to escape. Finally, metal anchors tie the brick wall to the frame wall.

Face brick should be chosen for both color and texture, since both affect the appearance of the house. Textures range from smooth to ribbed to very rough. Colors are various shades of brown and red, ranging from light tan to chocolate and from pale pink to dark red. Brick can also be bought in a few other colors, such as white, blue and yellow.

FIGURE 5–11.   Cutaway of brick-veneered wall.

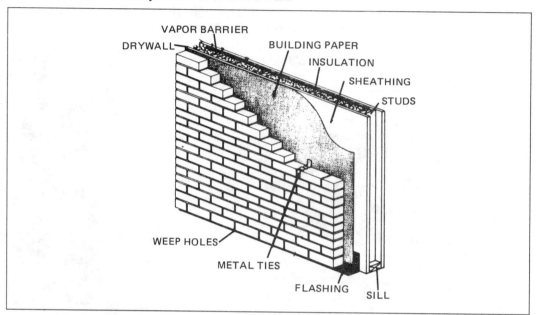

Stucco

A form of plaster, stucco is one of the most durable exterior sidings available for houses. It is an attractive, versatile and low-maintenance material that can be applied to such things as concrete block, clay tile or most commonly to metal lath attached to a wood frame. Stucco can be given a smooth finish or a rough texture. It can be left its natural color, which is light gray, it can be bought with color added, or it can be painted. Stucco surfaces that don't have waterproofing in the mix need to be sealed to prevent moisture from entering the wall. If moisture gets in, it can swell the wood and push the stucco away from the wall. Or, dry rot may result, ultimately causing the stucco to fall off.

INSPECTING THE SIDING

Siding is the most visible part of the exterior of a house, so look it over carefully. It may have problems, but generally there will be fewer than you might find on a roof because it is less susceptible to sun, wind and storm damage.

On wood siding, look at the paint job first. If you see extensive bubbling, cracking or peeling, it may mean that the house has insufficient vapor barrier protection. This can happen if the house is not insulated, or if the insulation does not have a vapor barrier on it. The vapor barrier is designed to stop the moisture in a house from moving through the walls where it may condense on meeting cold outside air.

Look for cracks in the exterior sheathing. Water can work its way through a crack to the inside of the wall and cause wood rot.

Check the trim around the doors and windows and at the corners of the house. It should be firmly in place and well caulked. There should be a tight seal where siding meets chimney masonry.

Aluminum siding has many advantages over wood. Very little upkeep is required. A good washing once a year should keep the home looking good. Colors will not fade or chip on aluminum. However, replacement costs can be considerable. Aluminum can be damaged or bent, so you need to check carefully for dents and scratches.

Brick is probably the sturdiest building material for outside walls. Barring a major disaster, it should last forever.

The basic maintenance problem with brick concerns the mortar that holds the bricks together. This can dry, crack and crumble through the combined effect of wind, rain, snow, stresses and strains in the walls and so on. Repair costs can be high. If you fail to replace crumbly mortar, leaks may occur inside the house, weakening the wall structure and causing damage to the finished interior. So look for cracked bricks and signs of mortar wear.

A stucco surface can be very attractive, but it too will require some looking after. Stucco can crack and peel and might need more than an occasional paint job. You should check all stucco surfaces for settlement cracks, which might indicate a problem in the structural wall. Look also for off-color patches in the stucco, possibly suggesting problem areas that may or may not have been cured.

WINDOWS AND DOORS

Windows and doors contribute to the overall tone of a house. Solid, heavy doors suggest stability, and large expanses of glass lend an open, airy feel to a house. Windows and doors have functional aims as well. Skillful placement of doors regulates traffic patterns through the house and secures it from intruders. Windows, in turn, admit light and a view from the outside.

WINDOW FUNCTIONS

A window serves three different functions: It lets in light, it provides ventilation, and it allows a view of the outside. Thanks to air-conditioning and improvements in the quality and intensity of artificial light, windows are no longer crucial for light and fresh air. But since house design has changed over the years to create more intimate indoor-outdoor relationships, the third function—to allow a view of the outside—has gained prominence. As we become more isolated in our daily living, we feel a stronger need to see what is going on outside of the house.

Windows do more for a house than admit light, air and a scenic view outward. They are also an important part of the architectural design of a house. Poorly proportioned, awkwardly placed windows can ruin an otherwise successfully designed house. There should be a balance of fixed picture windows and operating windows. An operating window can be closed to seal out unpleasant weather or opened to a cooling breeze, but a fixed window can never be opened. Climate and the orientation of the house on the site determine the best window placement and the degree of ventilation required.

The main parts of a window are shown in Figure 5–12.

TYPES OF WINDOWS

Windows come in a wide variety of types and sizes, both in wood and metal (usually aluminum). Wood is preferred where temperatures fall below freezing. Although metal windows require less maintenance than wood, the frames get colder in winter and panes frost up and drip from moisture condensation. Windows may be sliding, swinging or fixed (see Figure 5–13). A window will fit more than one category if part of it is fixed and another part slides.

FIGURE 5–12.   Parts of a window.

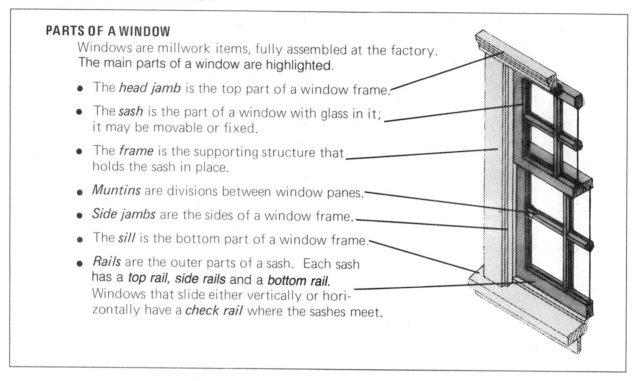

PARTS OF A WINDOW

Windows are millwork items, fully assembled at the factory. The main parts of a window are highlighted.

- The *head jamb* is the top part of a window frame.

- The *sash* is the part of a window with glass in it; it may be movable or fixed.

- The *frame* is the supporting structure that holds the sash in place.

- *Muntins* are divisions between window panes.

- *Side jambs* are the sides of a window frame.

- The *sill* is the bottom part of a window frame.

- *Rails* are the outer parts of a sash. Each sash has a **top rail, side rails** and a *bottom rail.* Windows that slide either vertically or horizontally have a **check rail** where the sashes meet.

Sliding Windows

The most commonly used window today is still the sliding window. And of the two typical types of sliding windows, the double-hung window is still most popular among builders, particularly in traditional houses.

Double-Hung Windows.   The double-hung window has both an upper and lower sash that slide vertically along separate tracks. This arrangement allows cool air to come in at the bottom and warm air to go out through the top. Double-hung windows are easy to fit with screens and storm windows, and they don't interfere with draperies and other window treatments. Unfortunately, only half the window can be opened at any one time for ventilation, and it can't be left open during a hard rain.

Horizontal Sliding Windows.   The horizontal sliding window moves back and forth on tracks. As with the double-hung type, only 50 percent of this window can be opened for fresh air. However, sliding windows usually provide more light and a better view of the outside.

Swinging Windows

Casements, awnings, hoppers and jalousies are four common types of swinging windows.

Casement Windows.   Casement windows are hinged at the side and open outward. Unlike double-hung and sliding windows, which have screens and storm windows on the outside, casements have a place for screens and storms on the inside. One advantage of the casement window is that the entire window can be opened for ventilation.

FIGURE 5–13. Window types.

Awning Windows. An awning window is hinged at the top and swings open at the bottom, providing good ventilation and protection from the rain. It is used most often in bathrooms and bedrooms, where privacy is needed.

Hopper Windows. A hopper window is hinged at the bottom and opens into the room, which can interfere with drapes and other window treatments. It is best suited to a basement, where the hopper opens above head level and there is little danger of bumping into it.

Jalousie Windows. Jalousie, or louver, windows consist of a series of overlapping horizontal glass louvers that pivot together in a common frame and are opened and closed with a lever or crank. In a sunroom or porch the jalousie combines protection from the weather with maximum ventilation. Insulating capabilities may be improved by inside storm panels, designed to be interchangeable with screens.

Fixed Windows

A fixed window (Figure 5–14) usually consists of a wood sash with a large single pane of insulated glass that cannot be opened for ventilation. It provides natural light and at the same time gives a clear view of the outside. Fixed windows are often used in combination with other windows. A fixed window in a living room or family room is sometimes flanked by a pair of casement or double-hung windows.

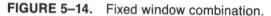
FIGURE 5–14. Fixed window combination.

Other Types

Bay Windows. A bay window projects from the side of the house, with two side windows on an angle and a center one parallel to the house wall. Bay windows add space to a room and provide more light and ventilation than a conventional window arrangement.

Triple-Track Windows. The triple-track window is self-storing. Glass and screen inserts slide vertically or horizontally along separate tracks mounted in a frame. The self-storing feature eliminates the need for switching storms and screens every spring and fall. They can be slid into place from inside the house.

Skylights. Skylights can bring both natural illumination and the heat of the sun into rooms. A skylight lets about five times as much daylight into an area as a window of the same size. As a result, a skylight can make a small space appear brighter and larger than it actually is. A skylight is also an excellent way to bring light into a room with an obstructed or unsightly view.

Because older skylights tended to be poorly insulated and badly placed, they were labeled energy wasters. But with a little guidance on purchasing and placement, they can actually save energy both in the winter and in the summer.

The local climate is the single most important factor in determining the right skylight for a house. In cold climates, heat loss through the skylight can be a problem; in warm climates, heat gain through the unit can translate into higher cooling costs. Therefore, skylights, like windows, should generally be installed on the south side of a house in a colder climate or on the north side of a house in a warmer climate.

In a predominantly cold climate, a clear, domed skylight combined with an insulating shade or storm window is the best choice. Conversely, in a warm climate, frosted or tinted skylights that open to vent excess heat and feature a shading device work best. Although the tint will slightly reduce illumination, it can also help to cut down on glare and heat gain.

LOCATION OF EXTERIOR DOORS

Exterior doors control passage in and out of the house. They are usually found in three locations around the house:

- The *main entrance door* is almost always the most attractive and most prominent door in the house. It serves as both a passage and a barrier and should be located on the street side of the house.
- The *service door* leads outside from rooms such as the kitchen, utility room, basement or garage. Service doors are important for good traffic flow in the house.
- The *patio door* is like the picture window in tying together indoors and outdoors. This door usually opens from a family room, living room, or dining area onto a patio, porch or terrace, and it fills the largest single opening in the wall of a house. The patio door often serves all the purposes that a door can—letting in light and air, allowing a view to the outside, and providing access between areas.

PARTS OF A DOOR

The main parts of a door are visible in Figure 5–15.

FIGURE 5–15. Parts of a door.

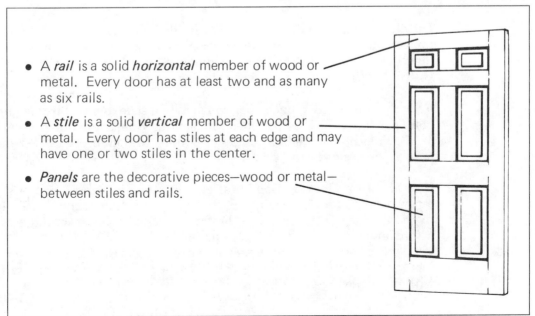

- A *rail* is a solid *horizontal* member of wood or metal. Every door has at least two and as many as six rails.
- A *stile* is a solid *vertical* member of wood or metal. Every door has stiles at each edge and may have one or two stiles in the center.
- *Panels* are the decorative pieces—wood or metal—between stiles and rails.

TYPES OF DOORS

Exterior doors are made from wood or metal and are available in many styles. Like windows, door styles must be compatible with the architectural design of the house. For example, the standard six-panel door is a popular choice for an Early American house.

Doors are most often classified by construction and appearance—the three prevailing types being flush, panel and sliding glass (see Figure 5–16). Panel and French doors fit best with traditionally styled houses, while flush doors blend better with the simpler lines of contemporary houses. Sliding glass doors, while contemporary in design, are appropriate to any style of house.

Flush Doors

Flush doors are most often made with plywood or hardwood face panels bonded to *solid* or *hollow* cores of light framework. Solid cores are generally preferred for exterior doors because they provide better heat and sound insulation and are more resistant to warping. Hollow-core doors are about a third as heavy as the solid-core type. They are used for interior locations, where heat and sound insulation are not critical.

Panel Doors

Panel doors consist of stiles and rails enclosing flat plywood, raised wood panel fillers or a combination of wood and glass panels. They are available in a variety of designs that are suited to both interior and exterior use.

Sliding Glass Doors

Sliding glass doors have at least one fixed panel and one or more panels that slide in a frame of wood or metal. Like a window sash, the door panels are composed of stiles and rails and may hold either single or insulating glass, depending on the local climate. Most glass doors provide self-storing screens in a separate track of the door frame. Snap-in muntins of wood or vinyl can be added to create a traditional appearance.

Other Types

Dutch Doors.   This type of door is divided horizontally in the middle so that the top can open independently of the bottom. A locking device holds the two sections together so that they can be opened as a single door. Although effective in design, Dutch doors are expensive to weatherstrip and screen properly.

French Doors.   A French door consists of a stile and rail frame enclosing a large glass panel that has been divided into smaller compartments by muntins (see Figure 5–17). French doors, either single or double, are often used in openings leading to patios, porches or terraces.

Combination Doors.   Combination storm and screen doors are hung outside exterior doors to provide additional weather protection in the winter and ventilation in the summer. They combine the functions of both storm and screen doors with interchangeable screen and glass panels.

Some types of combination doors have self-storing features where the glass and screens slide up and down so that weather protection or ventilation is possible without removing panel inserts.

INSPECTING WINDOWS AND DOORS

Doors

If doors are to work properly, they must be installed level and plumb. Open and close the main exterior door several times. Does it scrape the floor? If so, something is out of line. Either the door is improperly hung or the floor is not level.

Many door problems are caused by poor workmanship. If a door is out of level or out of plumb, rehanging may be required. Check the floor all around the doorway. In this area the floor is often unlevel, but unless the problem is severe, there is no reason to be concerned.

In most homes, cold drafts from underneath doors are a common problem. Exterior doors and doors leading to any unheated areas such as garages, basements and attics should be inspected for gaps at the bottom. These gaps should be weatherstripped.

Air leaks at the tops and sides of exterior doors are usually not as critical as those at the bottom. But these leaks also waste fuel, so all sides of exterior doors should be weatherstripped.

Do the hinges squeak when you open the door? The solution may be simple—like oiling the hinges. Or, the door may be warped, placing a strain on the frame. Warped doors that won't close tightly and that are beyond the help of weatherstripping should be replaced. If a replacement is needed, look for a prime door with insulation value as well as beauty. Doors with a polyurethane core insulate better than solid wood doors.

Look at the framework that surrounds the doors. Do you see any cracks? Cracks often indicate that the wood may not be in good condition. You obviously don't want trim work that is rotting or decaying.

Finally, check the locks on the doors to be sure they open and close easily.

Windows

Open and close every window in the house to find out how well they operate and fit. An out-of-plumb window will bind when you try to open and close it. Like doors, proper sizing and installation of prime windows are the real keys to performance.

Check the locks on the windows. Make sure they work easily to pull the sashes together. Broken locks need to be replaced. A broken lock can also mean that the window has been improperly installed. A window that is hard to close, for example, may place excessive stress on the lock, causing it to break.

Most houses have at least a few double-hung windows that are likely candidates for weatherstripping. Begin by checking the weatherstripping between the meeting rails of the two sashes—the most likely source of air infiltration. Make sure the window still operates easily after new weatherstripping has been installed.

The top, bottom and sides of a window may be drafty too. If so, weatherstripping should be installed in the window channels so it won't be seen when the window is closed.

Check horizontal sliding, awning and hopper windows to make sure they provide a tight seal when closed. However, if one of these windows is badly warped, it may need to be replaced—no amount of weatherstripping can save it.

While inspecting windows for weatherstripping, check for loose, cracked or even broken window panes; they can be the source of air leaks, as well as rain and moisture seepage that may cause damage. Loose panes can be reset with glazing compound, but cracked or broken panes will have to be replaced.

Look for evidence of any water stains or damage around the windows, especially at the sills—an almost sure sign of a leak.

FIGURE 5–16. Types of doors.

TYPES OF DOORS

PANEL

FLUSH

SCREEN DOOR

SLIDING GLASS

Storm Windows. A winter necessity in most parts of the country, storm windows fit either on the inside or the outside of the prime windows. Storm windows are usually made of aluminum, although older homes sometimes have wooden ones and newer homes may have the plastic type. Storm windows can reduce summer

FIGURE 5-17. Patio French doors.

air-conditioning bills as well as winter heating costs. Many homeowners who have air-conditioning now leave on their storm windows year-round.

There are two conflicting theories on how storm windows should fit: tightly, to avoid air leaks, and loosely, to allow ventilation and prevent the storm windows from fogging. In a way both views are correct, but a tight-fitting storm is preferable because it will save more fuel dollars.

If the outside storm windows are fogged or iced in cold weather, this usually means inside prime windows are leaking warm, moist air to the outside. Tightening the inside window with caulking and weatherstripping may eliminate the problem.

Homes in most parts of the country can benefit from double-glazed windows. But storm windows are not always the best way to provide double-glazing. If the prime windows are solid, storm windows are usually a good investment. However, if some prime windows are rotted, warped and beyond the help of weatherstripping, caulking and storm windows, they should be replaced.

THE GARAGE

Garages are either attached—part of the house framing—or detached—not connected to the house. Regardless of the type, a thorough inspection is needed to determine its condition. Like the house, the garage too can have serious structural defects or other problems. So, take the time and effort to check it as carefully as you would the house itself.

Inspecting the Garage

The detached garage has a roof of its own. It may also have gutters and downspouts that need to be checked. If you have a ladder and the roof is not too high, climb up to get a closer look at the shingles. If this is not possible, step back from the garage and use your binoculars. Inspect the roof shingles for broken, missing or deteriorating sections. Are the gutters in good shape? Or has water backed up and caused damage to fascia boards? Take your screwdriver and probe suspect areas. Pay close attention to the condition of the downspouts. Does rainwater flow away from the garage as it should? Or do the downspouts allow water to accumulate around the garage foundation?

As you walk around the garage, check the walls for any bowing or sagging. Because garages are sometimes not built with the same care that houses are, particularly older ones, you may find some structural defects.

Check the siding. Are all sections firm? Does the siding need to be painted or stained? Are there any missing or decaying sections? Check both the outside and inside walls for water penetration. Check the doors and windows. Are they difficult to open or close? Is there an automatic door opener? Does it work?

Because an attached garage is an integral part of the house, fire and safety hazards are of primary importance in addition to all the other inspection areas. For example, the entrance from the garage to the house should have a door that is fire resistant (metal clad), and one that has a tight seal to prevent garage fumes from entering the house. The garage floor should be lower than the house slab, again to prevent toxic gases from getting into the house. Walls and ceilings that are adjacent to living areas need to be covered with fire resistant materials, such as stucco or ⅝-inch wallboard.

Garage floors, like basement floors, should be checked for cracked or buckling sections. Minor hairline cracks are not serious, but they should be caulked and sealed to prevent water from coming in. Major cracks or buckling sections should be checked out by a professional to determine the cause and the possible solution.

INSPECTION CHECKLIST

Many salespersons begin the tour of a house with the exterior. The condition of the exterior can tell you a great deal about the general quality of the home, so it's worth a thorough going-over.

The following checklist will give you a general guideline of what the pros look at when they examine the outside of a house.

INSPECTION CHECKLIST

Exterior Materials

Roof Covering: asphalt shingles/wood shingles/wood shakes/tile/slate/other

Age of Roof: _____

Gutters
  and Downspouts: aluminum/galvanized metal/wood

Exterior Walls: wood clapboard/wood shingles/aluminum/vinyl/brick veneer/stucco/other

Type of Windows: double-hung/horizontal sliding/casement/fixed/triple-track/other

Storm Windows: yes/no

Window Frames: metal/wood

Exterior Doors: metal/wood/sliding glass/French/other

If Wood: solid core/polyurethane core/hollow core

Roof and Gutters	**Yes**	**No**
1. Look along the outer edges of the roof. Are the shingles firm (not curled or drooping)?	_____	_____
2. Are all shingles, slates or tiles in good shape (none missing, cracked or broken)?	_____	_____
3. Is the roof in good shape (no evidence of roof leaks)?	_____	_____
4. Are flashings on the roof-mounted members in good condition?	_____	_____
5. The greatest roof damage tends to occur in the valleys. Are the valleys undamaged and in good condition?	_____	_____
6. Is the roof free of dark patches indicating weak spots?	_____	_____
7. Are the wood shingles or shakes free of any signs of decay or rot?	_____	_____
8. Check the overhang of the roof. Is it free of any signs of wood rot?	_____	_____
9. Check inside the attic for leaks. Are all rafters free of water stains and any other signs of water penetration?	_____	_____
10. Does the house have proper roof ventilation?	_____	_____
11. Are roof vents free of any signs of water penetration?	_____	_____
12. Are there gutters and downspouts on the house?	_____	_____
13. Are the soffits, gutters and downspouts made of aluminum?	_____	_____
14. If not, have they been recently painted?	_____	_____
15. Did you see the house in the rain? (This is the best time to check the roof and the gutter-downspout system.)	_____	_____
16. Are all gutters free of leaks, cracks or weak spots?	_____	_____
17. Are the gutters firm (not sagging)?	_____	_____
18. Are the downspouts attached to the gutters, and do they carry water away from the house?	_____	_____

	Yes	No
19. Check the chimney. Are all bricks firmly in place? Is the chimney free of cracks?	_____	_____
20. Is the chimney flashing in good condition?	_____	_____

Siding

Wood

1. Are all sections of siding firm?	_____	_____
2. Is the siding in good condition (no peeling paint or faded colors)?	_____	_____
3. Has the siding been kept up so there are no missing or decaying sections?	_____	_____
4. Is siding in good shape (no splits)?	_____	_____
5. Do all joints fit tightly together (no gaps) to prevent water penetration?	_____	_____
6. Has the siding been nailed properly?	_____	_____
7. Is all sheathing concealed so that none shows between the boards?	_____	_____

Aluminum and vinyl

8. Is the siding firm?	_____	_____
9. Do all joints fit tightly together (no gaps) to prevent water penetration?	_____	_____
10. Is siding free of dents or scratches?	_____	_____
11. Is siding in good shape (no cracked or missing sections)?		

Brick

12. Is the brick in good shape (no cracked, broken or missing bricks)?	_____	_____
13. Is mortar in good shape (no sign of wear)?	_____	_____
14. Are walls straight (no bows)?		

Stucco

15. Is the stucco surface free of settlement cracks, which may indicate a problem in the structural wall?	_____	_____
16. Are the walls straight (no bows)?	_____	_____
17. Is the stucco firm (not pulling loose)?	_____	_____
18. Is the surface in good shape (no evidence of patches)?	_____	_____
19. Are the walls in good condition (no peeling paint or faded colors)?	_____	_____

Windows and Doors

1. Check all windows and doors. Do they all open and close easily?	_____	_____
2. Is the window glass in good shape (not cracked or broken)?	_____	_____

	Yes	No
3. Are all frames in good shape (not rotted or damaged in any way)?		
4. Are windows and doors free of water stains indicating leaks?		
5. Are the windows weatherstripped?		
6. Are all windows in good shape, so they will not need replacing?		
7. Are window locks in good shape (not broken)?		
8. Are window frames in good condition (no peeling paint or faded colors)?		
9. Are all doors in good shape (not warped, no signs of rot)?		
10. Do the door locks operate properly?		
11. Look at the framework that surrounds the doors. Is it clean and newly painted?		
Is the framework solid (not cracked)?		
12. Are the exterior doors weatherstripped?		
13. Are doors in good condition (no peeling paint or faded colors)?		
14. Are all storm windows and doors weathertight?		

Garage

	Yes	No
1. Check the roof shingles. Are they in good shape (no broken, missing or deteriorating sections)?		
2. Is the roof in good shape (no signs of leaks)?		
3. Are the gutters and downspouts in good condition?		
4. Do the downspouts carry water away from the garage?		
5. Are exterior walls straight (no bulges)?		
6. Is the foundation free of signs of defects?		
7. Are all sections of siding firm?		
8. Is the siding in good shape (no missing or decaying sections)?		
9. Are the siding and trim in good condition (no peeling paint or faded colors)?		
10. Is the garage floor free of major cracks?		
11. Is the floor sealed to prevent water penetration and stains?		
12. Are all walls free of water marks or other signs of water penetration?		
13. Do the doors open and close properly?		
14. Can the doors be locked?		

		Yes	No
15.	Is there an automatic door opener?	_____	_____
	Does it work?	_____	_____
16.	In an attached garage, inspect the door from the garage to the house. Is it fireproof?	_____	_____
17.	Are the interior walls and ceiling adjacent to living spaces fireproof?	_____	_____
18.	In an attached garage, is the floor of the garage lower than the house slab? (This placement prevents toxic gasses from entering the house.)	_____	_____
19.	Is there a piece of protective weatherstripping between the base of the door and the ground?	_____	_____
20.	Is the garage wide and long enough?		

Overall Rating	Good	Fair	Poor
Roof covering	_____	_____	_____
Roof vents	_____	_____	_____
Gutters and downspouts	_____	_____	_____
Exterior walls	_____	_____	_____
Windows	_____	_____	_____
Exterior doors	_____	_____	_____
Chimney	_____	_____	_____
Garage	_____	_____	_____

Major Problems: _____

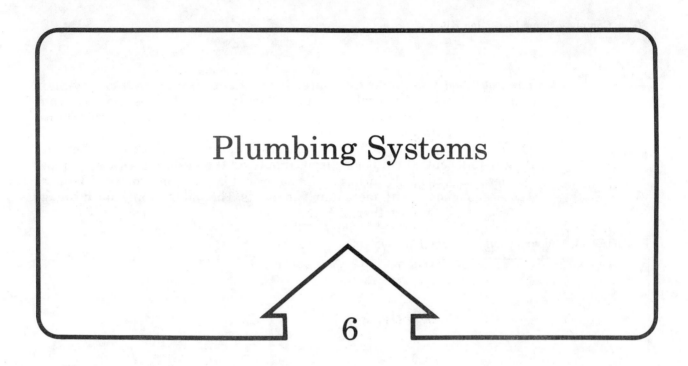

Plumbing Systems

6

EARLY BATHROOMS IN AMERICA

Cleanliness, hygiene and hot and cold running water are taken for granted by modern Americans. But not until the 1800s did bathing become an accepted and common practice.

Before germs were discovered, bathing was considered hazardous to health. Gradually, as people became aware that dirt breeds disease, bathing became fashionable. From the mid-19th century onward, bathrooms were status symbols for those wealthy enough to afford one.

The first bathrooms, or boudoirs, were converted bedrooms, usually located adjacent to the chambers of the mistress of the house. Places of luxury, they were lavishly decorated with green plants, Oriental rugs, rich silks and velvets and soft lighting.

Technological innovations in the mid-1800s brought the water heater and the toilet. Although a number of inventors share credit for developing the modern toilet, the Cretans had a version of it some 4,000 years ago.

For most of the country, however, hot and cold running water remained a dream. Until the first decade of the 1900s, only about 15 percent of American homes had plumbing. Most people bathed in crude tubs set in the kitchen. City folks could use public baths where 5 cents bought a hot bath complete with soap and towel.

Today, the trend is moving toward luxury bathrooms that offer quality, comfort, convenience and elegance—particularly in the master bedroom.

PLUMBING SYSTEMS

The plumbing system in a house is actually a number of separate systems, each with a special function.

- The *water-supply system* brings water to the house from a well or city main and distributes hot and cold water through two sets of pipes. Hot- and cold-water lines usually run close together. Water pipes are rarely larger than 1 inch in diameter.
- The *drainage system* collects waste and used water from fixtures and carries it away to a central point for disposal outside the building. Drainage pipes are never less than 1¼ inches in diameter and are at some points as large as 4 inches in a house with more than two toilets. The water-supply and drainage systems are shown together in Figure 6–1.

FIGURE 6–1.   Typical piping and drainage systems.

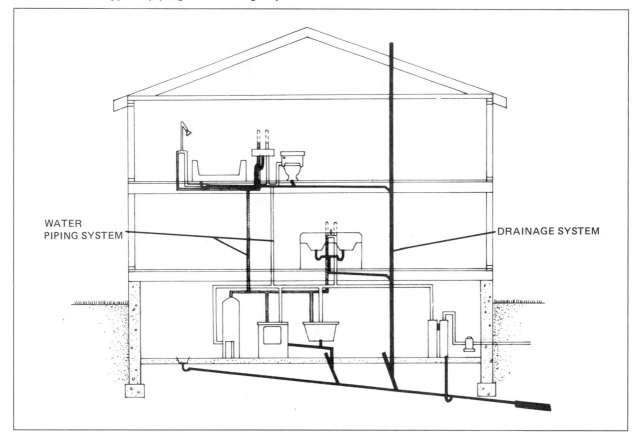

- The *vent piping system* carries only air. It operates as an interconnected part of the drainage system but serves a different function. It carries out of the house all sewer gases that develop in drainage lines. It also equalizes air pressure within the waste system so that waste will flow away and not back up into fixtures.
- The *waste-collecting system* is needed only when the main waste drain in the house is lower than sewer level under the street or when the house has more than one drainage system.
- The *house connection pipe system* is a single pipe. It is the waste connection from the house to the city sewer line, to a septic tank or to some other waste-disposal facility.

   Installation of all plumbing is governed by strict codes. Local codes may have their own plumbing sections, but almost all are based on the *Uniform Plumbing Code*, published by the International Association of Plumbing and Mechanical Officials

(IAPMO). You will find the IAPMO stamp of approval on many fixtures and fittings.

PLUMBING DRAWINGS

Most builders hire a plumbing subcontractor to install plumbing systems. The subcontractor can find information on the layout of plumbing in four places: floor plans, elevations, isometrics and detail drawings.

Floor Plans

The floor plan of a house always shows the location of bathtubs, toilets, water heaters, dishwashers, sinks and shower stalls. A thorough plan will also show floor drains, outdoor faucets and connections for gas lines and vacuum lines (Figure 6–2).

FIGURE 6–2.   Plumbing fixtures indicated in floor plan.

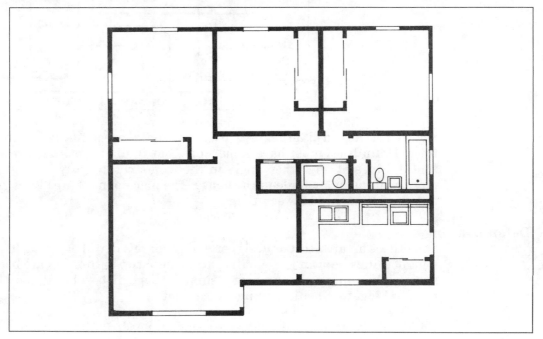

Elevations

Elevations of the exterior of a house usually show where outside faucets are situated. If the house is designed for a specific site, they may show the centers of lines to and from city utilities. Sometimes piping layouts are diagramed in elevation, as in Figure 6–3.

Isometrics

More often, however, piping layouts are plotted as isometrics so that the system can be viewed in three dimensions. A plumbing isometric can be very confusing at first sight because it shows the piping suspended in mid-air, with no walls or floors around it. But if you study a plumbing isometric with the floor plan next to it or superimposed on it (Figure 6–4), you will begin to see why a line turns, branches or connects where it does.

Vertical lines in the isometric represent vertical plumbing lines. Lines on the

FIGURE 6–3.   Elevation with interior piping layout.

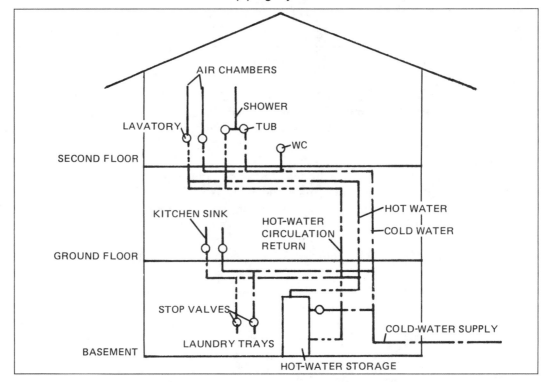

isometric that run at 30 degrees to the horizontal are actually horizontal plumbing lines. Drain lines must have some slope, but in diagrams they are shown as horizontal. Lines at any other angle in the isometric (usually 45 degrees) represent pipes running at an angle in the house. The placement of pipe lines gives the right-to-left relationship between them.

Detail Drawings

Sometimes an architect or designer will prepare a detail of piping in an area where a lot of things happen in a small space: where two bathrooms are back to back and share a plumbing wall, or where a sink, garbage disposal unit and dishwasher are plumbed together behind a kitchen cabinet.

Residential plumbing systems are not very complex. Today they are virtually standardized, so detail drawings are seldom needed. The plumbing subcontractor, who is responsible for following the local code, will usually make rough sketches of the proposed layout before excavation and footing work is done. The sketches guide the contractor in making an estimate and submitting a bid. He or she will then develop more finished layouts for approval from local authorities.

Symbols.   On floor plans all fixtures are designated by symbols that look much like the actual fixtures. A few of the more common ones are illustrated in Figure 6–5 on page 84.

In isometrics and elevations, plumbing lines are represented by solid and broken lines of varying thicknesses, as illustrated in Figure 6–6.

INSTALLATION

Plumbing is installed in three stages. The system begins outside the house, where water and drain lines are laid underground. The second stage consists of *roughing*

FIGURE 6–4. Plumbing isometric and floor plan.

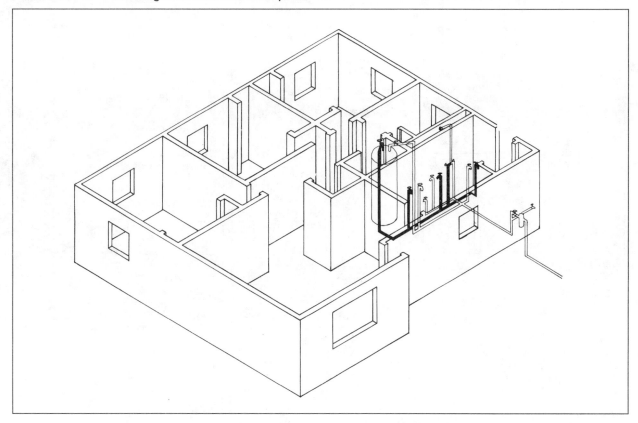

in water and drain lines. This means locating and installing piping and venting where they are hidden from view in walls and floors. The final stage is *finish plumbing*, which includes placing all fixtures except the bathtub and connecting these fixtures to the roughed-in plumbing. The bathtub is always the first fixture installed because connections have to be completed before you can finish the surfaces around the tub enclosure.

PLUMBING FIXTURES

Most rooms of a newly completed house look bare and cold until they are finished. Even draperies and carpeting don't help much until furniture and accessories are in place. When you show off a new house, about all you have to sell is the space. Two exceptions are the bathroom and the kitchen: both give the impression of a finished room as soon as the last bit of work is done. Because these rooms are such critical sales features of a house, and because fixtures are the only visible parts of the plumbing systems, it pays to buy good-looking, good-quality fixtures. The dollar difference between average fixtures and the top of the line is relatively small.

Bathtubs

Tubs come in three standard lengths—54, 60 and 66 inches. Most are rectangular and fit flush with the floor and the wall. The inside of a bathtub usually runs parallel to the outside, but some types run at a slight angle to the longest side to give a tall person a little more leg room while bathing and to reduce the amount of water used. Some tub bottoms are smooth, some are ribbed to channel the water toward the drain, and some are covered with nonskid strips.

84   Complete Home Inspection Kit

FIGURE 6–5. Plumbing fixture symbols.

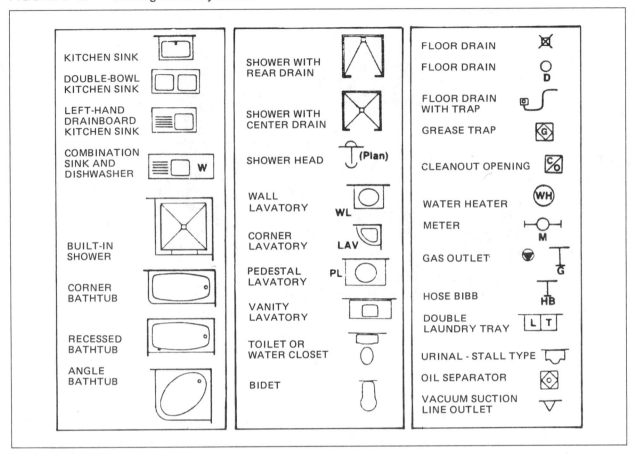

FIGURE 6–6. Plumbing line and connection symbols.

A recessed tub has walls on three sides, whereas a corner tub has walls on two sides (Figure 6–7). The drain is usually at the end of the tub nearest the water inlet, but some types have a drain in the middle of the tub at one side.

A square tub is difficult to fit into an ordinary bathroom unless the room was designed for that shape or is unusually spacious. Most square tubs require a 4-foot by 4-foot space and are only 12 inches deep at the rim. The bathing portion of the fixture runs diagonally across the unit, and there may be a shelf or low seat on one side or both.

Many of the old Roman baths were luxurious—very deep and large enough for several people. Luxury bathing is making a comeback that started in honeymoon

FIGURE 6–7.   Recessed bathtub.
(Courtesy of Kohler Co.)

FIGURE 6–8.   Shower stall.
(Courtesy of Kohler Co.)

suites of new hotels and motels. It has spread into more expensive houses, and you can now buy special tubs to satisfy almost any bathing desire.

Shower Stalls

Showers over bathtubs require a few extra fittings but no extra fixture. There are plumbing connections to the shower head and either a rod for a shower curtain or sliding doors across the tub rim. These doors have a sturdy metal frame and panels of plastic or tempered glass that may be clear, translucent or opaque. The bottom track is set in waterproof mastic, and the ends of the door frame are attached to studs or blocking with stainless-steel or chromium-plated screws.

Shower stalls are a complete unit in themselves, about 6 or 7 feet tall (Figure 6–8). Ready-made stalls of metal or plastic can be set into a framed compartment and may have lugs on the back and sides for attachment to studs. Like bathtubs, they are installed during the roughing-in stage. Shower stalls have no wall material behind them; they are designed so that the wall above can be finished flush with the top rim.

Drains are usually in the center of the stall floor, but some stalls drain to one side or to the rear. The floor of the stall is higher than the bathroom floor so that drain connections can be made easily. A 4-inch to 6-inch lip or dam below the doors separates the two levels.

Toilets

In the plumbing industry, toilets are classified by the method used to flush the water out of the bowl. The flushing efficiency is dependent on both the flushing mechanism and the bowl design. And as might be expected, the better a toilet functions, the more it costs. The quietest and most efficient toilet is the *siphon-vortex* type. Water from the rim creates a swirling action that washes the walls and flushes the water in the bowl by siphon action. Almost as quiet is the *siphon-jet* toilet, where water from the rim is propelled by a jet of water in the outlet. The *reverse-trap* type is similar but has a smaller bowl. The *blowout* is the most efficient toilet. It flushes quickly and uses the least water, but it is the noisiest type. The *washdown* toilet is the least expensive, but it too is noisy. Pressure of water filling the bowl from the tank causes the water to overflow and creates a siphon action.

The flushing tank on a residential toilet can be cast as one piece with the bowl, as in the photo at the left in Figure 6–9, or it can rest on a rear extension of the bowl, as in the photo at the right. The one-piece units are more complex and therefore more expensive. Most toilets are bolted to the floor through a gasket ring. The chief advantage of the type that hangs from the wall is that the floor under it can be cleaned more easily.

FIGURE 6–9.   One- and two-piece toilets. (Courtesy of Kohler Co.)

Lavatories

Of all plumbingware, you'll find the greatest variety in lavatories. Round, oval or rectangular, they range from 12 to 20 inches front to back and from 12 to 36 inches wide. They may fit in a corner, hang from the wall, stand on legs or be recessed into a countertop. They may be made of vitreous china, enameled cast iron, enameled steel or plastic. Some lavatories are self-rimming and others have a separated rim. There may or may not be a ledge at the back or sides for small storage.

The most popular lavatory today is the drop-in or countertop lavatory, often called a *vanity* (Figure 6–10). It fits into a hole cut in the top of the finished counter, and the edges or rims are set in sealant to prevent leakage. Connections to the water supply are made through holes pre-drilled in the unit within the circle. The countertops themselves are usually plastic laminate, but more expensive homes may use marble slabs, ceramic tile or molded plastic. In half-baths and powder rooms that are too small for a counter, you are more likely to find a wall-hung or free-standing unit.

Kitchen Sinks

Today, almost all sinks fit into a countertop and almost all are made of enameled cast iron, enameled pressed steel or stainless steel. Like lavatories, kitchen sinks may be self-rimming or rimmed with metal.

Many people feel that a single-compartment sink, no matter how large, is inadequate unless it has a drainboard for dishes. Even then, they prefer the conve-

FIGURE 6–10. Vanity lavatory.
(Courtesy of Kohler Co.)

FIGURE 6–11. Bidet.
(Courtesy of Kohler Co.)

nience and utility of a double sink without a drainboard—especially if the home is equipped with a dishwasher. At least one side of a two-compartment sink should have a large drain opening to accept a garbage-disposal unit.

Other Plumbingware

Laundry tubs are very serviceable plumbing fixtures. The deep tubs can be used for heavy cleaning or for soaking and laundering clothes. The fixture rests on a two-legged or four-legged stand and may be made of concrete, plastic, cast iron with porcelain enamel on the interior or soapstone—a quarried form of talc that has a soapy feel to it.

The *bidet* (pronounced bee-day), a common fixture in Europe and parts of Asia, is becoming more popular in this country (Figure 6–11). It is similar in size and shape to a toilet but has both hot and cold water connections. You sit in it to bathe a limited area of the body.

Water Heaters. Water is heated by gas, oil or electricity unless the house is heated with a hot-water system that uses the boiler as a source of hot water to plumbingware and appliances. Gas and oil water heaters are about 5 feet tall and slender; their diameter varies with the capacity of the heater. Electric water heaters are shorter but larger in diameter. Some electric units have the tank in a cabinet that fits under a kitchen cabinet and blends in with other appliances.

Water heaters come in several capacities, ranging from 17 gallons up to 82 gallons for residential use. Most families require a 40-gallon to 50-gallon tank, although 30 gallons is the minimum size for gas and oil models. Electric heaters should have at least a 50-gallon capacity, since they have a slower recovery rate than either gas-fired or oil-fired heaters.

Water heaters heat water to a predetermined temperature and automatically shut off. When hot water is drained off, cold water replaces it and the heating unit turns on automatically. Some water heaters are quick recovery heaters; they have special heating elements that turn on only when the tank has been almost drained of hot water to make a fresh supply of hot water available more quickly. This cuts down the size of the water heater required.

All water heaters have safety features. Most types have a sensing element in them that makes it impossible to start them for the first time before they are filled with water. They have a pressure-relief valve to prevent explosions. If the water heater continues to heat beyond the predetermined temperature, the valve bleeds off the steam pressure that builds up and warns you that something has gone wrong. The tanks that hold the water are made of heavy-gauge steel with a glass lining that water won't corrode. Pipe connections are usually, but not always, at the top of the water heater (Figure 6–12).

FIGURE 6–12.   Parts of a water heater.

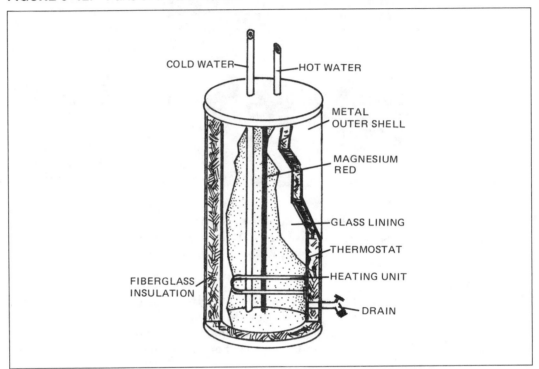

An electric water heater can be installed anywhere. Since a gas or oil water heater must be vented, it is usually located near the furnace and shares the same chimney. More important than sharing the same chimney, however, is closeness to rooms where hot water is needed quickly. This is almost always the bathroom. Nothing is more annoying than having to wait several minutes for hot water to reach a faucet or showerhead. In some two-story houses today, builders place a water heater in a closet on the second floor. The vent pipe (if needed) is short, and hot water reaches bathrooms almost instantly. A delay to the faucet is not as annoying in a kitchen, because the cooler water in the sink can be used for other purposes until the hot water arrives.

Hot-Water Softeners.   Much of the United States has hard water. Water is classified as hard when it contains over five grains of salts (carbonates and sulfates) per gallon. These salts tend to clog pipes, leave a scum on plumbingware when mixed with soap and complicate washing of clothing and glassware. They do help prevent rusting, however. The most common method of removing these salts is with a water softener (Figure 6–13). All water entering the house passes through the softener, which contains a bed of resin to absorb the salts. The resin needs to be regenerated every so often with common salt.

Water-softening systems usually consist of two tanks connected by a flexible hose. One contains the resin and a silica-sand filter, and the other contains brine—a salt and water mixture for regenerating the resin. Regeneration can be done by hand or can be automatically controlled by a meter and valve on the water-softener line.

FIGURE 6–13. Hot-water softener.

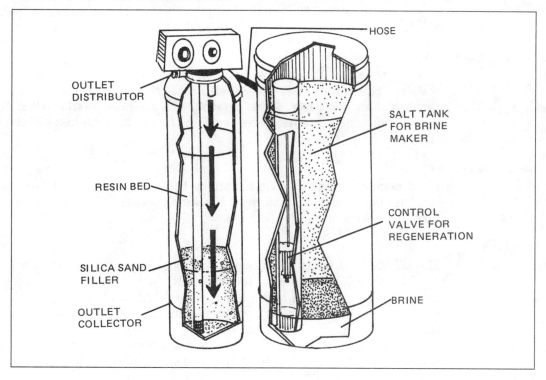

To solve the problem of frequent regeneration, and thus use less salt, some builders install the softener on the main supply line after water has passed through the water heater. This arrangement provides soft water for bathing and washing, but it is wiser to have both cold and hot water softened to prevent clogging and corrosion in the piping system.

MATERIALS

Plumbing fixtures are known in the industry as *plumbingware*. The materials used in their manufacture must be dense, durable, nonabsorbent and smooth. The five most popular choices are vitreous china, enameled cast iron, enameled steel, stainless steel and plastic.

Vitreous China

The word *vitreous* means glassy. Wet clay is poured into molds that absorb some of the water from the mix. After the clay has set, it is removed from the mold and baked, then coated with a porcelain enamel and rebaked. The baked enamel forms a glassy surface. Almost all toilets are made of vitreous china because the material is easy to mold, nonabsorbent and easy to clean. It has three disadvantages, though: it breaks easily, warps during the baking process and develops hairline cracks along its surface.

Vitreous glazed earthenware is a more expensive variety of vitreous china, one that won't break or crack. It is widely used in hospitals and other facilities where sanitation is crucial.

Enameled Cast Iron

Molten iron is poured into a mold to form a rough casting. This casting is smoothed, covered with at least three coats of porcelain enamel to a thickness of about ⅛ inch, and baked. The resultant glassy surface withstands most liquids, even acids, and resists hairline cracks. Except for toilets, most plumbingware is available in cast iron.

Enameled Steel

Steel fixtures are stamped out of sheets that are lighter and less expensive than cast iron. Each fixture is coated with a baked-on porcelain enamel. Steel is more flexible than cast iron, so its coating cracks more easily. Also, running water makes more noise against a steel surface than it does against vitreous china or cast iron.

Stainless Steel

Used primarily for sinks and laundry tubs that receive a lot of water, stainless steel is impervious even to most household acids. It will dent, but it won't chip, tarnish or scratch.

Plastic

Many lavatories today are made of durable plastic, a less expensive material that is also serviceable for sinks, shower stalls, bathtubs and toilet tanks. Plastics are available in low-sheen or high-gloss surfaces and in a variety of soft colors and textures worked into the material or the top coating. Some plastics will break under sharp impact, and abrasion is a big problem.

Plumbingware is one part of the house a buyer never expects to replace. An astute builder will look for good, classic design and durable materials.

INSPECTING THE PLUMBING

The plumbing system's ability to carry in water and carry away waste is obviously very important to the homeowner. Poorly made or poorly installed pipes and fixtures are common sources of problems.

To determine the quality of plumbing in the house, you need to check first on the condition of pipes and drains. Bad plumbing is usually a problem in houses with iron or steel pipes that are more than 25 years old. Copper, brass and bronze pipes, which were not introduced until about 1940, and the relatively recent polybutalene plastic pipes, will last much longer. You can use a magnet to discover what kind of pipes are in a house. Iron or steel will attract the magnet, but copper, brass and bronze will not.

Because most of the plumbing is hidden between walls or under floors, it is very important to check the exposed pipes located in the basement or crawl space. Signs of defects in water lines or drainage pipes can usually be found there. Examine the pipes for signs of leaks, corrosion or recent repair jobs. Look also for telltale watermarks in the basement—signs of flooding.

The best way to test for water pressure is to turn on all the faucets in the kitchen, bathrooms and laundry area. Faucets in an upstairs bathroom are the best indicators. Turn on all faucets and flush the toilets at the same time. There should be enough water pressure to provide a strong flow of water. This indicates that the pipes are clear of rust and corrosion. If the water trickles out, you can expect plumbing problems and, most likely, some expensive replacement work.

While you are testing the faucets for water pressure, check to see if they drip when they have been turned off. If so, then the washers or valves, or both, need replacing.

If the pipes make noisy, clanking sounds when you turn on the faucets, something is wrong. Vibrations in the pipes can loosen fittings, causing leaks to occur.

Improper venting is a defect often found in plumbing systems. One way to tell if there is no venting or improper venting is to listen for sucking or gurgling noises after a fixture is drained. These sounds often indicate that a fixture does not have a vent pipe extending to the outside, usually through the roof. Another way to tell whether a fixture is vented is to be cognizant of foul odors, most likely sewer gas, coming from the fixture itself. If you are in doubt about the venting, have a plumber double-check it for you.

Don't hesitate to give the toilets a thorough inspection. First, flush each toilet to see if it operates properly. If it drains slowly, there may be blockage in the line. Does the toilet have a separate shut-off valve? This allows you to cut off water to the toilet without turning the water off in the entire house. Sinks should also have shut-off valves for the same reason.

Check the floor around the toilet. Is there any water damage? If so, it was probably caused by a broken toilet seal.

Before leaving the bathrooms, be sure to note whether they include at least the following accessories:

- Large medicine cabinets, preferably two in each bathroom
- Storage for toilet paper, tissues and related items
- Shelves for towels
- Quality towel bars and toilet paper holders
- Enough electrical outlets for dryers, shavers, hot rollers and related appliances

The bathroom—the master bath in particular—should be an extension of the bedroom, which means that it ought to offer the same feeling of luxury and quality.

Check the water heater for signs of rust and leakage. Age and capacity are important, as is quality. Glass-lined water heaters are the most common. You can expect about 10 to 12 years of service from them.

Finally, find out what kind of waste-disposal system the house has—a public sewer system or a septic tank. An inadequate septic-tank system is another common source of trouble. The tank will require a good cleaning every two years or so, and any kind of repair work is expensive.

Of course, if you still have doubts about the plumbing, talk to a qualified professional. Your own inspection, no matter how thorough, cannot always guarantee that this extremely important system is in good shape.

INSPECTION CHECKLIST

The following checklist will help you to evaluate the condition of the plumbing in a house. Although you can't be absolutely certain that a pipe isn't ready to spring a leak, or whether hot-water lines to distant bathrooms are insulated, still, you can make some educated judgments about how well the systems work and about how long they will last.

INSPECTION CHECKLIST

Plumbing Information

Water pipes: copper/galvanized metal/polybutalene plastic/other

Drain lines: cast iron/plastic/other

Water heater: gas/electric/oil

Gallon capacity: _____

Age: _____

		Yes	No
1.	Check all exposed water pipes. Are they free of any signs of leaks, corrosion or deterioration in the water lines or their fittings?	_____	_____
2.	Are all drain lines clear, with no signs of deterioration?	_____	_____
3.	Are the pipes insulated?	_____	_____
4.	Is the basement free of any signs of sewage backup?	_____	_____
5.	Check the faucets for operation. Is there sufficient water pressure at each faucet?	_____	_____
6.	Is the water clear (no rusty water coming from any faucets)?	_____	_____
7.	Are faucets in good shape (no drips)?	_____	_____
8.	Check all sinks in the house. Do they drain properly?	_____	_____
9.	Check under the sink. Is this area free of signs of leaks or water damage?	_____	_____
10.	Are countertops in good shape (no need for repair or replacement)? Bubbling in the countertop around a sink might indicate that water has gotten under the lip and is causing damage.	_____	_____
11.	Do the water pipes have shutoff valves in the basement?	_____	_____
	In the kitchen?	_____	_____
	In the bathrooms?	_____	_____
12.	Do plumbing fixtures have proper venting?	_____	_____
13.	Is there sufficient storage in the bathrooms?	_____	_____
14.	Are there quality fixtures?	_____	_____
15.	Are there sufficient electrical outlets in the bathrooms?	_____	_____
16.	Flush all toilets. Does each one operate properly?	_____	_____
17.	Does each toilet have a water shut-off valve?	_____	_____
18.	Do all toilets flush quietly? (Make sure they're not excessively noisy.)	_____	_____
19.	After the toilet has been flushed and filled, does it stop running?	_____	_____
20.	Look at the floor around the toilets. Is it free of water damage?	_____	_____

	Yes	No
21. Look carefully at the ceilings beneath the bathrooms. Are they free of water stains?	____	____
22. Do the tubs and showers drain properly?	____	____
23. Do the tubs hold water without seepage?	____	____
24. Check the walls around the tubs and showers. Are they free of water damage?	____	____
25. Are tiles in good shape (not cracked or missing)?	____	____
26. Check the gallon capacity of the water heater. Does it meet your family's needs?	____	____
27. Is the water heater in good shape? (Check its age and for signs of rust and water leaks.)	____	____
28. If the house has a septic tank, is it free of strong odors coming from the tank area?	____	____
29. Is the septic tank area free of standing water?	____	____
30. Is the tank cover accessible?	____	____
31. Does the septic system work well? (Ask the owner how often the holding tank has been pumped out over the past several years. A septic system is very costly to replace.)	____	____
32. If there is a well, does it work well? (Ask the owner.)		

Overall Rating	**Good**	**Fair**	**Poor**
Overall plumbing system	____	____	____
Drainage	____	____	____
Water pressure	____	____	____
Water heater	____	____	____
Septic system (if there is one)	____	____	____
Well (if there is one)	____	____	____
Plumbing fixtures	____	____	____

Major Problems. _____

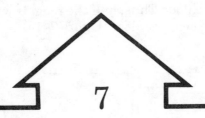

Heating and Air-Conditioning Systems

7

Prehistoric people made fires in the entrances to their caves to keep out the cold. When they began building shelters they brought the open fires in with them. Smoke—and a lot of heat—escaped through an opening in the roof. As civilization progressed, people learned to build fireplaces that would keep in the heat and let out the smoke. For centuries, the fireplace was the main source of heat.

EARLY HEATING IN AMERICA

Homes built in the American colonial period had a large central chimney with a single fireplace in the kitchen, where it was used for both heating and cooking. As construction techniques became more sophisticated, people demanded larger homes with a fireplace in every room, all feeding into that central chimney.

In the middle of the 18th century, Benjamin Franklin developed a cast-iron stove with metal surfaces that radiated heat in all directions, not in just a single direction the way a fireplace does. The stove sat on heavy legs and could be placed anywhere in a room as long as its smoke pipe could reach the chimney. The Franklin stove, improved of course, is still made today. It is often used in vacation homes where year-round heating is not required and low-cost heating is a factor.

Baseburners were invented about 50 years later. They burned coal, wood, peat, charcoal and even corncobs. Though much more efficient than fireplaces, these heaters were dirty and did not heat evenly. Fuel had to be carried into the house and ashes had to be carried out. The stove was later enclosed in a casing that made the unit a circulating heater. It also made the unit so large that it took up much of the space in the room. For this reason, the heating plant was moved to the basement and has remained there ever since. The next heating milestone was the gravity warm-air furnace. With its large circular ducts spreading out from the furnace toward registers in every room, it looked like an octopus sitting in the middle of the basement. It was the first central heating system, and it stimulated inventors and manufacturers to devise improvements for it while reducing the space it occupied. A central heating plant today takes up less than half the space it did only a generation ago.

At the same time that heating systems were being improved in design and efficiency, engineers were discovering more and more about heat movement and human comfort levels. Heat flows toward cold, but it also rises. This means that even though a heating system replaces heat as fast as it is lost, a person can still feel cold. Older homes, for instance, often have registers or radiators close to the floor or inside partitions. With this arrangement, runs of duct or pipe are short, so heat reaches the register or radiator at maximum temperature. It then rises toward the ceiling as it heads for the cold outside wall; infiltrating cold air from windows settles to the floor. Thus, half the room is warm above waist level and the rest is cold and drafty near the floor (Figure 7–1a).

FIGURE 7–1. Patterns of heat movement.

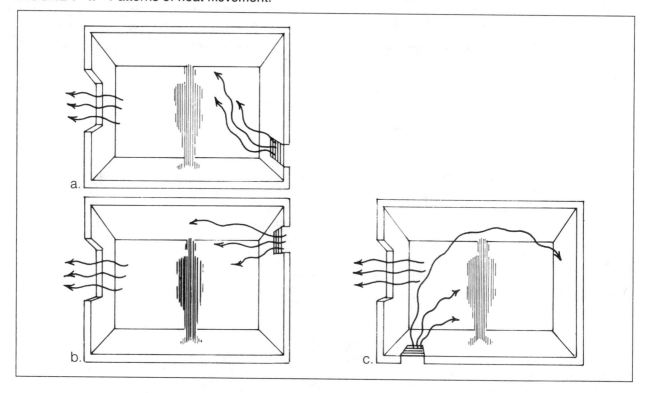

One improvement in the warm-air system was to put heating outlets high on the wall and cold-air returns on the outside wall under windows. While this flow of air warmed more of the room, it also increased draftiness near exterior walls (Figure 7–1b).

Today's heating systems correct this problem with heat outlets on outside walls under windows (Figure 7–1c). This system is called *perimeter heating*. A curtain of warm air flows up the outside wall, carrying with it infiltrating cold air from the wall and windows. This action fulfills the purpose of a heating system—to provide heat at the same rate as a healthy body loses it.

TYPES OF SYSTEMS

Broadly speaking, there are only two types of heating systems—central heating and space heating. They draw their heat from one of five sources: **warm air, hot water,** steam, electric wire and the sun. The systems are powered by gas, oil, electricity or such solid fuels as coal, coke, and peat. They are regulated by either central or zone controls.

Central Heating Systems

Central heating systems use one of two methods to propel heat from its central source to the point where it is needed. One is gravity circulation and the other is a forcing action that pushes the heat with a blower or pump.

Gravity Systems. There are four types of gravity systems, all of which require a separate air-conditioning system. They are gravity warm air, pipeless warm air, gravity hot water and steam heating.

The *gravity warm-air system* operates on the principle that warm air rises and cold air sinks. The furnace must be installed below the level of rooms to be heated, and it should be centrally placed to keep duct lengths at a minimum. The system requires a furnace, large-diameter warm-air ducts, warm-air registers (usually set in the walls), cold-air return grills placed in the floor of each room, large return-air ducts, a small fresh-air intake from outdoors and a humidifier (Figure 7–2).

FIGURE 7–2.   Air circulation in a gravity warm-air system.

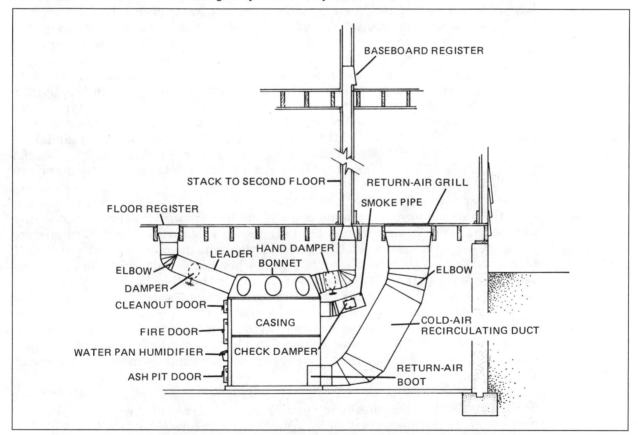

The advantages of a warm-air gravity system are simplicity of design, ease of maintenance and low initial cost. In a small, tightly insulated house an added advantage of the system is its low operating cost. It isn't practical for a large or sprawling house, though. Disadvantages of the gravity warm-air system are the amount of space required for the ducts, variable heat throughout the house and a tendency to draftiness.

The *pipeless furnace* is a gravity warm-air unit for small houses with low heating requirements. It is installed in the basement below a large grill set into the floor above. Between floor and furnace are two casings. Hot air flows upward through the center casing, while return air enters the outer casing around the edges of the same floor grill (Figure 7–3). Supply and return connections are separate, so it is possible to adapt the furnace to cold-air returns from other rooms.

To operate efficiently, a pipeless furnace must be located so that heat can circulate through several rooms. Interior doors must be left open to promote circulation or else cut short at top and bottom. Operating costs for this system are about the same as for a gravity furnace, but installation is cheaper. It is hard to maintain even temperatures with a pipeless furnace, and air tends to stratify. An added drawback of the system is the large floor register in the middle of normal traffic patterns.

The *gravity hot-water system* consists of a boiler, a piping system to carry heated water to radiators in each room, the radiators themselves that transfer the heat from the water into the air by radiation and convection, and piping to carry cooled water back to the boiler for reheating (Figure 7–4). Hot water systems are completely filled with water, and temperatures can be controlled to vary from 100 to 200 degrees Fahrenheit.

A gravity hot-water system is quiet and simple in operation, but it does not respond quickly to sudden rises or drops in outdoor temperatures. The pipes are larger than in other piped heating systems because water moves slowly by gravity. The boiler should be centrally located, preferably in the basement, but can go in a first-floor utility room as long as the connection for the returned water is lower than the lowest radiator in the system.

Gravity hot-water systems may be one-pipe or two-pipe systems. Hot water in the one-pipe system goes from the boiler to the first radiator, through it to the second radiator, and so on until it returns to the boiler for reheating. This type of system is not easy to control, and rooms that receive hot water first are often warmer than rooms at the other end of the system. In a two-pipe system, each radiator receives hot water directly from the boiler and returns it directly through a second pipe (Figure 7–4). Though more costly to install, this system provides more uniform heat to all rooms.

Steam-heating systems are efficient but noisy. Because they heat and cool quickly, they are practical for small commercial and public buildings that are occupied only part of the time. These systems are only partly filled with water. They operate when the water is heated to 212 degrees Fahrenheit, the boiling point at which it becomes steam. As a result, radiators are either hot or cold, and room temperatures vary more than with a hot-water system. On the other hand, a steam system responds more quickly to rapid changes in outdoor temperatures.

Steam heating also is available in one-pipe and two-pipe systems. In the one-pipe system condensed water returns in the same pipes that carry steam to radiators. Water in the two-pipe system flows back to the boiler in separate pipes (Figure 7–5). On the whole, these parts are much the same as those in a hot-water system.

Forced Systems.   Steam heating is a gravity system only. Warm-air and hot-water systems can operate either by gravity or by force.

Most homes today have *blower-forced warm-air heating systems* with continuous air circulation. The furnace is smaller than the one in a gravity system. Ducts also are smaller and are rectangular rather than round so that they can be placed between floor joists or close to the basement ceiling, where they don't encroach on basement space (Figure 7–6). Registers and grills are smaller, too, and they can be installed where they won't interfere with furniture arrangements and traffic patterns.

All of these advantages result from the addition of a blower into the air-distribution system. The blower forces the air through the ducts so that heat arrives

FIGURE 7–3. How air circulates from and to a pipeless furnace.

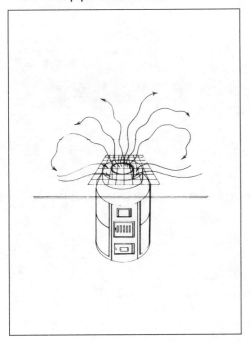

FIGURE 7–4. How water circulates in a two-pipe gravity hot-water system.

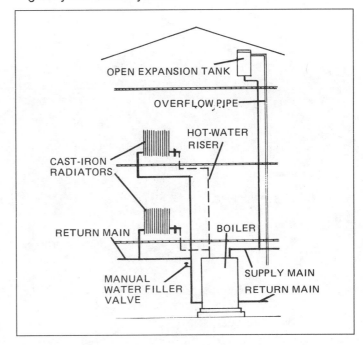

more quickly and disperses over a much larger part of each room. Since the system doesn't depend on gravity, you can place the furnace in a basement, in a crawl space, on the first floor or even in the attic. Air in a forced warm-air system is cleaner and more moist than in a gravity system because filters remove dust and lint from the air as it blows through. An automatic humidifier adds just enough moisture to keep the air comfortable.

The humidity of the air is as important as its temperature. You can be cold when the temperature in a room is 75 degrees Fahrenheit and humidity is 10 percent, yet comfortable when the temperature is 68 degrees Fahrenheit and humidity is 40 percent. Thus, a little moisture added to the air can reduce fuel costs. A well-built home with good insulation and vapor barriers requires little additional moisture. In fact, a small house with several young children living there might need a dehumidifier to cut down on condensation from laundry and bathing.

Most heating experts recommend letting the blower run all the time to provide continuous air circulation. While this does add a little to the cost of operation, it serves two important functions: It prevents stratification (layering) of the air, and it filters air more effectively. You may see stratified air when industrial smoke hangs in the sky on a windless day or when people smoke in a closed room. The blower in some continuous air-circulation systems runs at full speed while the furnace is giving off heat but at a quieter, slower speed the rest of the time to keep air moving gently within rooms. This movement keeps warm air from rising and cool air from dropping.

The pump-forced hot-water system has some of the same advantages as the blower-forced warm-air system. Both pipes and radiating devices can be smaller. The pump helps the system respond more quickly to a demand for heat and reduces the variation between the warmest and coolest temperatures in a heating cycle. It operates as long as the thermostat calls for heat. The system works well in large rambling houses—particularly if the house is divided into zones, each with its own thermostat and circulating pump. The boiler can be at ground level or above, and radiators can lie below boiler level.

Although forced hot-water systems can be adapted to air conditioning, it is

FIGURE 7–5. How steam and water circulate in a two-pipe steam-heating system.

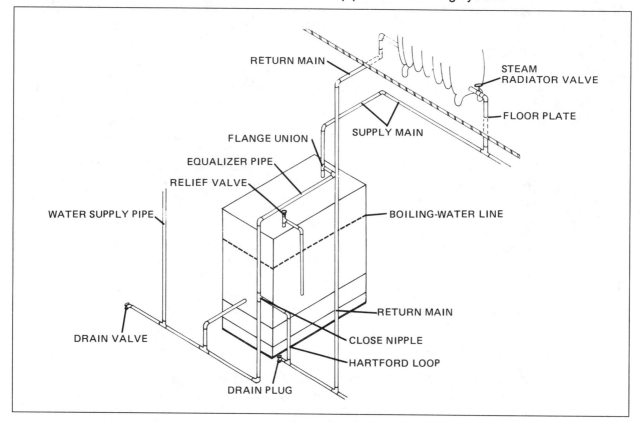

FIGURE 7–6. Warm-air perimeter system.

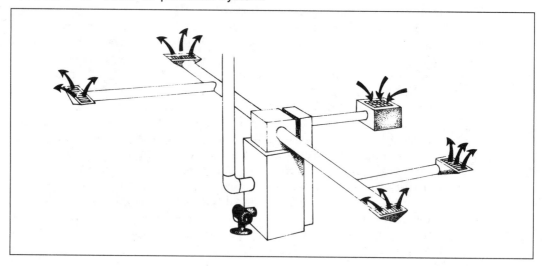

easier to do so with an air system. Some types of furnaces have heating and cooling systems combined into a single appliance, while others require separate furnaces and air conditioners that share the duct system. In most cases, chilled-water systems operate independently of hot-water systems.

Space Heating Systems

Space heaters are the simplest and least expensive of all heating devices. In this category are stoves, circulatory heaters, unit heaters, floor heaters, wall heaters and resistance heaters. In northern climates, central heating systems are often supplemented with space heaters in entryways, glassed-in porches, bathrooms and unheated garages used as workshops. A separate space heater in each room is sufficient where winter temperatures seldom drop to freezing.

Solar Heating

The increased demand for fossil fuels in recent years has forced builders to look for new sources of energy. One of the most promising sources of heat for homes is solar energy. Most solar heating units suitable for residential use operate by collecting heat from the sun's rays with devices called *solar collectors*. Ideally, collector panels should be installed on a south-facing roof and at an angle that places the panel surface in the direct path of sun rays.

The collector panels contain a series of pipes painted black to absorb solar radiation. A pump circulates water or air to be heated by the sun's rays through the panels. The heated water or air is then transferred to a heavily insulated storage tank until it is needed to heat the house.

Active and Passive Solar Systems.   There are two methods for gathering solar energy: active and passive. An active system uses motorized equipment to collect, distribute and store energy from the sun. A passive system uses no mechanical equipment to aid in heating or cooling. Today, most new homes feature many passive solar designs.

By insulating the ceiling in your house, you are contributing to a passive solar heating system. The reason: to work effectively, a collection system for passive solar heat must perform in an environment free of drafts or cold surfaces. Passive homes try to keep sun off the windows and encourage more openings for ventilation, higher ceiling spaces and clerestory windows to vent hot air. As you might guess, passive solar is considerably less expensive than active solar.

Many houses today are being heated and cooled by solar energy. However, these installations often furnish only supplemental energy and are accompanied by backup conventional systems needed for periods of high heat loads or poor sun conditions. To date, solar installations have also been relatively expensive. Nevertheless, as technology increases, it is expected that costs may be reduced sufficiently and a practical solar energy system, using a combination of active and passive, can be developed for single-family houses.

INSPECTING THE HEATING SYSTEM

The forced warm-air heating system is installed in three out of four new houses. The second most popular system, hot-water heat, is more expensive initially. Each of these systems can be fired with any fuel, which today is usually gas, oil or electricity.

Heating units on warm-air systems are called furnaces and hot water heating units are called boilers. Warm-air heat is distributed to the house through ducts, and hot water through pipes. When judging either system, examine the equipment and the heat distribution ducts or pipes.

A warm-air furnace with at least a 10-year guarantee has a thick, well-made heating chamber. A lower-grade furnace with a one-year guarantee is available at less cost. The air blower inside the furnace should be belt-driven with a pulley, much like an automobile's fan belt. Cheaper furnaces usually have a direct-drive blower; it is connected to the same shaft as its electric motor. The blower circulates the warm air from the furnace to the house. The 10-year guarantee and belt-driven blower mechanism are the major distinguishing features of a high-grade furnace.

The design and installation of the air-duct system are essential to good heating. The most effective duct design is called *perimeter duct distribution* and is recommended for warm-air heating in colder climates. The warm-air outlets are located around the exterior walls of a house (the house perimeter), usually under windows. The key to good heating is to supply warm air into each room at the source of the greatest cold. In general, there is at least one warm-air outlet register for every exposed wall. With warm-air heat, the system should be adjustable for continuous air circulation, and the air filter should be easily removable for cleaning.

Many older houses have furnaces that originally burned coal but have been converted to oil or gas. Look on the nameplate to see if the boiler is made of cast iron or steel. A cast iron one will usually last longer. Look inside the boiler for signs of cracking and around the exterior base for rust and deterioration.

If the house is less than 15 or 20 years old, it probably has the original heating equipment that was installed when the house was built. If the house is more than 20 years old, part or all of the system may need to be replaced soon. Keep in mind, however, that heating equipment may be inefficient not only because of its age, but also because of its old-fashioned design—especially when compared to today's energy efficient systems.

All heating systems need periodic inspection, cleaning and adjustments. As a general rule, gas and oil systems should be tuned-up every year before the start of the heating season to help cut fuel costs and prolong equipment life. Electric heating equipment doesn't require a tune-up, but it will require periodic cleaning and occasional lubrication of some of the components. Look for a service record attached to the furnace or boiler—a good indicator of how well the equipment has been maintained.

A heating unit that is too small for a house can also cause problems. The best way to check it is to visit the house on a cold day. Have the system turned on. Set the thermostat at 80 degrees Fahrenheit and listen for operating noises. A warm-air system should provide heat within 10 or 15 minutes, a hot-water or steam system within a half-hour.

CHIMNEYS AND FIREPLACES

Every house with a fireplace or a heating system fueled by gas, oil, coal or wood needs a chimney. To minimize fire hazards and to ensure efficient operation, building codes have strict design and construction standards for chimneys and fireplaces. For example, they must clear the house framework by at least 2 inches, and fire-resistant insulation should fill the space between the masonry and the woodwork.

HOW A CHIMNEY WORKS

The main job of a chimney is to supply fresh air to the fire and to carry off smoke and harmful gases. An upward flow of air is caused by the temperature difference from the heated air in the chimney and the cold air outside. This flow will continue as long as the furnace or fireplace is in operation. The height of the chimney and the wind conditions affect the direction of air flow, or draft. Figure 7–7 shows the two most common situations in which downdrafts occur, and how they can be avoided.

- When tall trees (Figure 7–7a) are obstructions and cause a downdraft, they should be trimmed to let air through (Figure 7–7b).
- A chimney placed at the low end of a house (Figure 7–7c) will receive a downdraft; it should be built at the highest ridge (Figure 7–7d).

CHIMNEY DESIGN AND CONSTRUCTION

Footing

A chimney constructed of masonry units is usually the heaviest single part of a house and must have its own footing. It should never be built directly on a basement floor

FIGURE 7–7. Prevention of downdrafts.

because the slab would not be strong enough to hold the weight. The footing should extend at least 6 inches beyond the chimney on all sides and should be 8 inches thick for one-story houses and 12 inches thick for two-story houses.

Flue

The flue is the opening in a chimney through which air, gases and smoke can pass. The best designed chimney has straight sides from the footing to the top, with flues also running vertically. Bends in a chimney or flue collect dirt and reduce the size of the flue area, thus restricting the draft. The number of flues and the size and shape of a chimney depend on how many fireplaces and fuel-burning appliances are in the house. Each unit should be connected to a separate flue; sparks that jump from one flue opening to another can cause fires.

Flue Lining. A lining, if installed correctly, gives the flue a smooth, interior surface, which helps it operate efficiently and safely. Rectangular fire-clay linings or round vitrified (glazed) tile are normally used in chimneys. Vitrified tile or a stainless steel lining is often required for gas-burning equipment. Local codes outline specific requirements.

Chimneys may be built without flue lining if the chimney walls are made of brick or unreinforced concrete at least 8 inches thick or of reinforced concrete at least 6 inches thick. However, linings are always used in well-constructed houses.

Chimney Location

The location of the chimney should be considered in terms of both cost and efficient operation. For example, the chimney that serves the furnace should also serve the fireplace. An interior chimney that rises through the roof costs less than one that rises on the outside of the house. When the chimney is on an outside wall, it needs face brick from the ground to the top, while an interior chimney needs face brick only above roof level.

The chimney must function properly. It should be built where a good flow of air will make it draw well. The height of a chimney usually depends on its location in relation to the ridge line. The lowest chimney flue must reach at least 2 feet above the highest point of the roof (Figure 7–8). Many building codes require 3 feet, which is always the minimum height above a flat roof. Sometimes a chimney has several adjacent flues. To prevent smoke pouring from one into another, the flues must have at least a 2-inch height difference.

Chimney Flashing

The installation of flashing around the chimney prevents water from entering the house. As seen in Figure 7–9, the intersection of the chimney and roof should be flashed with metal shingles which extend at least 4 inches under the roof shingles and 4 inches up the chimney. These shingles should overlap 3 inches to provide a watertight seal along the chimney. Counterflashing is installed over the top of the metal shingles, overlapping a minimum of 3 inches. The counterflashing is embedded a minimum of 1 inch into the masonry to prevent water from running behind the flashing and leaking into the house.

FIGURE 7–8.   Height of chimney.

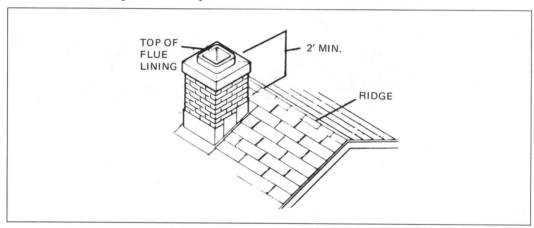

When the chimney is on the slope of a roof, a *saddle* (also called a *cricket*) should be erected to prevent a build-up of snow and water (Figure 7–10). The saddle is also flashed and counterflashed to make the junction with the roof watertight.

Chimney Cap

To prevent moisture from entering between the brick and flue lining, the top of the chimney is given a good watertight cap (Figure 7–11). The chimney can be capped with concrete, stone, brick or metal flashing. The most common cap is concrete, which should project 2 to 3 inches beyond the brickwork. The surface of the cap should be given a slight downward slope so that water will drain off easily.

Prefabricated Chimneys

Prefabricated chimneys bear a UL label (designating that they have been tested by *Underwriters Laboratories*) and are now approved by most building codes. One type of prefabricated chimney consists of two stainless steel casings separated by a special insulation. It requires a 2-inch minimum clearance from any combustible material as it passes through a floor, wall, or roof and can be used with furnaces, boilers and fireplaces. A different design has a flue lining encased in an insulating wall of light-weight cement, and an outside jacket of asbestos cement. This type is used with heating systems only and requires no clearance from combustible materials.

Both types of prefabricated chimneys are unaffected by temperatures, freezing and thawing or vibrations, and receive support from the floor or ceiling structure. They come as a complete package and can be installed after the house is finished. Compared to building a masonry chimney, installing a prefabricated one results in substantial savings of time and material.

FIGURE 7–9. Chimney flashing.

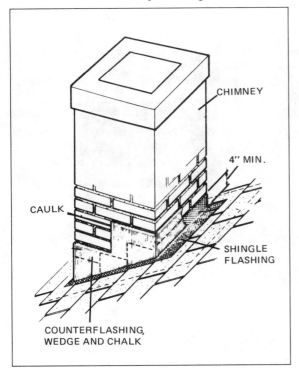

FIGURE 7–10. Chimney flashing with saddle.

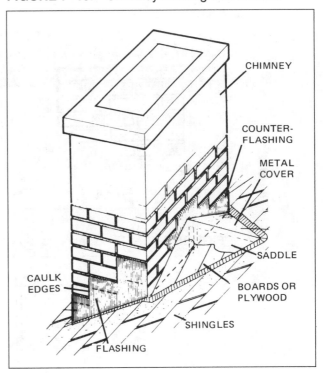

FIREPLACES

A masonry fireplace is expensive to build and is normally used less than any other feature of a house, even in cold climates. It is not too efficient either, because much of the heat goes up the chimney instead of into the room. In fact, only about 10 percent of fireplace heat makes it into the room. Yet, in spite of these drawbacks, a fireplace is an excellent sales feature in a house. Buyers will often give up other features rather than be without a fireplace (Figure 7–12).

FIREPLACE DESIGN

A well-designed fireplace should expel the smoke and harmful gases given off by the fire, while delivering the maximum amount of heat into the room. It should be fire-safe and should harmonize in detail and proportion with the room in which it is located.

Refer to Figure 7–13 as you read about the main parts of a masonry fireplace.

Hearth

The hearth is really an extension of the fireplace floor. It protects the floor area around the fireplace from sparks and ashes. The hearth may be at or above floor level, and must be made of noncombustible materials, such as brick or concrete.

Combustion Chamber

The combustion chamber is the space formed by the back and sides of the fireplace. Building codes usually require that walls of the combustion chamber be constructed of solid masonry or reinforced concrete at least 8 inches thick to withstand the high

FIGURE 7–11. Chimney cap.

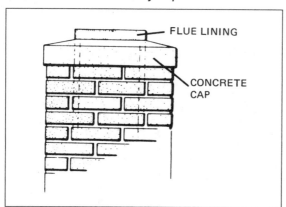

FIGURE 7–12. A typical fireplace.

FIGURE 7–13. Principal parts of a masonry fireplace.

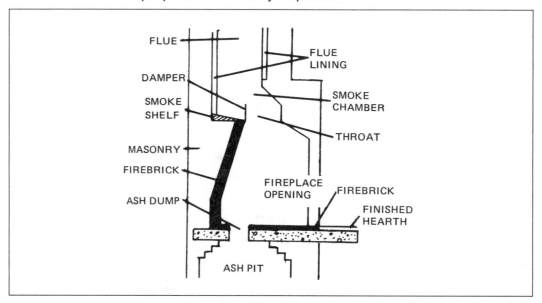

temperatures generated in this area. The walls must also be lined with firebrick or other approved noncombustible material not less than 2 inches thick or with steel lining not less than ¼ inch thick.

Damper

The damper, made of steel or cast iron, has a hinged lid that opens or closes to control the draft. The damper fits in the throat and extends the full width of the fireplace opening. When the damper is open, the lid forms a barrier that prevents downdrafts from entering the combustion chamber and deflects the air upward into the rising column of smoke. When a fireplace is not in use, the damper is closed to keep out drafts and dirt, and to prevent heat loss.

Smoke Shelf and Chamber

The smoke shelf prevents downdraft. This shelf is directly under the bottom of the flue, and extends the full width of the throat. The shelf should be horizontal, not sloped, to stop the downdraft. The space between the smoke shelf and the flue is the smoke chamber. The back wall is vertical and continues straight up the chimney. The side walls slope inward to meet the bottom of the flue lining.

INSPECTING THE CHIMNEY AND THE FIREPLACE

To get the most out of a fireplace, you need to first be sure the chimney is in shape to handle it. Most fireplaces and chimneys are seldom, if ever, cleaned and inspected, thus reducing their efficiency and safety. You should find out if the chimney had been cleaned recently, when the fireplace was last used, how often it was used, and if there were any problems.

The damper should be closed when the fireplace is not in use, otherwise the air you pay to heat or cool will escape through the chimney. Take a flashlight and see if there is a damper on the fireplace and what condition it is in. It should fit tightly, open and close easily, and have a handle that's not too difficult to reach.

Smoke in the chimney can back up into the room if the damper isn't operating properly, or if the chimney is clogged. You can check how well the chimney draws by lighting a piece of paper or by blowing cigarette smoke into the fireplace and observing whether it rises steadily and easily.

Carefully check the condition of the bricks and mortar joints on the facing of the fireplace. Are the bricks in good shape? Is the grout firm?

Next, poke around the firebricks with a screwdriver to see if any are loose, broken or chipped. Test the grout between the bricks. Darkened or burned firebricks tell you that the fireplace has been used frequently and probably works well.

Check the mantel. Is it level? If it isn't, it could mean that the footing is poor and the whole fireplace is settling unevenly into the ground.

AIR-CONDITIONING

A good air-conditioning system must do six jobs. In the winter it must heat the air and add humidity to it. In the summer it must cool the air and remove the humidity. The system also must circulate and filter the air. It takes good planning, good workmanship and good equipment to meet all these requirements.

Refining these requirements even further, a good system maintains constant daily temperature in the house. It should circulate air without drafts. Temperatures during the day should not vary much more than 2 degrees Fahrenheit in winter, and temperatures between rooms, unless the system is zoned otherwise, should not vary more than 4 degrees Fahrenheit. When outdoor temperatures are below freezing, there should not be more than a 5 degree difference between floor and ceiling air temperatures.

COOLING METHODS

Cooling equipment transfers the heat that is inside the house to the outdoors. It does this by expanding a liquid into a vapor, because when a liquid changes to a gas, it absorbs heat. Cooling equipment for residential air conditioning changes liquids to gas either by compression or by absorption.

Compression Cooling

This is the system used in your refrigerator and food freezer. At the heart of the system is a *compressor*, which forces a low-pressure gas, such as Freon, through a high-pressure line. The gas passes through a series of coils called a *condenser*. The condenser faces outdoors, and when a fan blows outside air over these coils, the gas loses heat and condenses into a liquid. This liquid flows into a reservoir, called a *liquid receiver*, then continues through an expansion valve, which regulates the flow, to an *evaporator*. The evaporator changes the liquid back to a gas at low temperature. Inside air blown across coils in the evaporator cools rapidly, then continues through ducts to various rooms. The path of the gas can be traced in Figure 7–14.

Water-cooled condensers are not practical for home use because they require large quantities of water.

Absorption Cooling

In an absorption system, the cooling cycle begins in a *generator*. Here a solution of water and lithium bromide (a substance similar to ordinary table salt) is heated to boiling. The solution, which is the *absorbent*, rises to a separator that draws off the lithium bromide and returns it to an absorber (Figure 7–15). The steam continues on to a condenser, where it turns back into water. The water flows into an evaporator, where it is turned into a very cold water vapor. This cold vapor, the *refrigerant*, is then pumped through coils in the furnace or boiler. Here it cools air or water that is forced to each room by blower or circulating pump. This system has no valves or moving parts and operates under a vacuum at all times. Absorption cooling works entirely on vapor-lift action, pressure differential and gravity.

AIR-CONDITIONING SYSTEMS

Homeowners can choose from seven different systems for summer air-conditioning. The most common is the single-duct, forced-air system. Others include the dual-duct system, the heat pump, panel cooling, fan-coil conditioners, the induction system, and room air conditioners. Dual-duct systems are used in hospitals; fan-coil conditioners are used in schools, motels and apartment houses; and induction systems are used in commercial buildings. We will discuss the residential systems in this chapter.

Central Forced-Air System

Most central forced-air systems operate on gas or electricity, although some use oil for fuel. Some types have the heating and cooling apparatus in two separate units, while others, like the year-round system in Figure 7–16, have the two systems built into a single unit. Most warm-air furnaces today are designed so that a cooling unit can be added at a later time. All types can use the same ducts, blowers and filters whether they are heating or cooling the house.

Wherever the condenser is located, it must drain off through a pipe of ¾-inch nominal dimension that carries it to a floor drain or outside the house. In addition, whenever the compressor unit or the air-conditioning unit is located above a habitable space, such as in an attic, most codes require that there be a watertight and corrosion-resistant pan underneath to catch any condensed water that might overflow from a clogged drain. From the pan runs another ¾-inch pipe that drains at some point where the amount of flow can be seen.

Equipment Size.   The size of a central cooling system is determined primarily by the square footage of living space in a house. In addition, the actual amount of heat that the house absorbs from the outside—influenced by such things as the number and size of windows, the amount of insulation, the layout of the house and the exterior shading—must also be considered. As a general rule, a house usually requires 1 ton of cooling capacity for every 600 square feet of air conditioned space. A typical 1,800-square-foot house, for example, would require a 3-ton system.

FIGURE 7–14. Compression cooling system.   **FIGURE 7–15.** Absorption cooling system.

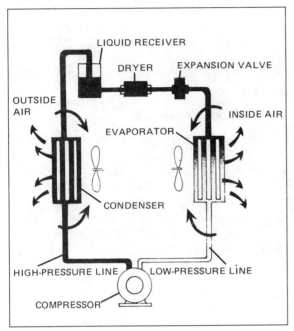

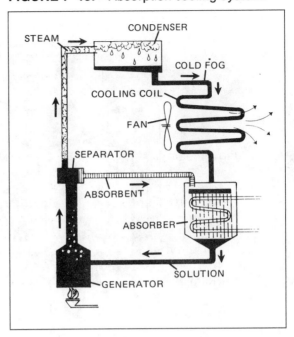

Water-Cooled Compressors

As we said earlier, most compressors are air-cooled, although a homeowner can enjoy the same flexibility of location with a water-cooled system. If the cooling unit will not fit next to the heating unit, it can be placed outside the house under cover, but this requires additional ductwork.

Central Hydronic System

There are fewer options available in cooling a house that is heated hydronically: you can install a chiller unit that sends air through a separate forced-air cooling system, or you can use individual room air conditioners.

Room Air Conditioners

In northern areas where the number of hot, humid days doesn't warrant the cost of installing central air conditioning, room air conditioners provide low-cost summer comfort. These units contain a compact compression cooling system. The condenser faces outdoors and removes the heat from the high-pressure hot gas. The evaporator faces the room, and a blower cools the room by drawing room air over the cold evaporator coils. Units operate on 110 to 120 volts, or 208-volt current.

The unit can be placed in a window, but it will defeat the window's purpose of providing light and ventilation. A far better idea is to frame the unit into an exterior wall below the window, just above floor level.

Heat Pumps

The heat pump is a special kind of year-round air conditioner. The principles on which it operates have been known for many years, and heating experts believe it will eventually replace conventional combination heating and cooling systems. Once installed, the heat pump operates very economically and requires little maintenance. It is most efficient in mild climates, but improvements make it adequate even in northern states. The main drawback to the heat pump is its initial cost.

The small heat pump is a single piece of equipment that uses the same components

FIGURE 7–16.   Diagram of a year-round air conditioner.

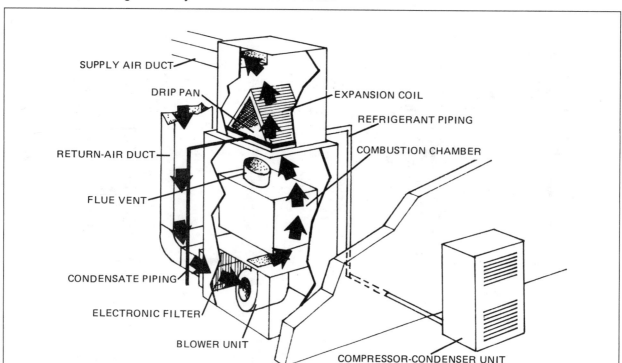

for heating and cooling. It doesn't need a flue or chimney. A *single-unit heat pump* may be installed outside or inside the house. As with other air-conditioning systems, a *two-unit heat pump* has a compressor unit that is set outside and a cooling unit for the inside.

Sources of Heat and Cold.   Heat pumps use the ground, air or water as their source of heat and cold, and either air or water as the means of distributing the desired temperatures to rooms (Figure 7–17). The most commonly used residential size heat pump takes heat out of the ground or air in winter and takes warm air out of the house in summer.

Because water contains more heat in winter and less in summer than does air, the heat pump uses less energy. But water corrodes the piping system, and it isn't always available in the quantity required. Disposing of the water that passes through the system poses an ecological problem, too.

Air is a much more plentiful source of heat than water, and it doesn't damage the pump. An air system uses more energy to obtain the proper BTU output; it also demands larger equipment and more complex controls than a water system. Frost and ice on the coils can be a problem, too.

The earth itself is almost as good a source of heat as water, and doesn't do the damage that water does. The controls are fairly simple, and use of energy is reasonable. The initial installation cost is higher, however, and good performance of the heat pump depends on the amount of moisture in the soil.

Distribution Systems.   Heat pumps that distribute heating and cooling through water in pipes work best in large buildings. Heat pumps, in most single-family houses, force air through a duct system sized for cooling.

How the Heat Pump Operates.   A heat pump, like a refrigerator, depends on the fact that gases give off heat when liquefied by pressure. In a ground-to-air heating

FIGURE 7–17. Reverse-cycle principle in heat pump operation.

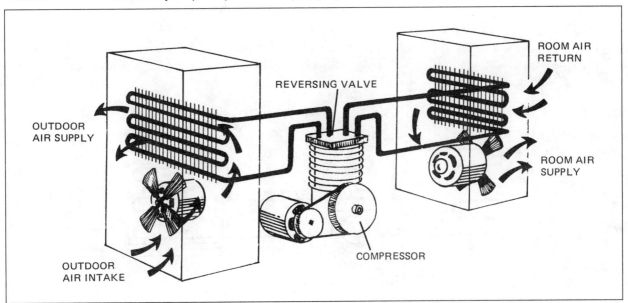

and cooling system, refrigerant (usually Freon) passes through coils of tubing buried in the ground (Figure 7–18). There it picks up heat, for the soil below frost level is always close to 50 degrees Fahrenheit. This heat moves to a compressor, which increases the temperature even more. At this temperature the heat moves into a coil in the indoor unit. The blower forces air over the coils, where it is heated; it then moves through ducts to the various rooms.

The cycle is reversed to cool the house in the summer. In the summer, inside air carries heat to the indoor unit, where the refrigerant in the coils absorbs it. This inside heat passes through the compressor on its way outdoors to the condenser (now acting as a chiller), from which it goes into the piping and dissipates into the cooler earth. Remember, warmth always moves toward cool—a scientific fact that makes the heat pump work in one direction in summer and in the reverse in the winter.

The principle of operation is the same for an air-to-air system. There is heat in air until it reaches absolute zero, which is –460 degrees Fahrenheit. Similarly, no matter how hot the air in summer seems to you, it can always absorb more heat.

Efficiency. A heat pump is adequate for cooling under almost any temperature conditions, because it is rarely called upon to reduce indoor temperature more than 20 degrees Fahrenheit below outdoor temperature. In the winter, however, when it may be called upon to heat 70 degrees inside when the outdoor temperature is below zero, the outdoor coil may gather frost and ice, which can obstruct air circulation. When this happens, the outdoor unit goes briefly into a defrost cycle that reverses the flow of refrigerant and melts the ice.

In extremely cold weather, the heat pump may have to struggle to supply all the heat required. Engineers solved this problem by adding electric-resistance strip heaters to the indoor unit. Under normal weather conditions, these heat boosters do not operate. When necessary, they turn on to make up the difference in temperature and reduce the strain on the heat pump.

Aside from initial cost of installation, the main drawback to the heat pump is that it becomes less efficient as the outdoor temperature drops. Because of this, you must build a tight house, weatherstrip all openings, and either double-glaze all windows or provide storm sash. These same fuel-saving steps should be taken with any type of heating system.

FIGURE 7–18.   Heat pump operation during heating and cooling cycles.

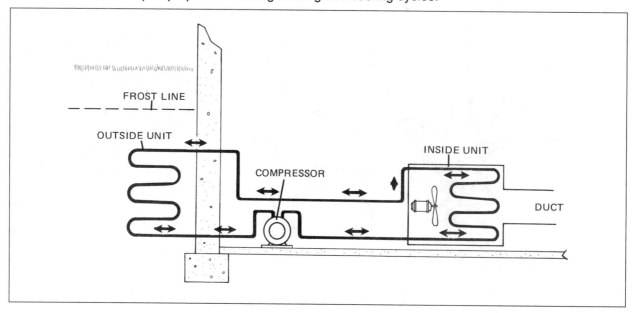

DUCT INSULATION

The purpose of ductwork in any air handling system is to effectively and efficiently distribute the conditioned air throughout the house.

Since bare, sheet-metal ducts offer little or no insulation and readily conduct heat or cold, air handling equipment must work harder to maintain indoor comfort. Metal ducts also leak air at the joints—a costly waste—and, when on the cooling cycle, sweat, drip and rust.

In many homes, heating ducts go through attics, under floors and through garages or other noninsulated areas. Ductwork, especially in these unheated spaces, should be insulated.

Because of the high temperature difference between the air in the attic and the heating ducts, these are the most important ones to insulate. Ducts in basements and crawl spaces should also be insulated, particularly if the floor above is heavily insulated.

If the house has a metal duct system already in place, all joints should be taped and the entire metal duct system wrapped with 2-inch-thick fiberglass duct-wrap insulation. Because fiberglass has a built-in vapor barrier, condensation problems are eliminated. And, heating and cooling equipment will operate more efficiently, creating continuous energy savings.

INSPECTION CHECKLIST

Type of System

Heating:	central forced-air/hot water/heat pump/other
Air-Conditioning:	central forced-air/heat pump/room AC/other
Fuel:	gas/oil/electricity

Age of equipment: _____

		Yes	No
1.	Does the heating and air-conditioning equipment use the least expensive fuel for the area?	_____	_____
2.	Does the house have energy-efficient heating and cooling equipment?	_____	_____
3.	Are the present utility bills acceptable for your budget?	_____	_____
4.	Do all rooms have air vents (or radiators)?	_____	_____
5.	Are the vent openings adjustable?	_____	_____
6.	Are the vents in the house clean and equipped with filtering devices?	_____	_____
7.	If the house uses a hot-water system, are radiators or piping free of leaks?	_____	_____
8.	Is sufficient warm (or cold) air reaching all rooms through the vents (or radiators)?	_____	_____
9.	Has the gas or oil furnace had an annual checkup?	_____	_____
10.	Is the Freon line in the central air unit free of leaks or other problems? (Ask the owner about any problems with the Freon. If there is too little, the unit will not cool properly. Too much Freon will cause the compressor to blow.)	_____	_____
11.	Do all ducts have dampers?	_____	_____
12.	Look at the joints connecting individual ducts. Are they properly sealed (no open gaps through which air is leaking)?	_____	_____
13.	Are the ducts (or pipes) wrapped with insulation?	_____	_____
14.	Is the heating and cooling equipment relatively new? (Check to see if they will need to be replaced soon due to age.)	_____	_____
15.	Does the equipment appear to be in good shape (no rust, dents, holes, etc.)?	_____	_____
16.	Is the condensation line for the air conditioner clear?	_____	_____
17.	Is the thermostat properly located (away from vents or ducts, etc., that may influence the temperature reading, causing the system to cycle on and off more than normal)?	_____	_____
18.	Is the size of the heating and cooling unit adequate for the number of square feet in the house?	_____	_____

	Yes	No
19. Has the owner properly maintained and serviced the chimney and fireplace?	_____	_____
20. Does the fireplace have a damper?	_____	_____
21. Is the damper tight-fitting and easy to open and close?	_____	_____
22. Does the fireplace draw well?	_____	_____
23. Are the face bricks on the fireplace solid (not coming loose from the wall)?	_____	_____
24. Are all firebricks firm?	_____	_____
25. Is grout firm (not loose or crumbling)?	_____	_____
26. Is the mantel on the fireplace level? (If not, be sure the reason is something other than a footing problem, which could be expensive to correct.)	_____	_____

Overall Rating

	Good	Fair	Poor
Heating system	_____	_____	_____
Air-conditioning system	_____	_____	_____
Fireplace and chimney	_____	_____	_____

Major Problems: _____

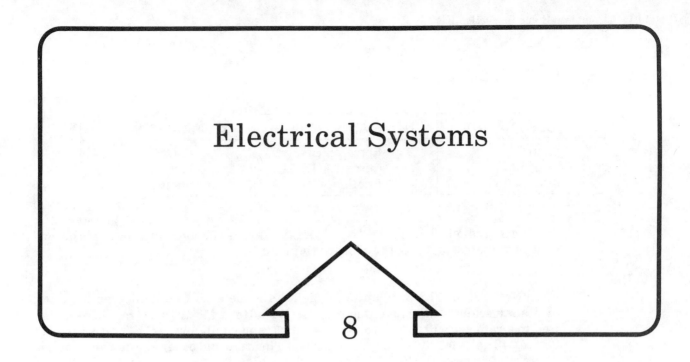

Electrical Systems

8

Electricity is a potent force. Errors or poor work can result in property damage and serious personal injury; hence all electrical work must conform to local codes and to the National Electrical Code (NEC).

Like plumbing, electrical work is divided into two phases: *rough-in work* and *finish work*. Rough-in work entails installing boxes for outlets, switches and fixtures and connecting them with the wiring. This work must be checked by a local electrical inspector before it is concealed in walls and ceilings. Switches, convenience outlets, cover plates and light fixtures are finish-work items. When they have been installed, the total job is rechecked by an inspector, who evaluates the electrical system in terms of three important characteristics:

- *Safety.* The system must meet all NEC requirements; each major appliance should have its own circuit, and lighting circuits should be isolated from electrical equipment that causes fluctuations in voltage.
- *Capacity.* The system must meet the home's existing needs and have the capacity to accommodate room additions and new appliances.
- *Convenience.* There should be enough switches, lights and outlets and they should be located so that occupants will not have to walk in the dark or use extension cords.

CHARACTERISTICS OF ELECTRICITY

Electricity behaves like water in many ways. Both move under pressure, at a rate of flow, and with some friction. The difference is that pressure (force) in the electrical line is measured in *volts*, not in pounds per square inch. Rate of flow (current) is measured in *amperes* instead of gallons, and friction (resistance) is measured in *ohms* (Figure 8–1).

Just as the size of a water pipe determines its resistance to the flow of water, the size of a wire determines resistance to electrical flow. You can't change one factor—volts, amperes, or ohms—without affecting the other two. The equation that

FIGURE 8–1. Electricity measurements.

DESCRIPTION	NAME AND SYMBOL	MEASURED IN
Pressure	Force (E)	Volts
Rate of flow	Current (I)	Amperes
Resistance to flow	Friction (R)	Ohms

expresses this relationship is $E = I \times R$, where E is the force in volts, I is the current in amperes, and R is the resistance in ohms.

Volts

The electrical unit known as the *volt* gets its name from Count Alessandro Volta, an Italian scientist who invented the electric battery. Most wiring in homes is limited to a range of 110 to 120 volts for lighting and small appliances and a range of 230 to 240 volts for stoves, dryers, baseboard heaters and other appliances that use electricity for heat. A 120-volt system consists of two wires: the hot wire carries the electricity, and the ground wire is neutral. A 240-volt system also has only two wires, but a 240/120-volt system has three: a neutral ground wire and two wires that carry power.

Amperes

The amount of electricity a wire can carry is measured in *amperes* (amps), named after André-Marie Ampère, a French scientist who discovered the relationship between electricity and magnets. One-hundred-amp service refers to the capacity of the service panel to supply 100 amps of current at a given voltage. A three- or four-bedroom single-family home should be equipped with a minimum 100-amp capacity—more if the home is heated electrically.

Ohms

Resistance to the flow of current is measured in ohms, an electrical unit named after German scientist Georg Simon Ohm. Ohm's law, his formulation of the relationship between current, electromotive force and resistance, is the basic law of current flow. The larger a wire, the lower its resistance. Similarly, the shorter the wire, the lower its resistance.

Watts

The fourth electrical measurement is the *watt* (w). Named after James Watt, a Scotsman who contributed to the invention of the steam engine, it is an expression of total power capacity. The equation for the watt is $P = E \times I$, where P is power in watts, E is the force in volts, and I is the current in amperes. Thus, a 100-amp, 240-volt power system can supply enough electrical current for 24,000 watts (100 amps $\times$ 240 volts). The only way to increase wattage is to increase amperes or volts, or both.

To determine the wiring requirements for a house estimate the total number of watts that are likely to be needed at any given time. A 30-amp, 120-volt circuit can supply 3,600 watts, which is usually adequate for lighting and small appliances. Major appliances need a 240-volt circuit at a higher amperage.

Since a watt is a relatively small unit, power supply is normally measured and sold in 1,000-watt units known as *kilowatts* (kw). One thousand watts used for one hour equal one kilowatt hour (kwh). Two 100-watt bulbs will consume 1 kwh of electricity in five hours. Electric bills are figured at so much per kwh, as in Figure 8–2.

FIGURE 8–2. Wattage.

DESCRIPTION	MEASURED IN
Total power capacity 1,000 watts 1,000 watts per hour	Watts (w) Kilowatt (kw) Kilowatt-hour (kwh)

Horsepower

Horsepower is a measure of power usage by motors. One horsepower (hp) is equal to 746 watts, so a power tool with a ¾-hp motor will use about 560 watts.

TYPES OF CURRENT

Batteries operate on direct current (dc); that is, the current always flows in one direction. Early experiments with electricity used dc batteries for power. Except in some isolated rural and mountain areas, all electric current today is ac, *alternating current*. Alternating current flows in one direction then reverses and flows in the other direction—hence its name. The movement in one direction and back again is called a *cycle* and occurs 60 times a second. Such current is referred to as 60-cycle ac.

WIRE SIZES

There are only three basic wire sizes used in homes and they are measured by the numbers 10, 12 and 14. The smaller the number, the larger the wire; and the larger the wire the more watts it will carry.

- Number 10 wire is used for appliances such as stoves, clothes dryers, electric heating and electric water heaters—all requiring at least 220 volts.
- Kitchen outlets should have number 12 wire because appliances there require high wattage and are used frequently.
- Number 14 wire is often used in rooms other than the kitchen, where low wattage electrical devices such as lights, alarm clocks, televisions and so forth are found.

TYPES OF WIRING

The NEC allows five different types of wiring systems: flexible armored cable, nonmetallic sheathed cable, special sheathed cable, conduit (rigid or flexible) and knob-and-tube wiring. Codes in many rural areas and small towns permit all five types of wiring, but most larger cities permit wiring only in conduit or nonmetallic cable.

Flexible Armored Cable

Almost all residential codes today permit flexible armored cable, also called *BX cable*. The cross-section in Figure 8–3 shows that this type of cable consists of two or more wires insulated from each other and a protective cover of flexible, spiral galvanized steel. The cover protects the wires inside against accidental damage, but it is not watertight and can be punctured by nails, screws or staples. BX cable, then, is not meant to be used outdoors or underground. Armored cable with a water-proof lead or plastic cover is more suitable for such purposes.

BX cable is flexible, which makes it easy to draw through partitions and bend around corners. The cable may have a small extra wire between the insulation and the cable cover that acts as a ground to maintain a complete circuit through the metal covering. Because it needs grounding, BX cable requires steel junctions, outlets and switch boxes.

Nonmetallic Sheathed Cable

Nonmetallic sheathed (NM) cable, commonly called *romex*, is similar to BX cable except for its exterior cover. Instead of a flexible metal sheath, the insulated wires are wrapped with various fibrous materials that resist heat and moisture (Figure 8–4). NM cable is less expensive than metallic cable, so it is generally used to wire garages and farm buildings rather than houses. It may be exposed or concealed, but it can't be used outdoors, underground or in masonry walls or partitions.

FIGURE 8–3.   Flexible armored cable is often used in frame construction.

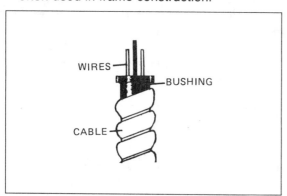

FIGURE 8–4.   Nonmetallic sheathed cable.

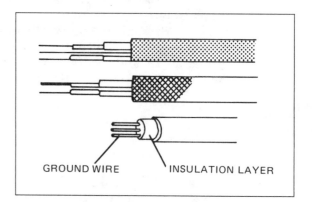

Because its exterior covering does not conduct electricity, NM cable can be used with steel, porcelain or plastic switch boxes. It can be attached to structural members and pulled through partitions or joists. One drawback of the NM cable is its stiffness; another is the fragility of its exterior covering.

Special Sheathed Cable

Early types of fibrous coverings deteriorated slowly under certain conditions. In response to this problem and the problem of stiffness manufacturers have developed a wide variety of durable, water-resistant jackets, a few of which appear in Figure 8–5.

The most common types of special sheathed cables are NM, NMC, and UF (Figure 8–5). Type NM (nonmetallic cable) has thermoplastic insulated conductors and a more flexible braided cover than regular sheathed cable; it may be used indoors, either exposed or concealed. Type NMC (nonmetallic corrosion-resistant cable) is similar to NM, but the exterior covering resists corrosion and fungus; it can be used in a completely grounded system with three-wire tools or appliances in a laundry, workshop or garage. Type UF (underground feeder cable and branch circuit) has a tough thermoplastic jacket and insulation wires that allow you to use it indoors, outdoors, underground, in masonry or where ice, moisture or fungus would cause ordinary sheaths to deteriorate. A variation of UF cable has a lead sheathing. It weighs about five times as much as UF cable, but it is flexible and completely waterproof.

Conduit

Wiring systems using conduit (a pipe or tube for protecting electric wires) are more expensive and time-consuming to install. They are also the safest systems and are required by many city codes in all new construction.

Rigid Conduit.   In rigid conduit the insulated wires are enclosed in metal pipe or tubing similar to water pipe but somewhat softer to bend more easily. Galvanized rigid conduit is suitable for almost any installation. Enameled conduit, however, is restricted to indoor use. Of all the wiring systems, rigid conduit is the only one that permits new wires to be installed or old wires replaced without tearing out the entire system.

Thin-Wall Conduit

Thin-wall conduit, also called EMT (electrical metallic tubing), is similar to rigid conduit except that walls are thinner. Thin-wall conduit may be used in exposed or concealed work where it is not subject to damage. It also may be buried in a concrete slab or carried in masonry.

Knob-and-Tube Wiring

Knob-and-tube is the oldest and least expensive method of wiring. The system consists of individual insulated wires strung between nonconductive insulators of porcelain, glass or composition (Figure 8–6). The insulators may be knobs, cleats or through-tubes. Knob-and-tube wiring is concealed when the wiring is installed between walls, between floors or in an attic; it is exposed on the surface of walls and ceilings.

Many local codes do not permit knob-and-tube wiring. Where it is allowed, it is found only in frame houses. This type of wiring is commonly used to bring a temporary power supply to construction shacks, roadside stands and carnival rides. Actually, knob-and-tube wiring has only one advantage over sheathed cable; it dries out quickly, so it isn't as easily damaged by moisture. It costs only a little less than sheathed cable and is no easier to install.

WIRING DIAGRAMS

Most electrical specifications, like the ones in Figure 8–7, are for performance, not materials. Their main purpose is to point out nonstandard items, such as the post light in section 1d, and to establish standards for appliances, as in sections 3c, 3d and 3e.

Symbols

The electrical plan shows the location and capacity of electrical outlets, built-in electrical equipment and the arrangements of circuits and switching. As with other mechanical systems, much of this information appears in symbols. You may find them confusing at first, but you should learn to identify them because they are standard throughout the country. Figure 8–8 displays the most widely recognized symbols.

The amount of detail on working drawings varies considerably. Floor plans, for instance, locate switches, the lights they operate, ordinary convenience outlets, telephone outlets and power outlets for high-wattage fixtures.

Switches.   An *S* on a drawing along a wall indicates a switch at that point. An *S* by itself denotes an ordinary single-pole switch. The *S* is always connected by a solid or dotted curved line to the light or receptacle it activates.

FIGURE 8–5.   Special-purpose nonmetallic
sheathed cable.

FIGURE 8–6.   Knob-and-tube wiring.

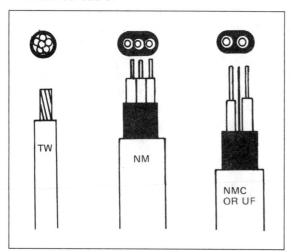

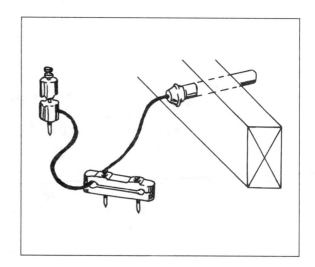

An S_3 indicates a three-way switch—one of two switches that operate the same light or a group of lights. An S_4 indicates a four-way switch—one of three switches that operate the same light. You will most often find four-way switches in hallways. Three-way and four-way switches allow you to turn on the lights as you enter a room at one point and turn them off at another point when you leave the room.

FIGURE 8–7.   Typical electrical specification establishes standards and notes exceptions.

Sec. 1. Scope. This division includes all interior electrical wiring, fixture installations and related items required to complete the work indicated on the drawings and specified.

a. The work under this division shall commence at the point of attachment at the service entrance equipment.

b. Electrical service supplied to the structure will be 240 volts, 3-phase, 60-cycle, 3 wire.

c. Allowance of $400.00 for selection of light fixtures by owner.

d. Bath receives ceiling exhaust fan. Electric post light by garage.

Sec. 2. General Requirements. Electrical system layouts indicated on drawings are diagrammatic and locations of outlets and equipment are approximate.

Sec. 3. Materials and Appliances.

a. Materials and appliances of the types for which there are Underwriter's Laboratories standard requirements, listings and labels shall have listing of Underwriter's Laboratories and be so labeled or shall conform to their requirements, in which case certified statements to the effect shall be furnished, if requested.

b. Materials other than those listed herein shall be the size, type and capacity indicated by the drawings and the specifications. Insofar as possible use one type and quality.

c. Hood over surface unit to be Nutone 1600, 30 inch, or equal.

d. Surface unit and oven to be General Electric, or equivalent model.

e. Dishwasher to be Kitchen-Aid KDI-17A or equivalent model.

Switches for special purposes have a subscript letter(s) beside them, such as S_d. The subscript letter indicates the item being operated—in this case an automatic door switch.

Outlets.   The standard convenience outlet has two receptacles for plugging in lamps, appliances or extension cords. Their symbol is a circle with two parallel lines running through it to the wall. If the symbol has an S beside it, that receptacle is operated by a switch. Two S's means both receptacles are operated by the same switch. If the symbol has a 3 beside it, the outlet has three receptacles in it instead of the usual two. An outlet with any letter except S beside it is a special-purpose outlet. GR denotes a grounding outlet, WP a weatherproof exterior outlet, and T a television hookup. A special-purpose outlet in a 240-volt line may appear

FIGURE 8–8.   Standard electrical symbols.

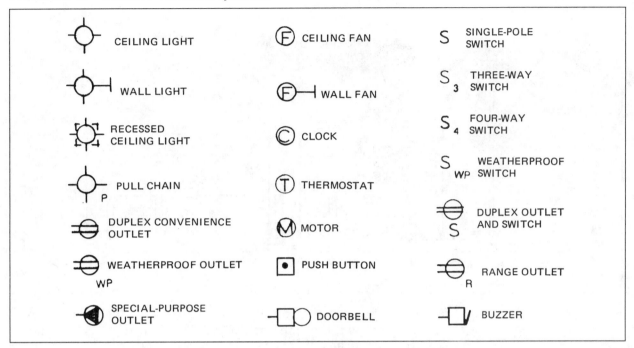

as a circle with three lines running to it or as a circle with a solid triangle in it. The special purpose is described in the electrical specifications.

Lights.   An outlet for a lighting fixture is represented by a circle with four lines radiating from it. When one line extends beyond the others and connects to the wall, the symbol is describing a surface-mounted wall light. A light by itself in the middle of the room on a floor plan indicates a fixture mounted on the surface of the ceiling. The same symbol with dotted lines around it calls for a recessed fixture; the shape of the dotted lines shows the shape of the fixture. A light symbol with a *P* beside it means the light is operated by a pull chain rather than a switch, as are many closet lights in older homes.

Other Symbols.   Most of the remaining symbols look like the fixture they represent—push button, clock, doorbell and buzzer.

SERVICE TO THE PANEL

In the early 1920s, 30-ampere service was standard. The standard doubled by the 1940s, and by 1950 the use of electricity and of appliances requiring 230-volt power had increased so rapidly that 100-amp service became the recommended standard. Today, 100-amp service is the minimum recommended by the NEC for houses that use gas for heating and cooking. Many all-electric homes have at least 200-amp service.

The Service Entrance
When the power needs of a house have been determined, the power company will check all calculations and will bring power to the house over a line called a *service entrance*. The size of this power line is based on the electrical amount needed; it also limits the energy available to the house. The service line to the house and the main service panel must be large enough to handle present power needs, with a

FIGURE 8–9. Clearances required for service drops.

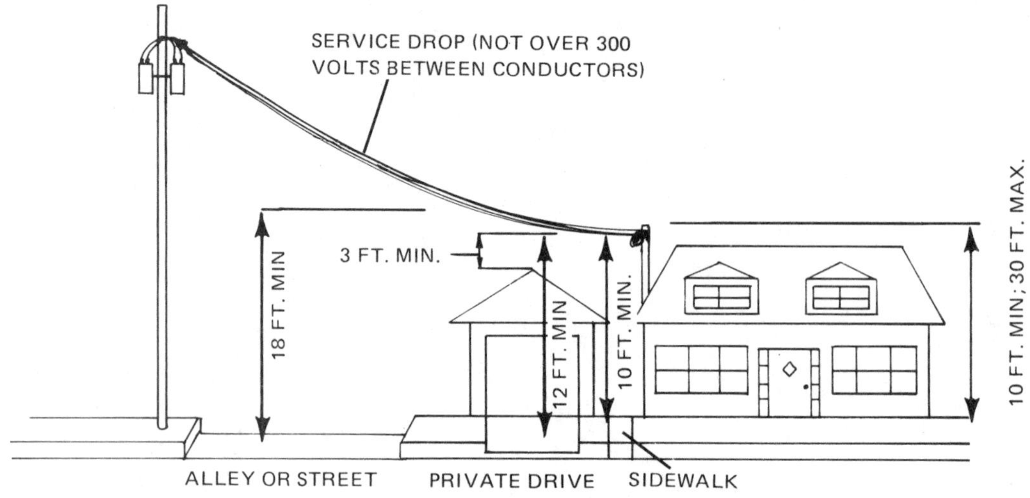

comfortable reserve for future use. Even if more circuits are added to the service panel, they won't do any good if the amperage of the service entrance is too small.

The service entrance reaches the house in one of two ways—overhead or underground. The *service drop*, a typical overhead service entrance, consists of three wires running from a power pole to the house. These wires must clear obstructions by distances specified in the NEC. They must run at least 12 feet above driveways; 10 feet above walks, porches and balconies; and 3 feet above the highest point of any low-pitched roof between the power source and the wall (Figures 8–9, 8–10).

The wires are heavily insulated; they may be attached directly to the house with nonconductive insulators or to a *mast*, which is usually a metal pipe that rises above the roof and continues downward onto the exterior wall. In both types of installation the entrance head is higher than the incoming wires. The raised head and loosely draped wires prevent water from draining into the electrical system. This is a code requirement.

Electrical power in many new residential developments is in underground lines and comes to the house underground. If the meter is in the basement, the service entrance ends at the meter, as it does in Figure 8–11. If the meter is outdoors, or if the house is over a crawl space or on a concrete slab, the service entrance rises on the outside wall. In all cases, the service entrance ends at the service panel.

The builder's contribution to the electrical system begins at the service entrance. He or she provides the insulators, brackets, clamps, entrance head, entrance cable or wired conduit, and, in many cases, the meter itself. The builder is responsible for all wiring from the entrance head on.

The Service Panel

The service panel is the distribution point for all electrical power brought into the house. No connections can be made into the line between the meter and the service panel.

Types of Service Panels. There are only two types of service panels in common use: the fused panel and the circuit-breaker panel (Figures 8–12, 8–13). Equipment, which is usually housed in one metal box, consists of a main disconnect switch and individual fuses or circuit breakers for each circuit in the house and sized to the capacity of that circuit. The neutral ground wire is never fused.

Excessive current can make a wire so hot that the insulation will burn. When

FIGURE 8–10.   Service entrance to a wall.

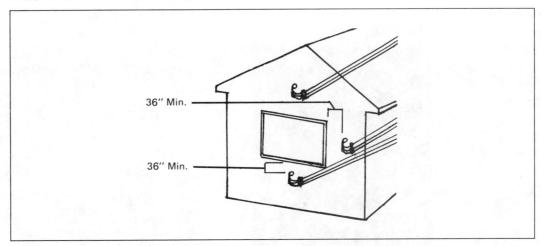

the insulation between conductors fails, you have a short circuit and a power failure. You also have an electrical hazard. To regulate the flow of current, you need something that will shut off the power, like a shutoff valve in a water line. Two devices serve this purpose: a fuse and a circuit breaker.

FIGURE 8–11.   Underground service to a basement.

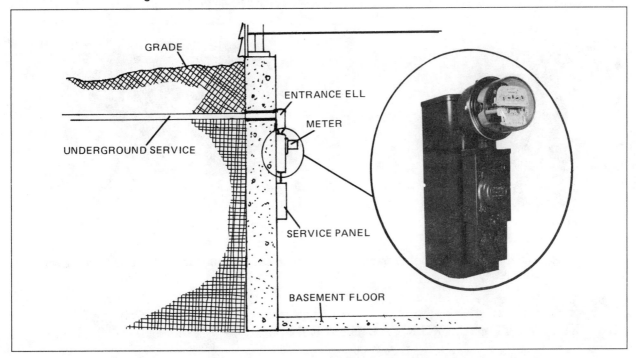

A fuse (Figure 8–14) is a small device that either snaps or screws into position in a fuse panel. Current flows across the fuse through a thin metal strip with a low melting point. When any current above the rated amperage of the fuse passes through that fuse, the metal strip melts and stops the flow of current. The plug-type fuse, which screws into a socket, is used in most residential service panels. The cartridge type is used when service is more than 300 volts.

A *circuit breaker* has a tripping mechanism that opens a switch when current exceeds rated amperage. In many respects a circuit breaker works like a switch. It stays in the *on* position as long as current flow is not excessive. It automatically

FIGURE 8–12.   Breaker-type service panel.

FIGURE 8–13.   Circuit breaker.

FIGURE 8–14.   Fuse.

switches to *off* when current flow is too great. When flow returns to normal, you have to reset it.

INSPECTING THE ELECTRICAL SYSTEM

Check the wiring, especially in older houses. Is it adequate? The electrical wiring should be supplied by a 220- to 240-volt three-wire feed from the power pole to a 220- to 240-volt service panel in the house. The panel should have a capacity of at least 100 amperes. A larger 150 to 200 or more ampere service may be needed if there is electric heat, an electric range, or if the house has more than 3,000 square feet. New wiring will be required if the existing board is only 30 or 60 amperes in capacity. If there are fewer than eight or ten circuits, you are likely to need more. Each individual circuit is represented by a separate fuse or circuit breaker. A house with a lot of electrical equipment may require 15 to 20 or more circuits. A separate circuit should be provided for each of the following appliances:

Correct fuse or circuit breaker size for appliances

Electric stove	50 amp
Clothes dryer	30 amp
Water heater	30 amp
Washing machine	20 amp
Dishwasher	20 amp
Garbage disposal	20 amp
Furnace	15 amp

Check the kind of material wiring in the house is made of. *Copper wire* is best. It is pliable and durable—and the most expensive. *Aluminum* wiring, used in homes primarily between 1964 and 1972, heats up much more quickly than copper and is a poor conductor of electricity. Because of its poor safety record—it creates a fire risk approximately 40 times greater than copper—it might be prudent to walk away from a house that has total aluminum wiring. Copper-clad aluminum wire (aluminum wire with a thin coating of copper) is a reasonable compromise and appears not to have the problems associated with 100 percent aluminum wire.

Check the number of electrical outlets, particularly in the kitchen. Are there enough light switches throughout the house?

REMEMBER: Under no circumstances should you touch any exposed wiring or probe with tools in electrical panels. Electricity is technical, complicated and dangerous. If you are in serious doubt about any aspect of the house's electrical service, consult with a professional home inspector or a licensed electrician before giving the house further consideration.

INSPECTION CHECKLIST

Electrical Information

Service Drop: two-wire/three-wire

Service Panel: fused panel/circuit-breaker panel

Wires: copper/copper-clad aluminum/aluminum

Ampere Service Capacity: _____

Number of Circuits: _____

		Yes	No
1.	Do the living areas of the house have sufficient electrical outlets?	_____	_____
2.	Are all outlets in good working condition?	_____	_____
3.	Are all switches and outlets properly grounded?	_____	_____
4.	Are there outside electrical outlets?	_____	_____
	Do they work?	_____	_____
5.	Are the covers over outdoor outlets weathertight?	_____	_____
6.	Are all outlets three-holed? (The third hole is the grounding connection.)	_____	_____
7.	Are all switches and outlets in good shape?	_____	_____
8.	Do appliances have their own separate circuits?	_____	_____
9.	Is there a main disconnect switch?	_____	_____
10.	Pull the main disconnect switch. Does it shut off all electrical circuits? (If not, a serious defect exists in the system.)	_____	_____
11.	Are there enough circuits to serve your needs?	_____	_____
12.	Does the wiring meet the code?	_____	_____
13.	Has copper or copper-clad aluminum wiring been used (instead of 100% aluminum)?	_____	_____
14.	Are all light fixtures working?	_____	_____
15.	Are all circuit breakers working?	_____	_____
16.	Are all fuses or circuit breakers cool to the touch? (If they are warm, a serious defect may exist.)	_____	_____

Overall Rating	**Good**	**Fair**	**Poor**
Wiring	_____	_____	_____
Ampere service capacity	_____	_____	_____
Number of circuits	_____	_____	_____
Number of electrical outlets per room	_____	_____	_____
Number of light switches per room	_____	_____	_____
Average dollar amount of electric bills	_____	_____	_____

Major Problems:_____

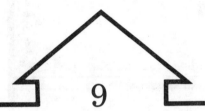

Insulation, Interior Walls and Ceilings

9

A house without enough insulation allows a needless waste of heat and air conditioning. Since fuel prices continue to climb steadily, it is senseless to let warm or cool air escape through an uninsulated roof, floor or wall.

How much insulation a home should have depends on the climate, the cost of fuel and your family's comfort. In general, however, homes with electric heat need more insulation than homes where heat is supplied by gas or oil—and more is needed in homes with air conditioning. Each climatic area makes different energy demands on a house. Homes in very warm or very cold climates need more insulation than do homes in temperate climates.

INSULATION AND R-VALUES

Most houses built before the 1940s were constructed without any insulation. From World War II up to about 1955 many houses were built with attic insulation but little or no wall insulation. Since 1955 most houses have been built with both wall and ceiling insulation, though not necessarily enough. Regardless of age, houses with masonry or brick walls usually have no wall insulation.

The effectiveness of insulating materials is not related to thickness, but to resistance to heat flow, known as the *R-value*. (*R* stands for *resistance* to heat flow.) The higher the insulation's R-value rating, the better it will prevent heat from leaking out of the house. The minimum R-value for walls is 11; for ceilings, 19; and for floors over crawl spaces, 13. In colder climates and for homes heated by electricity, higher R ratings may be called for. In general, R-19 should be sufficient for walls, R-33 for ceilings and R-22 for floors. However, check with local authorities for the insulating needs in your area. In colder climates, higher R ratings may be called for, and builders sometimes suggest thicker insulation for homes heated by electricity.

In an inspection of a house, you'll need to find out the extent of the insulation throughout the building. To reduce heat loss during cold weather in most climates, all walls, ceilings, roofs and floors that separate heated from unheated spaces should be insulated. Figure 9–1 shows the areas where insulation is required.

FIGURE 9–1. Areas that require insulation.

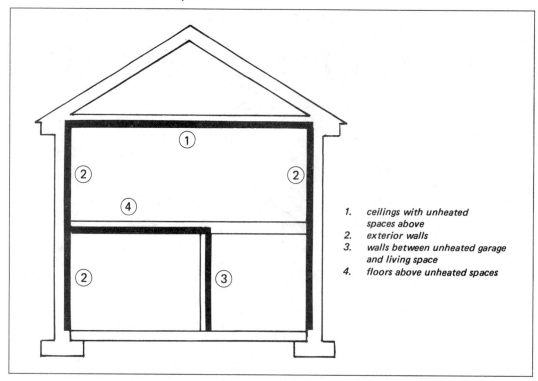

1. ceilings with unheated
    spaces above
2. exterior walls
3. walls between unheated garage
    and living space
4. floors above unheated spaces

Types of Insulation

Insulation products come in many different types, qualities and thicknesses. For instance, two products with differing thicknesses may have the same R-value, as shown in Table 9–1.

TABLE 9–1. R-values for various thicknesses of insulation.

| | Batts-Blankets | | Loose and Blown Fill | | | | |
R-value	glass fiber	rock wool	glass fiber	rock wool	cellulose fiber	vermiculite	perlite
R-11	3½ in.	3 in.	5 in.	4 in.	3 in.	5 in.	4 in.
13	4	3½	6	4½	3½	6	5
19	6	5	8½	6½	5	9	7
22	7	6	10	7½	6	10½	8
26	8	7	12	9	7	12½	9½
30	9½	8	13½	10	8	14	11
33	10½	9	15	11	9	15½	12
38	12	10½	17	13	10	18	14

A house usually contains more than one type of insulating material. However, the most popular types are batts and blankets, which come in preformed rolls of R-11, R–13, R–19, and so on. Batts and blankets can be used in more parts of a home than any other insulation. There are, of course, other materials that can be used. For example, a typical house might have sheet insulation and batting for exterior walls, batting for floors and some ceilings, and blown-in insulation for attics and ceilings.

If a house has less than two inches of insulation, more insulation must be installed; if the house has less than four inches, installing more is strongly recommended.

Upgraded Insulation Guidelines

The United States Department of Energy (DOE) has recently upgraded its insulation recommendations to homeowners, increasing its minimum R-value suggestions for the country's various climates. The new R-values are now specific to zip code areas and take into account climate, heating and cooling needs, types of heating used and energy prices. The DOE estimates that 50 to 70 percent of the energy used in the average American home is for heating and cooling. Yet, most of the houses in the United States are not insulated to recommended levels. In an attic insulation study, for example, it was found that the average insulation level in attics is about R-20. But the DOE now recommends an average of R-40. The new guidelines cover other areas of the home as well, including ceilings, floors, exterior walls and crawl spaces. Since insulation is relatively inexpensive, the cost-benefit ratio makes increased insulation levels worthwhile.

Asbestos and Urea Formaldehyde

Two kinds of insulation to avoid in homes are asbestos and urea formaldehyde. Asbestos insulation, embedded in ceilings and walls by builders of another era, is no longer used because it is believed to cause cancer if its fibers get into the lungs. Urea formaldehyde may also be a potential health hazard and its use has been banned in most parts of the United States. It often emits noxious odors and toxic fumes, causing nausea and other irritations to those who inhale it. If you are interested in a house that you suspect has either asbestos insulation or urea formaldehyde, don't take any chances. Bring in a qualified inspector to examine all questionable areas. It would probably be in your best interest to avoid homes with these kinds of insulation.

WALLS

As soon as the house is under roof; once the carpentry, plumbing, heating and electrical rough-in work is completed and inspected; when the walls are insulated and sheathed and the window frames are installed, the builder is ready to start covering exposed studs and ceiling joists. Interior walls may be made from a number of different materials—gypsum wallboard, plaster, prefinished paneling and solid wood paneling.

GYPSUM WALLBOARD

Gypsum wallboard, also called plasterboard, Sheetrock or drywall, is used today on more walls and ceilings in residential construction than any other material (Figure 9–2). Essentially, wallboard consists of a gypsum filler (commonly called plaster of paris) that is mixed with water, poured between two sheets of specially manufactured paper, and baked to rock-like hardness. It is produced as a 4-foot wide continuous ribbon that is cut in lengths of 8 feet to 16 feet after the gypsum core has set. Thicknesses vary from ¼ inch to ⅝ inch.

The backside of the board may be thin cardboard, special water-resistant paper to be used in bathrooms and kitchens or as a base for applying tile, or metal foil that provides reflective insulation. The exposed face paper may be a patterned or textured vinyl that requires no further finishing or an ivory-colored paper that is specially treated to take paint or wallpaper.

The face paper on all gypsum wallboard is wrapped around the long edges to reinforce the board, but the core is exposed at the ends. The edges may be beveled or slightly rounded so that one panel can be butted to the next without finishing. They also may be tapered for further finishing with joint cement and paper tape to give a smooth surface.

FIGURE 9–2. Installation of drywall. (Courtesy of United States Gypsum Co.)

FIGURE 9–3. Aluminum-backed wallboard. (Courtesy of United States Gypsum Co.)

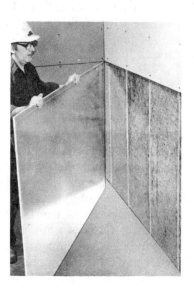

Gypsum wallboard has some limitations. The ¼-inch board, for example, must have a backing; it is used primarily in covering old wall and ceiling surfaces. The ⅜-inch board should not be used in single thickness when stud or joist spacing is greater than 16 inches on center. It is typically used in a double-wall system made up of two layers on ⅜-inch wallboard to form a ¾-inch-thick wall. The ½-inch and ⅝-inch thicknesses are the most common in houses.

Wallboard is heavy: a sheet ½ inch by 4 feet by 8 feet weighs about 60 pounds. Wallboard also can be damaged in movement. It is easy to snap a corner, and the thinner boards can break in two if handled roughly. Once in place, wallboard is quite sturdy, though not as hard as a plastered wall. There are many advantages to wallboard, too. It is a low-cost, fire-resistant material that is easy to cut, fit and apply. As a building material, gypsum wallboard is a relative newcomer compared to plaster and wood. Like many new products, it was not perfect when it first came on the market, but since then research has overcome all problems except poor workmanship.

Regular Wallboard

Regular wallboard is commonly used for ceilings and walls. It comes in thicknesses from ¼ inch to ⅝ inch, in 4-foot widths, and in lengths from 6 to 14 feet. Its face paper is ivory-colored, the backing is cardboard and the edges along the length are tapered. On walls, it is strongest when applied horizontally; on a ceiling it is strongest when applied across joists.

Predecorated Wallboard

Predecorated wallboard has been available for years, but the finishes have improved steadily. Early surfaces were attractive but didn't stand up to the wear and tear of a household full of small children. Today, almost all decorative facings are durable, easy-to-clean vinyls. Available in thicknesses from ⅜ inch to ⅝ inch and in 8-foot and 10-foot lengths, predecorated panels come in solid colors and in wood-grained, marbleized and textile patterns.

Insulating Wallboard

Insulating wallboard is made by the same process as regular wallboard, except that it is backed with aluminum foil instead of cardboard. It comes in ⅜-inch to ⅝-inch thicknesses, 8-foot to 14-foot lengths, and with tapered or eased edges. The aluminum foil insulates and acts as a vapor barrier (Figure 9–3). Panels are fastened with the foil side against studs or furring strips, but an airspace of at least ¾ inch must be left behind the foil for it to be effective. The reflective insulating value is roughly equal to ½ inch of fiberboard insulation.

Water-Resistant Wallboard

Water-resistant board was developed for rooms with high humidity, such as bathrooms, kitchens and utility rooms. It too is made like regular wallboard, but its components are different. The thicker back and face papers are chemically treated to withstand moisture, and the gypsum core has asphalt mixed into it to make it water-resistant. It comes only in ½-inch and ⅝-inch thicknesses, in 8-foot and 12-foot lengths and with tapered edges.

PLASTER

Steady improvements in drywall construction have all but done away with plaster as a wall and ceiling material except in the most expensive homes, or where required by code.

Compared to drywall, the main disadvantages of plaster are its expense, long application and drying time, and the amount of moisture that penetrates the air and wood framing members during drying. Plaster is valued for its plasticity, which allows it to conform to any contour, its hardness and its durability. It is also fire-resistant and soundproof.

Many of the fine homes built before 1950 had ornamental plaster work. As drywall grew more popular, ornamental plastering (and the craftspeople capable of doing this work) almost disappeared. It is now making a strong comeback, primarily in public buildings.

There are many types of plasters. Some contain wood fibers for improved workability and added strength against cracking; some are fine-grained for hard, dense surfaces; others, like some concretes, have high early strength. There are acoustical plasters with lightweight or fibrous materials to absorb sound and there are pliable, white molding plasters.

Plaster Bases

Plaster is applied to a base. Until recently, that base was most often wood lath—strips of wood 4 feet long that absorbed moisture from the plaster and formed a mechanical bond with it. But wood lath shrank and expanded, and plaster tended to crack in the winter. Metal lath was the first replacement, followed by gypsum lath, which is now the prevailing plaster base for both walls and ceilings.

Gypsum Lath. In some ways, gypsum lath is like gypsum wallboard: it has a gypsum core sandwiched between layers of paper and a cardboard or foil backing that serves as a vapor barrier. For stud or joist spacing of 16 inches on center, a ⅜-inch thickness is used. For 24-inch stud or joist spacing, and for better-quality jobs, the thickness should be ½ inch or ⅝ inch.

Most gypsum lath is 16 inches wide and 48 inches long with square edges. It may be solid, or it may be perforated to improve its bonding capabilities and thus increase the time it will remain intact when exposed to fire. The gypsum core is faced with several layers of paper. The outer layers absorb water quickly so that plaster sticks to the lath before it begins to slide. The inner layers, on the other hand, are chemically treated to resist moisture that would soften the gypsum core and cause it to sag after the board is in place.

Metal Lath.   Metal lath plaster base is sheet metal that has been slit and expanded to form a mesh with many small openings. The meshes can assume a variety of patterns (Figure 9–4).

FIGURE 9–4.   Metal lath mesh patterns.

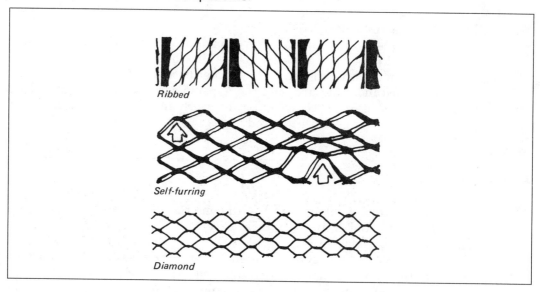

Metal lath comes in sheets 27 inches wide and 96 inches long. One of these sheets covers more than three times the wall area that gypsum lath does, but the openings in the mesh consume considerably more basecoat plaster.

WOOD PANELING

The warm, rich look of wood adds a soft, textural quality to a room that can't be matched by any other wallcovering. There are basically two types of wood paneling: prefinished and solid wood—but quite a difference exists between the two.

Prefinished Paneling

Prefinished paneling is made from a number of materials, but hardboard and plywood are the usual choices (Figure 9–5).

Hardboard is a manufactured product, but don't think it isn't real wood. Hardboard is an all-wood panel made from regular logs that have been converted to chips, then to wood fibers. The fibers are bonded together into sheets under heat and pressure. Wood-grain hardboard is printed with grain to match the color and texture of oak, mahogany, walnut and many other woods. It is also available in brick and marble patterns and solid colors.

Toughness is the principal characteristic of hardboard. You can't realize how tough it is until the first time you have to cut it. Hardboard thicknesses range from ⅛ inch to ⅜ inch, with standard thicknesses of ⅛ inch, 3/16 inch, and ¼ inch. The

FIGURE 9–5. Types of paneling.

standard panel size is 4 feet by 8 feet. Because of its comparative hardness, hardboard endures abuse better than some other types of paneling. It doesn't crack and it takes paint well.

A popular variety of hardwood, called *pegboard*, is perforated to receive hooks and hanging hardware. When fitted with metal or plastic accessories, perforated wall panels create storage space for tools, kitchen utensils and other loose items.

Prefinished plywood paneling is just a step away from natural wood, since it is made up of layers of wood glued together. Plywood with hardwood facing is available in more than 80 different woods, including birch, oak, maple, cherry and walnut. The cost of the panel varies with the wood and the thickness of the panel. Prefinished plywood paneling is manufactured in sheets 4 feet wide, 7 or 8 feet long, and between 5/32 inch and 1/4 inch thick.

Solid Wood Paneling

Solid wood paneling is lumber milled from trees, with all the natural texture, warmth, fragrance, color and grain subtleties of wood. Although solid wood paneling can be made from any kind or grade of hardwood or softwood lumber, most is manufactured from western pine lumber. Some heavily knotted pine lumber is manufactured into the familiar knotty pine paneling. Besides the many standard patterns of solid wood paneling, it can be made in special patterns if required. Interior wood paneling is usually installed vertically, but it can also be put on horizontally, diagonally or in a combination of directions to obtain special effects (Figure 9–6).

FIGURE 9–6.   Decorative effects with interior wood paneling.

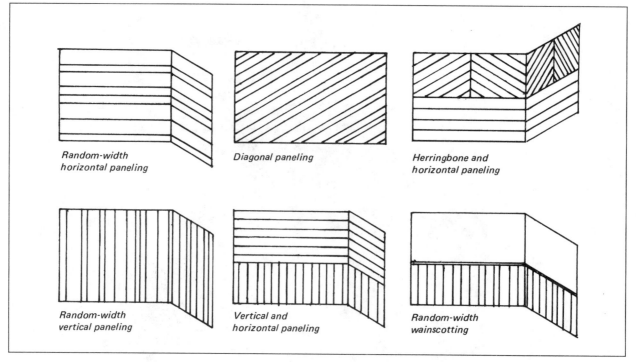

Random-width horizontal paneling

Diagonal paneling

Herringbone and horizontal paneling

Random-width vertical paneling

Vertical and horizontal paneling

Random-width wainscotting

DECORATIVE FINISHES

Most walls and ceilings of gypsum wallboard or plaster receive no further decorating treatment except paint or, perhaps, wallpaper. Homeowners who want more can choose from several materials to decorate and soundproof drywall and wetwall (plaster) surfaces.

Ceiling Tile

Ceiling tiles, inexpensive and available in designs that blend with almost every decorating period, are designed to absorb sounds within a room. Acoustical ceilings are made of wood fiber tile or mineral fiber tile (Figure 9–7). Wood tiles are a form of fiberboard about ½ inch thick with a painted surface. The tiles may be plain, finely perforated to improve sound absorption, or highly decorated. Mineral tiles are made out of rock that is heated until it is molten, then blown into 1-inch thick sheets. These tiles are almost white and, unlike wood tiles, they do not burn.

The most popular sizes of acoustical ceiling tiles are 12 inches by 12 inches and 12 inches by 24 inches. Edges may be square, beveled, shiplapped, tongue-and-grooved or slotted.

WARNING: Acoustical ceilings in homes built before 1979 may contain asbestos. Any deterioration or disturbance may release hazardous asbestos fibers into the air. Be sure to ask both the owner and the real estate agent whether such materials were used in the house you are inspecting.

Cork

Cork is a lightweight, dark substance that comes from the outer bark of the cork oak tree, which grows primarily in Portugal, Spain and Algeria. While cork is inexpensive in its natural state, by the time it is shipped and processed it costs more than other materials that serve the same purpose. Nevertheless, it is valued for its

FIGURE 9–7.   Acoustical ceiling tiles. (Courtesy of United States Gypsum Co.)

quality. It is an excellent insulator in addition to being sound-resistant and water-resistant.

At one time, cork was used in its natural state for flooring and as an ingredient in linoleum. Today, it is most often seen as a feature material on one wall or part of a wall, for its texture and color.

Cork may be purchased in tiles or sheets. Tiles are either 9 inches by 9 inches or 12 inches by 12 inches and vary in thickness from ½ inch up to 2 inches. Sheets of cork are thinner (less than ¼ inch) and may have a burlap backing. Both are applied with adhesive.

Wallpaper

Cheers for the Chinese. In 200 B.C., they decorated rice paper squares and stuck them on walls, and the wallpaper industry was born. The Chinese established a home decorating tradition that is strong today. The Europeans imported papers from the Orient in the 16th century. The French found wallpaper a cheap and pleasant substitute for tapestries, and the American colonists carried wallpaper to the New World to cheer it up.

Wallpaper was once the hallmark of an elite house. It declined in popularity during the 1940s but slowly revived in the 1950s. But wallpaper has changed. So has the term. Now we say *wallcovering* because 80 percent of what we paste up isn't paper at all. It's vinyl, suede, grasscloth, mylar, silk, foil, linen, burlap, cork or tooled leather.

Today, wallcovering is a more desirable interior treatment than ever—and, from the standpoint of design and decor, a more imaginative one (Figure 9–8). It's relatively inexpensive, and it offers instant changes that can have a remarkable effect on the background mood and identity of the room. In addition, modern wallcoverings have other advantages, such as acoustical properties for better insulation. They are also fire-resistant and easy to clean.

FIGURE 9–8.   Wallpapered room.

INSPECTING THE INSULATION, INTERIOR WALLS AND CEILINGS

Insulation

Insulation can serve the double purpose of heating and cooling a house. If attic space is not meant to be used as a living area, the floor of the attic is insulated; otherwise, the attic ceiling is insulated. All outside walls should be insulated, as should floors over unheated areas such as a crawl space. Insulation can be applied in the form of blankets or batts that are stapled between the studs, loose insulation that is blown into floor and wall spaces, or rigid fiberboard materials that are used structurally as sheathing or wallboard.

While it is not difficult to determine the amount of insulation in an older home, blown-in insulation is not easily detected unless it is evenly distributed. Blown-in insulation can be exposed by removing wall outlets at several places. Insulation beneath the floor is not as easy. A floorboard can be pried up with a crowbar, the insulation measured and the floorboard carefully replaced. Another way is to drill a hole through the floor and insert a pencil through the hole. If a mark is made on the side of the pencil where it first touches the insulation below, and where it touches the base of the insulation, the distance between the two marks will be the thickness of the insulation. The hole in the floor can be repaired with a section of dowel.

Walls and Ceilings

Things to look for on painted walls or ceilings are cracks or bulges. Holes or depressions that have been carefully filled are not serious; a single coat of paint will restore the beauty of the wall or ceiling. However, long or prominent cracks and bulges may indicate deeper problems.

Plaster cracks are common; plaster, like stucco, is stiff and brittle and will show the slightest movement. Cracks can be caused by such things as shrinking lumber, poor diagonal bracing, foundation settling, earthquakes, wood rot or termite damage. Large cracks should be checked to see if the plaster is pulling away from the wall or ceiling. Bubbles or raised portions are sure signs. One cause of plaster pulling away from a wall or ceiling is moisture—perhaps from a slight leak that eventually results in decay of the lime in the plaster.

Wallboard cracks are a different story. Straight cracks are usually found at joints and are generally caused by poor taping. Large diagonal cracks, on the other hand, are caused by extreme shifting or settling. It takes a severe movement to break wallboard diagonally.

Frequently you will find cracks on either side of a doorway or window at the top of the opening. These are header cracks caused by shrinkage of the wood and are not serious. Once the shrinkage has stopped, the cracks can be filled and repainted.

In some cases, wallcovering or paneling could be hiding some faults in the wall itself. If you have any suspicions—for example, about discoloration or an uneven surface—be sure to find out the cause.

You should test wallboard surfaces by rapping on the wall. If the sound is thin and hollow, the boards are probably less than ½ inch thick. Thicker boards (½ inch to ⅝ inch) will keep out the noise that the thinner and less expensive ones let in.

Check the ceilings for signs of leakage. You are not likely to spot actual holes through which rainwater runs. Look instead for water marks with discolored edges. These spots are where the water collects and where it will ultimately drip through.

Make sure that plaster ceilings are in good condition. Since ceiling plaster has to withstand a constant pull of gravity, the weaker sections may eventually crumble and fall to the floor. The cost of replastering or covering the ceiling is relatively high.

INSPECTION CHECKLIST

Types of Insulation, Walls and Ceilings

Interior Walls: wallboard/plaster/wood/wallpaper/other

Ceilings: wallboard/plaster/wood/tile/other

Insulation: batts or blanket/loose fill/rigid board/other

R-Value: floors _____   walls _____   ceilings _____

		Yes	No
1.	Has an energy audit been done on the house?	___	___
	If so, were the results positive?	___	___
2.	Are the basement walls fully insulated?	___	___
3.	Is the attic adequately insulated?	___	___
4.	Are unheated areas such as garages and crawl spaces insulated?	___	___
5.	Are the exterior perimeter walls insulated?	___	___
6.	Does the house have good quality wall and ceiling insulation?	___	___
7.	Do the insulation materials have vapor barriers?	___	___
8.	Is the house free of asbestos insulation?	___	___
	Is the house free of formaldehyde insulation?	___	___
9.	Are interior walls in good shape (no major defects)?	___	___
10.	Are wallboard or plaster walls free of cracks?	___	___
11.	If no, are these cracks narrower than ¼ inch? (Larger cracks, particularly those in corners or next to window or door framing, may indicate structural failure.)	___	___
12.	Are walls straight (no unsightly bows)?	___	___
13.	Is all wallboard secured?	___	___
14.	Are plaster walls in good shape?	___	___
15.	Are walls free of holes?	___	___
16.	Are all wood panels solidly attached and in good shape?	___	___
17.	Are walls free of water stains or other signs of leakage?	___	___
18.	Does all wallpaper appear in good condition (not curled at the edges or faded)?	___	___
19.	Are ceilings free of cracks?	___	___
20.	If no, are these cracks narrower than ¼ inch? (Larger ones may indicate structural failure.)	___	___
21.	Are ceilings free of water stains or other signs of leakage?	___	___
22.	Is wall and ceiling paint in good condition (no peeling paint or faded colors)?	___	___

	Yes	No
23. Are the plaster ceilings in good condition (no bubbles or raised portions)?	_____	_____
24. Are all ceiling tiles in good shape?	_____	_____
25. Push back suspended ceiling panels to examine hidden areas. Are they in good shape (no signs of deterioration in ceilings or walls)?	_____	_____

Overall Rating	Good	Fair	Poor
Interior walls	_____	_____	_____
Ceilings	_____	_____	_____
Insulation	_____	_____	_____

Major Problems: _____

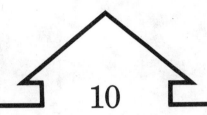

Finish Flooring and Interior Trim

10

With the house fully enclosed and interior wall and ceiling finishes completed, plans can be finalized for the type of flooring that will be used in various locations. Homeowners today are fond of hardwood strip or parquet floors, wall-to-wall carpeting, resilient flooring and hard surfaces such as ceramic tile, brick, slate and stone for special areas.

HARD FLOORS

Hard floors can be either wood or made of natural materials such as slate, brick, marble, terrazzo, stone and ceramic tile. All of them are expensive to install, are permanent yet almost impervious to damage.

Wood Flooring

During the last two decades more and more homeowners have become interested in real hardwood flooring—once the hallmark of every fine home. They are uncovering old wood floors that have been covered with carpet or tile for years, and sanding and refinishing the wood to restore its original luster and beauty.

Wood flooring continues to be popular in many rooms, especially the family room or den. There has been a growing preference for darker wood tones and specialty boards such as pegged planks. Oak is used most extensively for flooring, but maple and pecan are also common choices.

Wood flooring can be bought in prefinished blocks and in prefinished or unfinished strips.

Prefinished Blocks.   Of the three, wood block is the most expensive. The standard size is 9 inches by 9 inches, like most thin tile, but you can sometimes find 8-inch, 10-inch, and 12-inch squares; rectangles; and special shapes. Thickness ranges from 5/16 inch up to 3/4 inch. The thinner block is set in adhesive over concrete or plywood subfloors, while the thicker block must be nailed to wood or plywood subflooring. Less expensive wood blocks are hardwood veneer laminated under pressure to a core of plywood. Top-quality blocks are made of solid hardwood.

Most blocks have tongues on two sides and grooves on the other two, so that they can be laid in a straight pattern or as a parquet floor (Figure 10–1), with the grain of each block at right angles to the grain of adjoining blocks. Tongues are drilled for nailing. Some have a groove for metal splines on the back to keep the block from cupping; others have resilient foam backing with self-stick adhesive for fast installation.

FIGURE 10–1.   Parquet floor.

FIGURE 10–2.   Prefinished strip flooring.

Mastic is the usual adhesive for setting block flooring. It is similar to the adhesive used for thin floor tile but has a lower moisture content.

Prefinished Strip Flooring.   Prefinished strip flooring is less expensive than block flooring but more expensive than unfinished strip flooring. Prefinished strips save from 3 to 5 days of work in the average house, and the floor is ready for use as soon as it is laid.

Unfinished strips have square edges, while prefinished strips have slightly beveled edges. This difference does not affect application, but it does make cleaning a little harder.

A popular variation of strip flooring is prefinished planking. As its name implies, plank flooring comes in boards—usually in random widths, and usually with tongue-and-groove edges and ends so the boards interlock when installed.

Often called *ranch plank* or *pegged flooring*, the wood planks are usually 2¼ or 3¼ inches wide and are laid in alternate strips to simulate old Colonial-type plank flooring. Factory-installed walnut pegs or plugs (Figure 10–2) near the ends of each board look like the wood dowels used with early floors. Thickness ranges from ⁵⁄₁₆ inch to 1⅓ inches.

Ceramic Tile

Cork is one of the few materials that can be used on both walls and floors. Ceramic tile is another.

Ceramic tile is one of the oldest building materials known. Some 5,000 years ago the Babylonians used glazed tile to protect the sun-dried brick with which they built their temples. Even then, tiles were made in bright colors and gaudy designs that were sometimes laid in intricate patterns called mosaics. Although the process for making ceramic tile and the product itself have become more sophisticated over the years, the basic process—firing clay at high temperatures and baking on a decorative finish—is much the same today as it was then.

Ceramic tiles are available in a wide variety of designs and colors that can be used with all except the most formal furniture styles (Figure 10–3). Grouting, which is applied between the tiles after they have been laid, comes in colors so it's possible to create interesting effects by setting off different areas within a room.

With their history of good performance, ceramic tile walls and floors have won lasting acceptance in new homes and are a key sales feature in older homes. Ceramic tile continues to be the most popular bathroom floor and wall covering.

Shapes and Sizes.   Ceramic tiles range in nominal size from ⅜ by ⅜ inch up to 16 inches by 18 inches. The smaller sizes are suitable for decorative flooring, while the larger rectangular sizes are used as an exterior or interior wall material in commercial and public buildings. Typical wall-sized tiles are 4¼ inches square.

Rectangular tiles (1 inch by 2 inches, 3 inches by 6 inches, 6 inches by 9 inches) can be interspersed with square tiles to form decorative patterns. There are also hexagonal and octagonal tiles available in 3-inch and 4¼-inch overall dimensions.

Other Hard Flooring

Brick, stone, mozaic tile, slate and marble make beautiful flooring materials and are most practical for entryways, bathrooms, family rooms and perhaps kitchens. They are dangerous when wet, however, and are often used in conjunction with an area rug that is firmly secured to prevent slipping.

RESILIENT TILE

Resilient floor tile is manufactured from an almost endless variety of materials, including asphalt, vinyl, reinforced vinyl, cork, rubber and inlaid vinyl.

Reinforced vinyl, also called vinyl-asbestos, is the most versatile and is currently the best selling resilient floor tile. Asphalt is the least expensive but is not recommended where it is likely to become a target for grease or solvents (Figure 10–4). Solid vinyl is durable but costly. Also fairly expensive is cork, which is rich looking and comfortable underfoot but must be sealed for easier maintenance.

Except for cork, resilient tiles are thin—from less than ⅟₁₆ inch up to about ⅛ inch. Most thin tiles are made in 9-inch or 12-inch squares.

RESILIENT SHEET FLOORING

Resilient floor covering (Figure 10–5) is also manufactured in sheet form, available in 6-foot, 9-foot, and 12-foot-wide rolls. The wide rolls allow installation of a continuous one-piece floor surface. Inlaid vinyl, also referred to as linoleum, is the most commonly used kitchen floor covering today. Sheet flooring comes in a wide variety of patterns that resemble everything from pebbles to carpeting.

A recent innovation is to inset one color in another. This trend is strongest in large rooms, such as game rooms, where most of the furniture is around the walls. These patterns personalize a room and add flair to it.

FIGURE 10–3.   Ceramic tile entryway.

FIGURE 10–4.   Asphalt tile floor.

CAUTION: All vinyl flooring *contains some asbestos*, so care must be taken during its installation or removal.

FIGURE 10–5.   Resilient floor covering.

CARPETING

There is nothing quite as luxurious as wall-to-wall carpeting in a room—and probably nothing quite as expensive either. It adds elegance, warmth and softness, and has become a popular living room and bedroom treatment over the past 30 years. Stain-resistant carpeting is now found in family rooms, dining rooms, and even kitchens.

Although carpeting is generally selected for its comfort and decorative values, it also absorbs sound and reduces sound reflection in a room—much like acoustical ceiling tile.

Wall-to-wall carpeting is available in an enormous range of colors, patterns, thicknesses, fiber contents and costs. A good-quality pad underneath the carpeting is almost as important as the quality of the carpet itself. Padding adds to the "bounce" of the carpet and prolongs its wear life.

INTERIOR TRIM

Trim has a number of meanings in the building industry. In a broad sense, the term refers to any item—from a doorknob to a sink rim—that finishes off something else. Also called *molding*, trim usually describes the pieces used to finish walls around openings, at corners and where two different materials meet. Figure 10–6 pinpoints places where trim is required and identifies the piece of molding used in each location.

FIGURE 10–6. Moldings and trim locations.

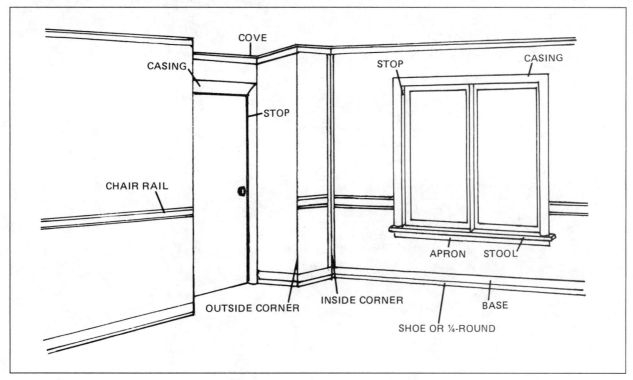

Virtually every home has molding trim around doors and windows and as "kickboards" where walls meet floor. However, *chair rail* (a single piece of trim that rims the walls at chair height) and *crown* molding (the trim that separates—and integrates—ceiling and walls) went out of fashion altogether some years ago. Now the cycle is changing, and such moldings are coming "in" again.

Crown moldings top off walls and tie them to a room's ceiling with a flourish. The accent added to a wallpapered room in this way helps create a warmer, cozier feeling by "bringing down" the ceiling—joining it visually more closely to the walls.

Chair molding divides a room, circling it at a height of about 32 inches, usually at the top of a wainscot panel or between wallpapered and painted portions of a room.

Most interior trim is made of Ponderosa pine and Idaho white pine. Trim for painting is milled from pine, gum, poplar and similar woods; trim for staining is more likely to be a decorative hardwood such as oak, walnut, chestnut, birch or mahogany. Millwork is shaped from woods that are clear (free from knots and other defects) and kiln-dried to a low moisture content.

Although wood is still consumers' number one preference, hardboard and vinyl moldings are the latest substitutes.

INSPECTION CHECKLIST

Floor Finishes

Kitchen: linoleum/vinyl tile/wood/carpeting/ceramic tile/other

Bathrooms: ceramic tile/linoleum/vinyl tile/other

Living room: carpeting/wood/linoleum/vinyl tile/other

Family room: carpeting/wood/vinyl tile/linoleum/brick/other

Bedrooms: carpeting/wood/vinyl tile/linoleum/other

Entryway: wood/vinyl tile/ceramic tile/slate/carpeting/other

Hallways: carpeting/wood/vinyl tile/ceramic tile/other

Wood Flooring	**Yes**	**No**
1. Are the floors finished and sealed correctly?	_____	_____
2. Is the floor finish in good condition?	_____	_____
3. Are floors free of squeaks? (A squeak may simply indicate a need for renailing, but it may also be part of a more serious structural problem.)	_____	_____
4. Is the floor firm? (An unusual spring to the floor as you walk across it could indicate a subfloor problem.)	_____	_____
5. Is flooring in good shape? (Make sure there is no rotting, which usually occurs at bathrooms or door thresholds.)	_____	_____

Resilient Flooring		
1. Is the linoleum or tile smooth? (Bumps or hollows may indicate the subfloor wasn't properly prepared.)	_____	_____
2. Are linoleum surfaces free of cracks, tears or noticeable marks? (If not, the only possible correction is total replacement of the flooring.)	_____	_____
3. Are individual tiles in good shape (not cracked, loose or curled)? (Remember, however, that these can be replaced fairly easily.)	_____	_____

Hard Tile Flooring		
1. Are tiles in good shape (no cracked, loose or missing tiles)? (Several cracked tiles could be the result of house settlement, perhaps indicating a serious structural problem.)	_____	_____
2. Is grout firmly in place?	_____	_____
3. Is the flooring level? (High or low spots could pose a safety hazard.)	_____	_____

	Yes	No

4.   Is this type of flooring—particularly brick, slate, and marble—in areas that do not receive a lot of water? (These materials are slippery when wet.)   _____   _____

Wall-to-Wall Carpeting

1.   Are there good quality carpets in the house? (In general, the tighter the twist of the yarn and the closer together the individual tufts in a row, the better quality the carpet is. In shags, however, density is not an important factor.)   _____   _____

2.   Is there good quality padding underneath the carpets?   _____   _____

3.   Are the carpets in good condition?   _____   _____

4.   Are the carpets tightly stretched? (Any looseness will cause the carpet to wear much faster.)   _____   _____

5.   Is the carpet free of worn or torn spots?   _____   _____

6.   Are seams inconspicuous?   _____   _____

7.   Is the carpet free of stains?   _____   _____

8.   Are all carpets relatively clean? (Cleaning may not help excessively dirty carpets.)   _____   _____

Trim

1.   Are the decorative moldings around the house in good shape?   _____   _____

2.   Is the paint or stain on the moldings in good shape (no peeling paint, no faded colors)?   _____   _____

Overall Rating	**Good**	**Fair**	**Poor**
Wood flooring	_____	_____	_____
Resilient flooring	_____	_____	_____
Hard tile flooring	_____	_____	_____
Wall-to-wall carpeting	_____	_____	_____
Trim	_____	_____	_____

Major Problems: _____

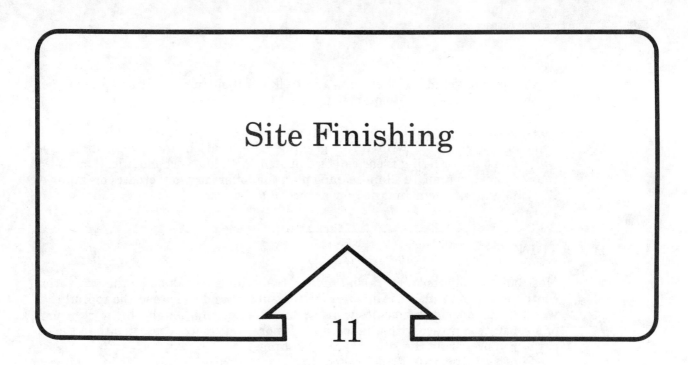

Site Finishing

11

While finishing the inside of the house, the builder can turn his or her attention to the finishing touches on the site. Before staking out the house, the builder made a plot plan that located not only the house, but also the driveway, walks, outdoor living areas and large trees to be kept. At the time, the builder may have had in mind a general picture of just what landscaping would be required to set off the new house to its best advantage. The landscaping around a house is one of its most important assets—or liabilities—and can add or subtract 5 to 10 percent of the value of the house.

THE SITE PLAN

Site planning should be reviewed after the house has taken shape. Then you can see in three dimensions what could only be seen in two dimensions on a plot plan. Things will be seen that hadn't been obvious before—a bare spot that needs shrubbery, a wall that looks higher than it did on working drawings, or a fast-growing tree that wasn't noticed originally.

A good starting point in final site planning is to take another look at the plot plan and reevaluate the three areas of the site—the outdoor living area, the service area, and the public area. Ask yourself these questions:

- Does the land slope so that rainwater and melted snow drain *away* from the house and outdoor living areas?
- Is the view best from the living and working areas most often occupied during daylight hours?
- Are outdoor living areas screened from public view?
- Is the play area clearly visible from the kitchen, family room and main living areas?
- Is the service area, where trash is kept, hidden from view?
- Is the driveway laid out so that its slope, turns and width are adequate for safe movement of cars?

- Can people get out of their cars and walk to all entrances without stepping on the grass or falling into planting?

The answers to these questions will determine your next steps. Most drainage problems can be corrected with finish grading. The location and size of driveways, walks and outdoor living areas can be adjusted. With any such modifications out of the way, you can prepare a landscaping plan that offers privacy, creates or improves the view and complements the appearance of the house.

FINISH GRADING

Most builders subcontract finish grading. Sometimes it is done by the excavation contractor, who returns to finish-grade the subsoil and to spread the topsoil that was piled to one side when site work began. More often, though, this work is part of a separate contract with a landscaper. He or she is more interested than the excavator in preparing the site for growing things.

Finish grading usually is limited to the top 6 inches of subsoil. The topsoil isn't spread until the ground is ready for seeding or sodding.

DRIVEWAYS AND WALKS

A good solid driveway from the main road to the house is essential for deliveries and for the convenience of the family.

There are two main points to consider in planning a safe driveway. First of all, it should not slope too steeply to the road; it should be as level as possible. Another safety factor is to provide enough room at the end of the drive or at some other point so that a car or small truck can be turned around. The driveway and turnaround in Figure 11–1 allow the driver to back out of a single or double garage into the turn and proceed to the road in a forward direction. In areas of heavy traffic this is much safer than having to back into the road. Concrete gives the best surface for a driveway, but brick, asphalt, crushed rock and gravel are also popular.

Main walks should extend from the front entry to the street or front sidewalk or to a driveway leading to the street. They should be pitched so that water drains off quickly. A 5-percent grade is considered maximum for walks. When slopes to the house are greater than a 5-percent grade, stairs or steps should be used. Walks should be wide enough for two abreast to walk, a minimum of 4 feet, preferably 5 feet.

THE LANDSCAPING PLAN

Landscaping design looks easier than it actually is. In fact, it is one area in which many good builders go wrong. Builders constructing more expensive houses often use the services of a landscape architect, who has specialized knowledge of architecture and building materials. This individual knows how to use planting, walls and fencing to hide flaws in the house's design and to emphasize its good points.

Like any exacting job, good landscaping starts with a plan (Figure 11–2). The plan locates what is already fixed—the house, large trees, driveway, walks and outdoor living areas—and from that point on indicates the following:

FIGURE 11–1. Driveway turnaround.

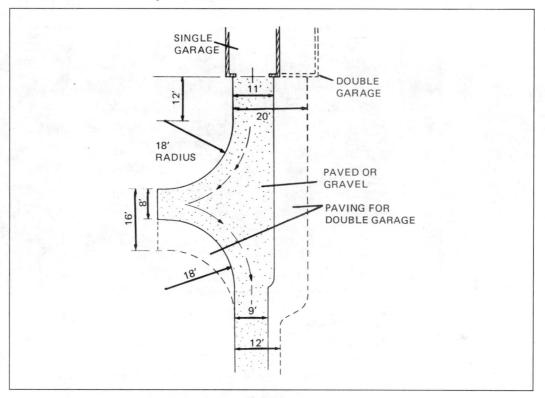

- Planting around the foundation to soften the baseline of the house
- Planting to edge and define walks, driveways and outdoor living areas (also locates lighting for these areas)
- Hedges or tall shrubs along the side lot lines to define the property yet exist as "friendly fences"
- Evergreens that will add a touch of green all through the gray-brown winter
- Planting to hold the soil of steep banks in and keep it from washing away, and walls to separate levels or to balance irregular contours
- Planting to frame a beautiful view or to screen out a less attractive one
- Trees that will shade the patio, break the wind or keep the house cool on a hot summer day
- Locations of swimming pools, rock and flower gardens, underground sprinkler systems and sheds
- Locations of gates, fences and other visual space dividers

A landscaping plan is usually drawn at a scale of 20 feet to the inch (1 inch = 20 feet) and may show contour lines if the site has irregular topography. Like architects, engineers and others who draw plans, landscape architects have symbols for types of planting (Figure 11–2).

Good landscapers consider several factors that are often overlooked by homeowners. Landscaping must help the appearance of the house when it is new, but must still look good many years later. Proper spacing of shrubs and trees is critical. Landscaping should also provide a variety of textures and colors; a good plan has something in bloom somewhere on the site from early spring until late fall. By supplementing existing trees and creating a pattern of shade and shadow, landscaping can soften the rectangular lines of the house.

There is no right or wrong landscaping design. A landscape plan depends

FIGURE 11–2. Landscaping plan and typical landscaping symbols.

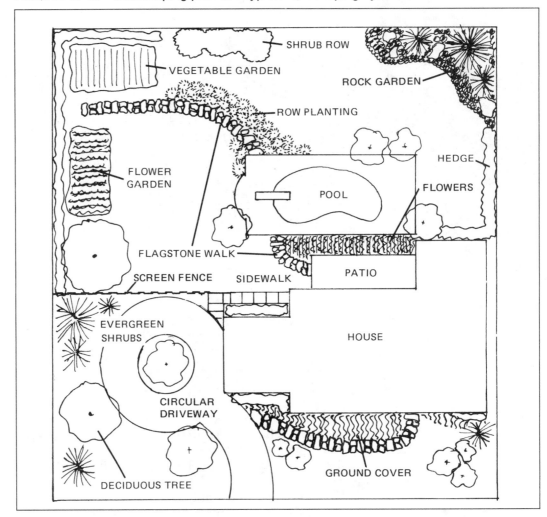

on personal and aesthetic preference. There are certain principles of design that, when followed, add to the beauty of a house and affect its market value.

Now let's look at some areas that can benefit from landscaping. The three photographs on the following page illustrate several approaches to landscaping design.

Main Entrance

Planting can highlight the main entrance door (Figure 11–3). If the house is low, the planting should be kept low. Planting that grows slowly and that grows outward rather than upward should be selected. If the house is tall or if the entrance door is above grade, taller plants are appropriate.

Corners

The corner of a house looks bare until it is provided with some landscaping to soften it. Just as entrance planting frames the doorway, corner planting frames the entire front of the house. Taller and fuller plants can be used here, as long as they don't shut off light from windows near the corner.

Base Planting

Good base planting is low at most points, but it should vary in height to relieve the monotony of a horizontal planting line. Planting beneath windows should be kept

FIGURE 11–3.   Entryway landscaping.

FIGURE 11–4.   Border planting and young trees.

FIGURE 11–5.   Lawn landscaping.

low so that it does not prevent light from entering the house. On the other hand, planting under windows is most effective if it can be seen from inside the house and thus provide a bottom frame for a view.

Care should be taken, however, to see that trees and shrubs are not planted too close to the house—a small juniper or yew can grow into a 6-foot circle within 10 years.

Borders

Annuals and perennials are better than trees and shrubbery for borders along walks, driveways and patios (Figure 11–4). An *annual* is a flowering plant that lasts for only one season. A *perennial* is a flowering plant that lives through the winter and blooms again the next spring. Annuals and perennials are colorful and easy to control and they help to create an attractive setting.

Hedges are also excellent borders and low screens. With proper pruning, almost all shrubs and some types of trees can be used as hedges. In choosing a suitable hedge, consider its height and fullness.

Privacy Screens

A privacy screen can be created with planting, a wall or a fence when local ordinances allow it. The screen may be solid or open. A solid screen affords greater privacy, but it may also shut out or reduce sunlight and the flow of air.

Though privacy depends on personal preference, the desire for it generally increases with the size of the community and decreases with the size of the lot. A large lot in itself provides privacy. On a narrow city lot, with neighbors on all sides, people want a place where they can be outdoors without being in full view of even friendly neighbors.

Planting As a Screen.   A live privacy screen can be created with a high hedge or trees. This type of screen isn't as practical as a wall or fence because a tall hedge is difficult to trim, and a screen of trees—ideal for breaking the wind or forming a backdrop for the house—is not solid enough to provide real privacy.

Walls.   Walls of brick, stone or concrete are the best solution to most problems of slope and are also good privacy screens. A wall keeps a steep bank from washing away. It also provides a point of interest in a landscaping plan and, when it is heightened with border planting, can be a screen.

Fences.   Some fences are designed for security and control. The most common of these is the chain-link fence. Other types are primarily used for decoration or to define property lines, gardens or recreation areas. Another common use for fences is, of course, for ensuring privacy. Such fences are usually made of wood, but expanded metal mesh, exterior hardboard, plywood, and other sheet materials that will withstand weathering are also used. Privacy fences are normally 6 feet high, may be open at the bottom for ventilation, and are supported on 4-by-4 posts spaced 4 or 8 feet apart. In all cases, fences should be attractive from both sides in the interest of good neighborhood relations.

Trees

A tree can serve four purposes. By its very shape it provides beauty. It also affords protection, shade and, in some cases, food. Trees are expensive; a house surrounded by tall and beautiful trees can add to the dollar value of a piece of property. For this reason, developers try to save all trees that are healthy and do not interfere with the use of the land.

Some trees can be troublesome, however. For example, a tree may be planted so close to the house that its root structure will eventually damage the foundation. Also, tree roots near walks and driveways, in time, can lift up the surface, creating hazardous conditions and ultimately will result in costly repaving. In addition, overhanging branches can cause serious damage to roofs, gutters, and the siding on a house.

Are there any dead or dying trees on the property? Dead trees can be dangerous and should be removed. All it takes is a strong gust of wind and a heavy branch could break off and strike the house—or even worse, cause injury to someone walking below. Remember, too, tree removal is expensive.

Lawns

Preparing a lawn is usually the final step in completing site work (Figure 11–5). It's best to wait until all construction on the site is over, so that the new lawn has a chance to grow undisturbed. Before the lawn is seeded, the site should be finish-graded and the top soil spread.

Sodding is a quicker but more expensive way to establish a lawn. Select only sod that contains perennial grasses and lay the strips of sod on topsoil that has been prepared for seeding. Tamp the strips firmly onto the topsoil. Early spring is the best time to plant sod. The ground is still very moist and the sod is more firmly rooted by the time hot, dry weather comes along. Sod laid in the fall requires more watering and a richer mixture of topsoil.

INSPECTION CHECKLIST

Begin your inspection by surveying the grounds and the house from a distance to get an overall impression of the landscaping, driveway, walks, patios, decks, fences and other structures. Keep in mind, however, that it is rare to find a property landscaped and laid out to perfection. But, at the same time, you want to be sure the grounds are in reasonably good shape before you consider buying the house.

A landscape that has been carefully thought through not only adds beauty to the property but can also influence the climate around and in the house—even the energy bills. In addition to their aesthetic value, plantings can provide shade in the summer, windbreaks in the winter, and can also cut down on soil erosion.

The following checklist can be used as a guide when you examine the grounds around the house.

INSPECTION CHECKLIST

The Grounds	Yes	No
1. Is the landscape style compatible with the architectural style of the house?	_____	_____
2. Is the overall landscaping plan visually appealing?	_____	_____
3. Have the grounds been well maintained?	_____	_____
4. Does the land slope so that water drains away from the house and outdoor living areas?	_____	_____
5. Are trees and shrubs far enough away from the house? If they are too close, overhanging branches can cause serious damage to roofs, gutters and siding.	_____	_____
6. Are trees far enough away from the house so that roots cannot penetrate cracks in the foundation or lift up the paving on driveways and walks?	_____	_____
7. Are trees healthy?	_____	_____
8. Will landscaping maintenance require minimal work?	_____	_____
9. If not, will these maintenance requirements be convenient for you?	_____	_____
10. Has proper landscaping been done to prevent soil erosion?	_____	_____
11. Does the driveway slope away from the house or garage?	_____	_____
12. Is the driveway in good shape?	_____	_____
Are the walks in good shape?	_____	_____
Is the patio in good shape?	_____	_____
13. Is the driveway exit unobstructed?	_____	_____
14. Does the driveway provide a turnaround?	_____	_____
15. Are outdoor living areas screened from public view?	_____	_____
16. Are fences in good shape (no signs of deterioration—wood rot, insect damage or rust)?	_____	_____
17. Are wooden members of patios, decks or porches free of rot or insect damage?	_____	_____
18. Are walks, driveways or patios free of cracks that could cause accidents?	_____	_____

Overall Rating	Good	Fair	Poor
Landscaping	_____	_____	_____
Slope of land	_____	_____	_____
Walks	_____	_____	_____
Patios	_____	_____	_____
Decks	_____	_____	_____
Porches	_____	_____	_____
Fences	_____	_____	_____

Major Problems: _____

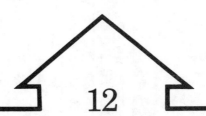

The Energy-Efficient House

12

An energy-efficient house has the potential to provide comfort and convenience on far less energy than a conventional house. Climatic conditions, utility rate structures and construction approaches determine the energy-saving potential of a house. With steady mounting fuel and utility service costs, energy-saving installations may be well worth the added initial investment. The day may not be very far off when documentation of a house's past performance in energy usage may have a real impact on its resale value.

If a house is still under construction, a homeowner may be able to influence such things as insulation R-values, weatherstripping and caulking applications, window locations, heating and cooling equipment size and performance efficiencies, and fireplace design. Even if construction is completed, many of these considerations can be kept in mind for remodeling.

AIR-INFILTRATION CONTROLS

Air infiltration is the uncontrolled movement of air into or out of a house. It occurs constantly and for many reasons—wind action, pressure differences and even the operation of furnaces and fireplaces. Most houses have significant air-infiltration problems that account for 40 percent or more of the total energy required for heating and cooling.

Cold air that penetrates warm space must be heated to maintain a constant inside temperature. If warm, moist air invades air-conditioned space, heat and humidity must be removed to maintain comfort levels. Air infiltration cannot be completely stopped in a house, but it can be controlled. The bar graph in Figure 12–1 will give you a good idea where air infiltration normally occurs in a house with its windows and doors securely closed. As you can see, wall outlets on both exterior and interior walls are responsible for a great deal of the air infiltration in standard house construction. Outside air follows the wiring through the studs and cavities of the walls and comes in through the switch plates. Proper caulking around the wiring can alleviate this major problem.

FIGURE 12–1. Air leakage test results for average home of 1,728 square feet.

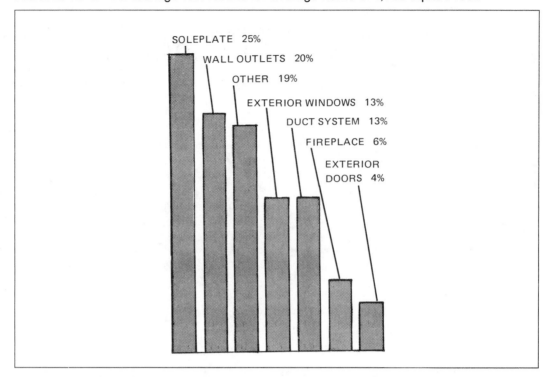

Figure 12–2 shows some key points for controlling infiltration in conventional framing. The exterior of the house should be examined carefully for points of air infiltration. Look for cracks in the masonry or gaps in the siding and make sure that the windows and window frames have been tightly caulked and weather-stripped. A tiny ¹⁄₁₆-inch crack along the sides and top of a typical doorway is equal in surface area to a 4-inch by 4-inch hole in the wall.

Efficient Ductwork

Ductwork is the air-delivery system for central heating and cooling. It presents very important requirements for both air-infiltration control and insulation. Ductwork should be tightly sealed and insulated. Since you are paying to heat or cool the air, you don't want it to leak out of the ducts before it can be delivered to the living areas, and you don't want the lining of the ductwork to become much hotter or colder than the air you are trying to move.

One of the most important considerations in designing an energy-efficient heating and cooling system is the length of the ductwork. A design that cuts the length of the ductwork in half may also cut duct energy losses in half.

ORIENTATION OF THE HOUSE

A house will be easier and less expensive to cool in the summer if it is shaded from the sun (Figure 12–3). Anything that stops the sun before it gets in through the glass is several times more effective than blinds and curtains on the inside. Since most heat comes through the east and west sides of the house, you will want to shade those sides. Trees and vines that bloom in the summer and lose their leaves for the winter are a pleasing solution and a welcome sight in an urban setting.

FIGURE 12–2.   Key points for controlling infiltration in conventional framing.

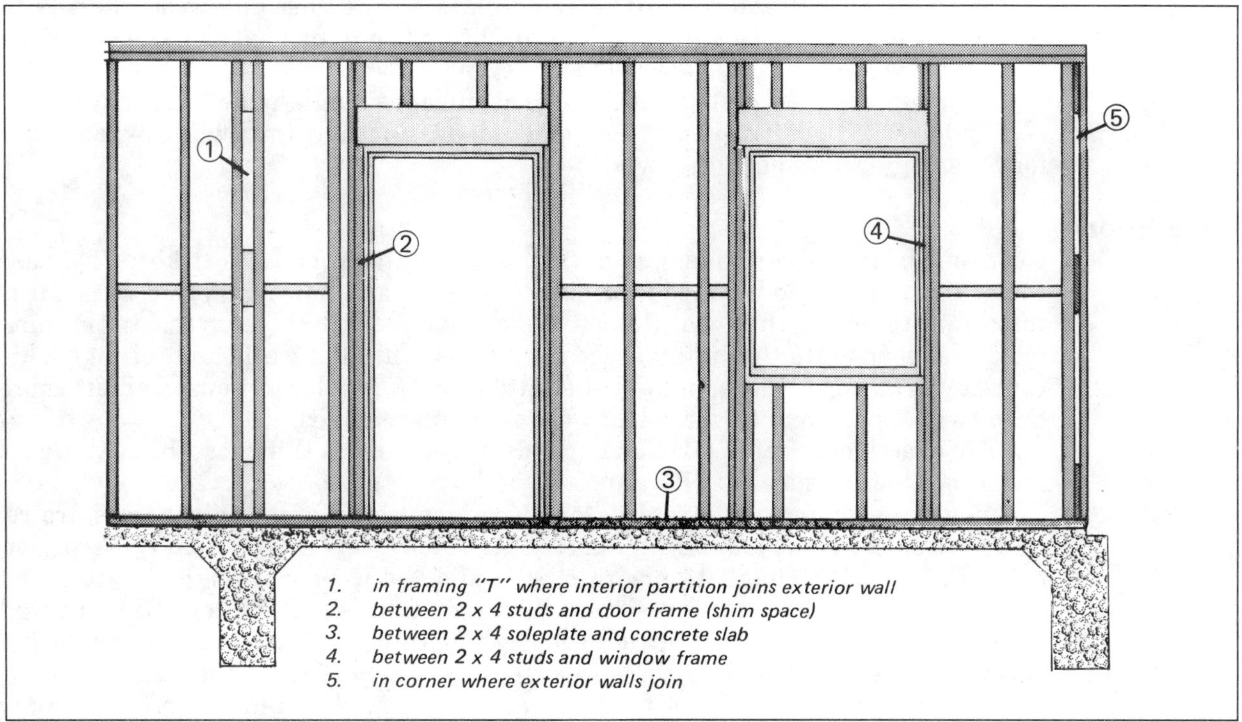

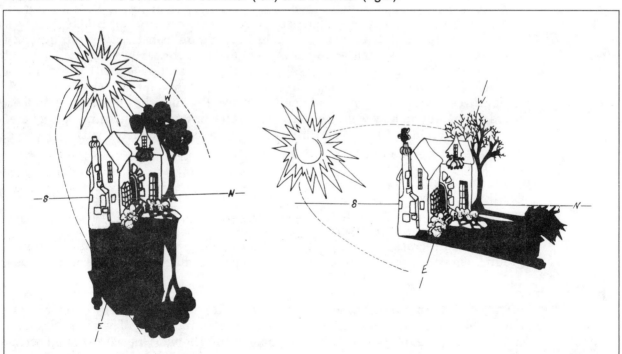

1. *in framing "T" where interior partition joins exterior wall*
2. *between 2 x 4 studs and door frame (shim space)*
3. *between 2 x 4 soleplate and concrete slab*
4. *between 2 x 4 studs and window frame*
5. *in corner where exterior walls join*

FIGURE 12–3.   The sun's arc in summer (left) and in winter (right).

Window Size, Location and Treatment

Single-pane glass will allow as much as 15 times more heat to move through the house by conduction and radiation than would flow through a comparable area of a well-insulated wall. For this reason, windows should be planned carefully. If the house is to be cooled by air-conditioning, use as little glass as possible, and face it to the south; there should be little or no glass on the east and west sides. With proper design, the house will permit sunlight and radiant heat to come in during the winter when the sun is lower in the sky.

Double-pane glass costs almost twice as much as single-pane but it pays for itself in decreased utility bills. Storm windows are another worthwhile expenditure for an energy-conscious homeowner.

Insulation

Good insulation is permanent and virtually maintenance-free. It keeps a house cooler in summer and warmer in winter. To understand how insulation works, it is important to realize that heat flows from warmer areas to cooler areas. In the summer, heat seeps into the living spaces of a house through walls and ceilings adjacent to the garage, the attic and the outdoors. Uninsulated houses admit more than twice as much of this summer heat as insulated ones.

The effectiveness of insulation depends not just on its thickness, but also on its resistance to heat flow—its R-value.

Insulating materials have different R-values, so different thicknesses are required to do the same job. Minimum standards for federally financed construction call for R-11 or R-13 insulation within the walls and R-19 or R-22 in the attic. The larger the R-value, the more resistant the insulation is to heat flow. Higher rated insulation is needed in the attic because hot air rises, and without insulation sheetrock would be the only thing between the inside of the house and the attic. R-values are additive. If you already have an R-13 rated insulation in a particular location and you want to upgrade it to R-35, you can use a layer of R-22. The numbers on the map in Figure 12–4 show insulation recommendations for six different climate zones. The first number in each case is the R-value for ceilings, the second is for walls and the third is for floors above crawl spaces or other cold areas.

It is easy to insulate exterior walls during original construction, but quite difficult later on; then the material has to be blown into the walls or injected through small drilled holes or large cavities. The insulation can be loose-fill mineral fiber, cellulose or a foam material such as the controversial urea formaldehyde, currently under investigation as a potential health hazard. Because the effectiveness of loose fill is dependent on how well the contractor can work around mechanical and electrical obstructions, it is vital to hire an experienced contractor with the proper equipment.

Weatherstripping and Caulking

Caulking and weatherstripping go hand in hand with insulation. All share the same objective: to stop the movement of heat and cold. It doesn't make sense to pad walls if openings in the exterior of the house are admitting heat and cold. Sometimes, though, cracks and openings in the exterior wall are not visible from the ground. They may go unnoticed until a water leak damages the inside of the house.

The Fireplace

Mistakes and omissions during construction can reduce the energy efficiency of a house below its true potential. Many of these are minor, but a few are so devastating that they negate the total energy-efficiency of a house. One of the more destructive oversights is the failure to equip a fireplace with a tight-fitting damper.

A fireplace can enhance the charm and value of a house, but a fireplace without a high-quality damper can impair the effectiveness of the heating and cooling systems. Unless the damper is securely closed when the fireplace is not in use, the air you pay to heat or cool will be drawn continuously up the chimney. In fact, an ill-fitting damper can actually waste more heat than an open window.

FIGURE 12–4. Insulation recommendations for different climate zones.

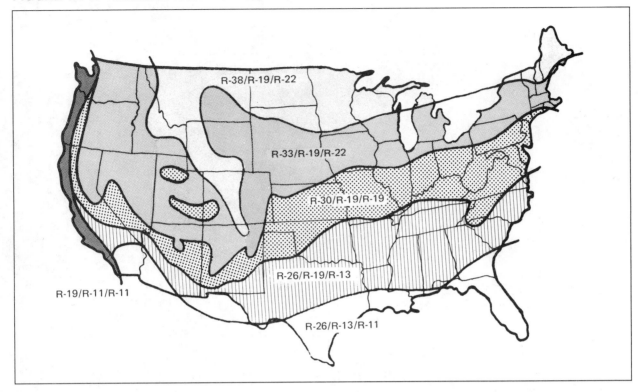

In addition to a high-quality damper, there are other optional pieces of equipment that can turn a fireplace into an energy asset (Figure 12–5):

● An *outside air intake to the firebox* will enable the fireplace to pull its combustion air from outside the house, instead of from the living area.
● *Glass doors* shut off most of its access to air from the living area. This will increase the draw of air from the outside vent, and the glass front will actually help the fireplace radiate heat into the house.

PROPER EQUIPMENT SIZING

The old guidelines for determining the proper size for air-conditioning and heating units don't apply to energy-efficient houses. These houses can be cooled and heated with smaller equipment that consumes less energy. This lowers operating costs for the building and allows the homeowner to recover part of the expenses incurred for insulation and storm windows. Equipment sizing is crucial, for oversized units do not run at peak efficiency. They waste a great deal of energy cycling on and off, and the homeowner of course pays the price for this wastefulness.

Energy-Efficiency Ratio (EER)

It was once cheaper to buy a less efficient air conditioner that used somewhat more energy, but this is no longer true. Modern air conditioners can operate on 25 to 30 percent less energy than older models—an important advantage, considering utility costs.

The more efficient an air conditioner is, the higher its EER, which represents the amount of heat that one watt of electricity will remove from the air in one hour.

FIGURE 12–5. Energy-saving fireplace options.

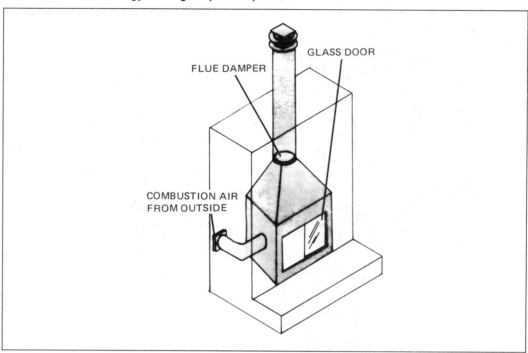

It is calculated by dividing the number of BTUs required for cooling purposes by the number of watts needed to run the cooling system.

A 36,000 BTU (3-ton) air conditioner that requires 6,000 watts to operate has an EER of 6.0 (36,000 ÷ 6,000). A 3-ton unit that needs 4,300 watts to operate has an EER of 8.4. The unit with the higher EER needs less energy to do the same job. Even though an EER of 6.0 to 7.0 is acceptable for air-conditioning in most states, an energy-efficient house should have an EER between 8.0 and 10.0.

ENERGY-EFFICIENT WATER HEATING

Next to heating and air conditioning, the biggest consumers of energy in a house are water heaters and lights. Water heating for a typical house now accounts for approximately 17 percent of the total annual energy bill. This may sound high, but consider the many ways hot water is used—showers and baths, shaving, laundry, dish washing, general cleaning and food preparation. To conserve energy, wrap the hot-water pipes throughout the house with insulation. Of course, if the house was built with its hot-water pipes in the slab, the opportunity to insulate the pipes was lost after the concrete was poured.

The location of the water heater also is important from an energy-efficiency standpoint. It should be placed as near as possible to bathroom and kitchen faucets to cut down on the total length of the plumbing in the hot-water system. The greater the overall length of the hot-water plumbing system, the more it will cost initially and the more water and energy it will waste through the years.

OTHER WAYS TO MAKE A HOUSE MORE ENERGY EFFICIENT

Location of Air Conditioner
The location and type of trees and shrubbery can be a plus in reducing both cooling and heating energy costs—or they can create maintenance problems. With home

cooling and heating energy costs up, it makes sense to adhere to both sound land-scaping practices and recommended equipment maintenance schedules (Figure 12–6).

FIGURE 12–6.   This location of an air conditioner or heat pump lets the house protect the unit from prevailing winds. A tree shades it from the summer west sun.

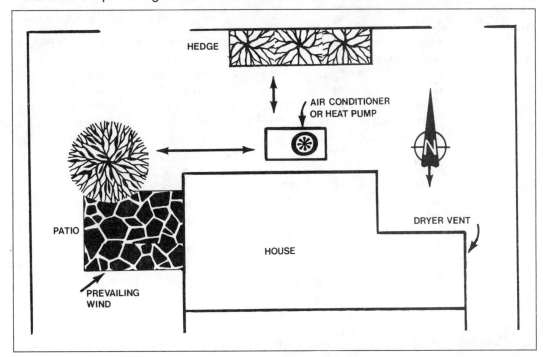

If you are planning to install a new air-conditioning or heat pump system, the outside equipment should be located where it will be protected from prevailing winds. The unit should be kept away from a clothes dryer vent—since hot vapor increases the load on the air conditioner and lint might cause damage.

Letting the house protect the air-conditioning equipment is desirable but not always possible, particularly with existing installations. A solution could be strategically planted trees or shrubbery or a sun fence. But deciduous trees or shrubs should be kept at least 10 feet away from the unit so that leaves and twigs are not sucked into it.

Shade trees (or a sunscreen) can perform another energy-saving function: They can reduce the load on an air conditioner (or heat pump in its summer operating mode) by shading the equipment from the south and west sun.

Foundation plantings also play a role in keeping a house cool, but those near the outdoor air-conditioning or heat pump unit should be trimmed back to maintain proper air flow through the grille. Plants serve both as insulation and a natural air conditioner.

Lighting

Efficient use of lighting in your home does not mean groping around in relative darkness. What it does mean is following certain energy saving tips that will keep your living space bright and at the same time cut down on energy use and monthly bills.

Home lighting accounts for about 5 percent of the total electric energy load nationally. Quality lighting is designed to give the most useful light output for each unit of energy input. A 25-watt fluorescent bulb, for example, gives off as much light as a 100-watt incandescent bulb but uses one-fourth as much energy. A homeowner can save energy and money simply by having the builder install fluorescent fixtures in the kitchen, bathrooms and garage work areas.

Outdoor Living Areas

A homeowner may want to limit the square footage of heated and cooled space by substituting outdoor living areas such as porches, patios, decks, verandas, gazebos and breezeways. In many parts of the country, a screened-in porch or patio can be enjoyed almost all year. It costs less to build than an enclosed living area and, of course, less to heat.

Equipment Maintenance

Seasonal maintenance of equipment is another priority item for stretching cooling and heating energy dollars.

Heating and air-conditioning units should be checked and cleaned by a qualified service representative. Coils should be cleaned. This is a job some homeowners can undertake themselves, but first they should observe an expert doing it.

Clean filters are essential and should be checked once a month. Disposable filters should be thrown away, and permanent filters should be washed with a garden hose.

Life-style and Household Schedule

Life-style and household schedule also play a role in conserving on air-conditioning expenses:

- Run appliances such as the clothes dryer in early morning hours.
- Keep curtains, drapes, shutters, etc. closed on sunny windows during the day.
- Turn up the thermostat while the family is gone during the day. With a properly sized air-conditioning system, it takes only an hour to bring the temperature down to the comfort zone.

Air-Conditioning and Heating by Zones

Zoning can save energy and money by giving you control over the square footage you actually heat or cool. For example, you could zone the bedrooms of the house separately from the living and kitchen areas.

Evaporative Coolers for Low-Humidity Areas

In areas where high humidity is not a problem, window-mounted evaporative coolers—which require much less energy than air conditioners—can be just as effective as the more expensive refrigerated systems. With special installation, these units can also be used with ductwork systems to provide whole-house cooling.

Attic Fans

An attic fan is another alternative to the high energy consumption of refrigerated air conditioning. Normally, a house retains heat, so there is a lag between the time when the outside air cools after sunset on a summer night and the time when the interior of the house cools. As Figure 12–7 indicates, an attic fan speeds up the cooling of the house by pulling air in through open windows, up through the attic and out.

INSPECTION CHECKLIST

High fuel prices have driven many homeowners to add more insulation, block out drafts, caulk cracks, install tighter windows, and generally seal up their houses. The object, of course, is to contain skyrocketing heating and cooling costs. The following checklist will help you determine the energy efficiency of the house you are inspecting.

FIGURE 12–7. Attic fan.

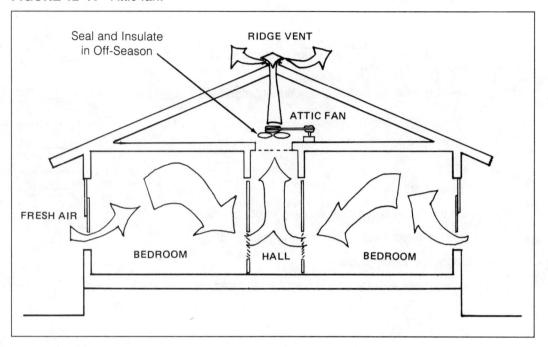

INSPECTION CHECKLIST

		Yes	No
1.	Has an energy audit been done on the house? If so, were the results positive?	_____	_____
2.	Does the house have sufficient insulation in:		
	ceilings?	_____	_____
	floors?	_____	_____
	walls?	_____	_____
	basement?	_____	_____
3.	Do the insulation materials have vapor barriers?	_____	_____
4.	Is all ductwork tightly sealed and insulated?	_____	_____
5.	Are water pipes insulated?	_____	_____
6.	Is there sufficient ventilation in the attic and crawl space?	_____	_____
7.	Does the house have an attic fan?	_____	_____
8.	Are all windows tight and free from air leaks?	_____	_____
9.	Do the windows have double-pane glass?	_____	_____
10.	Are all exterior doors tight fitting?	_____	_____
11.	Does the house have storm windows?	_____	_____
12.	Does the house have storm doors?	_____	_____
13.	Is the house free of any significant air-infiltration problems?	_____	_____
14.	Does the air conditioner have an EER higher than 7.0? (8.0 and above is considered energy efficient.)	_____	_____
15.	Is the heating and cooling unit properly sized for the number of square feet in the house?	_____	_____
16.	Is the heating or cooling system in good working order?	_____	_____
17.	Is the outside portion of the air conditioner in a shady location with free air circulation around it?	_____	_____
18.	Does the fireplace have a high-quality, tight-fitting damper?	_____	_____
19.	Does the fireplace have a glass front?	_____	_____
20.	Are there deciduous trees and bushes on the south and west sides of the house to provide shade against the summer sun?	_____	_____
21.	Are there evergreen trees and bushes on the north side of the house to act as a break against winter winds?	_____	_____
22.	Are there ceiling fans throughout the house?	_____	_____
23.	Check with the owners about the energy bills during the past year. Do they seem reasonable?	_____	_____

OVERALL RATING	**Good**	**Fair**	**Poor**
Total energy efficiency rating	_____	_____	_____

APPENDIX A: House Diagram

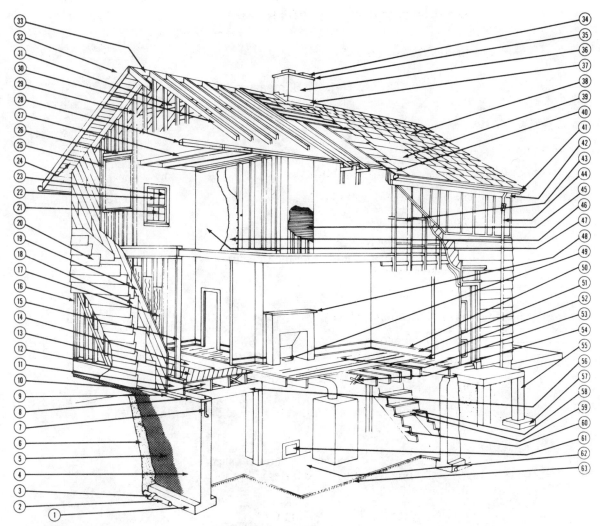

1. FOOTING
2. FOUNDATION DRAIN TILE
3. FELT JOINT COVER
4. FOUNDATION WALL
5. DAMPPROOFING OR
   WEATHERPROOFING
6. BACKFILL
7. ANCHOR BOLT
8. SILL
9. TERMITE SHIELD
10. FLOOR JOIST
11. BAND OR BOX SILL
12. PLATE
13. SUBFLOORING
14. BUILDING PAPER
15. WALL STUD
16. DOUBLE CORNER STUD
17. INSULATION
18. BUILDING PAPER
19. WALL SHEATHING
20. SIDING
21. MULLION

22. MUNTIN
23. WINDOW SASH
24. EAVE (ROOF PROJECTION)
25. WINDOW JAMB TRIM
26. DOUBLE WINDOW HEADER
27. CEILING JOIST
28. DOUBLE PLATE
29. STUD
30. RAFTERS
31. COLLAR BEAM
32. GABLE END OF ROOF
33. RIDGE BOARD
34. CHIMNEY POTS
35. CHIMNEY CAP
36. CHIMNEY
37. CHIMNEY FLASHING
38. ROOFING SHINGLES
39. ROOFING FELTS
40. ROOF SHEATHING
41. EAVE TROUGH OR GUTTER
42. FRIEZE BOARD

43. FIRESTOP
44. DOWNSPOUT
45. LATHS
46. PLASTER BOARD
47. PLASTER FINISH
48. MANTEL
49. ASH DUMP
50. BASE TOP MOULDING
51. BASEBOARD
52. SHOE MOULDING
53. FINISH MOULDING
54. BRIDGING
55. PIER
56. GIRDER
57. FOOTING
58. RISER
59. TREAD
60. STRINGER
61. CLEANOUT DOOR
62. CONCRETE BASEMENT FLOOR
63. CINDER FILL

APPENDIX B: Measurement and Metric Conversion Tables

TABLE B–1. U.S. measure.

Measures of Length			Measures of Surface (Square Measure)		
1 foot (ft.)	=	12 inches (in.)	1 square foot (sq. ft.)	=	144 square inches (sq. in.)
1 yard (yd.)	=	3 feet (ft.)	1 square yard (sq. yd.)	=	9 square feet (sq. ft.)
1 rod (rd.)	=	5½ yards	1 square rod (sq. rd.)	=	30¼ square yards (sq. yd.)
1 rod	=	16½ feet	1 township	=	36 sections
1 mile (mi.)	=	5,280 ft.	1 section	=	1 square mile (sq. mi.)
1 mile	=	320 rods (rd.)	1 square mile	=	640 acres
1 chain	=	66 feet	1 acre	=	43,560 square feet
1 chain	=	4 rods	1 acre	=	10 square chains
4 rods	=	100 links			
1 link	=	7.92 inches			

TABLE B–2. Metric measure.

1 millimeter (mm)	=	.001 meter (m)	1 milligram (mg)	=	0.001 gram (g)	1 milliliter (ml)	=	0.001 liter (1)
1 centimeter (cm)	=	.01 meter	1 centigram (cg)	=	0.01 gram	1 centiliter (cl)	=	0.01 liter
1 decimeter (dm)	=	.1 meter	1 decigram (dg)	=	0.1 gram	1 deciliter (dl)	=	0.1 liter
meter (basic unit)			gram (basic unit)			liter (basic unit)		
1 decameter (dkm)	=	10 meters	1 decagram (dkg)	=	10.0 grams	1 decaliter (hl)	=	10.0 liters
1 hectometer (hm)	=	100 meters	1 hectogram (hg)	=	100.0 grams	1 hectoliter (hl)	=	100.0 liters
1 kilometer (km)	=	1000 meters	1 kilogram (kg)	=	1000.0 grams	1 kiloliter (kl)	=	1000.0 liters

TABLE B–3. Measurement conversion.

Metric to U.S.		U.S. to Metric	
Common Measures of Length			
1 centimeter	= 0.3937 inch	1 inch	= 2.54 centimeters
1 meter	= 39.37 inches	1 yard	= 0.9144 meter
1 meter	= 1.093 yards	1 mile	= 1.609 kilometers
1 kilometer	= 0.621 mile		
Common Measures of Capacity			
1 liter	= 1.056 quarts	1 quart	= 0.946 liter
1 liter	= 0.264 gallon	1 gallon	= 3.785 liters
Common Measures of Weight (Mass)			
1 gram	= 0.0352 ounce	1 ounce	= 28.35 grams
1 kilogram	= 2.2046 pounds	1 pound	= .4536 kilogram
1 metric ton	= 2204.62 pounds	1 ton	= 0.907 metric ton

APPENDIX C: Radon

Radon is a naturally occurring radioactive gas found in soil. It has been blamed for as many as 20,000 lung cancer deaths annually in the United States.

FIGURE C–1.   Radon entry routes.

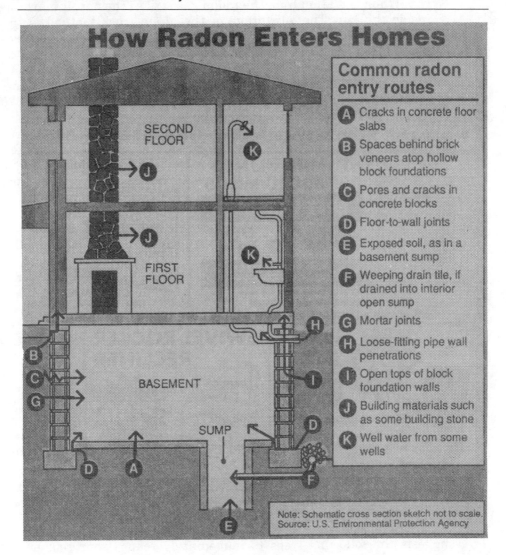

You can test for radon gas in your home by getting a radon detector kit, which is available in many local stores in your area. Whichever kit you choose, make sure it has been tested for accuracy by the Environmental Protection Agency (EPA).

Here are three general methods to detect radon:

1. *Charcoal canister.* The majority of homes checked for radon undergo this test. It consists of placing a small, charcoal-containing canister about the size of a 35mm film case in your home, usually in the basement, where radon levels are likely to be highest. The charcoal absorbs gamma radiation from the radon gas,

much the same way that a box of baking soda absorbs odors from the refrigerator.

Windows, doors and other openings to the house must be closed for at least 12 hours before starting the test and kept closed as much as possible during the test. The cost ranges from $10 to $20 per canister and they need to be exposed to the air in your home for three to seven days.

After the specified time period, the detector is sealed and sent to a laboratory, designated in the instructions, for analysis.

2. *Alpha track or track etch*. This detector ($20 to $40) looks like a small plastic pill box. When radiation from the radon gas strikes the box, it marks a plastic strip inside the box. The advantage of the alpha track method is that it gives a longer-term reading of radon levels. The disadvantage is that the detector must remain in place for at least a month and preferably two or three months.

3. *Continuous radon monitor*. The most expensive test is one conducted by a technician who will come to your house with an electronic detector. This radon monitor is about the size of a clock radio, and at anywhere from $75 to $150 per day, is the most expensive to operate.

The continuous radon monitor is used for about two days; results are available a few days later. This device is most often used in real estate transactions in which a sale is contingent on the radon levels in a house. Aside from cost, the drawback to this test is that it gives a reading for a very brief period of time, which most experts say is not indicative of long-term exposure levels.

If the radon analysis reveals concentrations above a certain level, the EPA recommends corrective action that can run from a few hundred dollars to several thousand.

Typical radon levels for a house are about 1.5 picocuries per liter, a measure of the amount of radiation in the air. *Pico* means one-trillionth and a *curie* is a unit of radiation.

The EPA sets the following guidelines to help homeowners gauge their radon levels:

- For less than 4 picocuries per liter, no remedial action is probably required in your home.
- For between 4 and 20 picocuries per liter, some remedial action may be required during the next year or so.
- For between 20 and 200 picocuries per liter, remedial action may be required within the next several months.
- For levels above 200 picocuries per liter, remedial action should be taken within the next several weeks.

If your measurement is significantly higher than 4 picocuries per liter, the EPA suggests the following steps to immediately reduce your risk from exposure to radon:

1. Stop smoking and discourage smoking in your home.
2. Spend less time in areas with higher concentrations of radon.
3. Whenever practical, open windows and turn on fans to increase air flow through the home.
4. If your home has a crawl space underneath it, keep the crawl space vents on all sides of the house fully open all year.

APPENDIX D: The Value of Home Improvements

Homeowners spend a lot of money improving their houses each year. If you are one of them, you would do well to take a close look at the kind of improvements you're planning—to see whether the job is really a good investment.

You can see from the table below that many home improvements, such as patios, saunas and greenhouses, do not recapture their original cost.

On the other hand, most projects that add square footage or substantially upgrade rooms, such as kitchens and baths, will usually add most of their cost to the overall value of the house.

TABLE D–1.   How much home improvements increase house value.

IMPROVEMENT	Average Cost	% of Cost Added to Value
Roofing:		
nail over old roof	$60–$80/square (100 sq ft)	100
tear off and replace roof	$85–$200/square	100
Room Addition	$50–$75/sq ft	100
Kitchen Remodeling	$3,500–$16,500	100
Bath Remodeling	$3,500–$11,000	75–100
Garage into Living Space	$8,000–$11,000	100
Fireplace	$2,500–$5,000	90–100
Solar Hot Water	$3,500	100
Insulation	$2,000–$4,500	100
Skylight, Insulated	$550–$700	70
Swimming Pool	$13,500–$16,500	50–60
Patio/Deck	$2,500–$4,500	25–35
Greenhouse	$5,500–$9,000	25
Basement Rec Room	$8,000–$11,000	20–25
Sauna	$2,500–$3,500	20

APPENDIX E: Special Building Requirements

Much of the construction industry throughout the United States today relies on standardized materials and practices, but climate, geography and geology will always promote regional differences in building design and construction. Homes in the north central states, for example, are made with roofing and insulation that will withstand blizzards and keep occupants comfortable in below-zero temperatures. In contrast, homes along the Gulf Coast must be solid enough to endure hurricane winds and well-insulated to remain cool. Homes in earthquake-prone areas are subject to special stresses that designers and builders must take into account. Although building codes have brought about improvements in construction techniques, code requirements are often enforced only after building failures have made them imperative.

Most of the special requirements mentioned in this appendix are not easily discernible. A building may be in perfect compliance with local codes and still be a bad investment, especially for a buyer who is unaware of the risks of a particular geographic location. By knowing the right questions to ask about a proposed or completed building, and what to look for in one under construction, buyers can avoid costly and potentially disastrous situations.

DANGER FROM SNOW AND ICE

The mountain states and the north central and northeastern areas of the United States always expect heavy snow accumulation, and recent winters have taught homeowners to anticipate other extreme conditions as well.

Although few buildings suffer an actual roof cave-in, the mere threat of roof collapse can cause accidents, as worried homeowners try to shovel the snow from the roofs of their houses. The greatest immediate danger from snow accumulation is not to residences, but to commercial structures that combine large roof areas and inadequate reinforcement.

In terms of their destructive potential, ice storms are worse than snowstorms. Telephone and power lines can snap under the weight of a heavy load of ice. When ice from intermittent thawing and refreezing of snow collects on the eaves of a roof, water from thawing ice and snow above it backs up under eaves and shingles. Figure E–1 illustrates how ice accumulation can effectively dam a roof eave: Melted snow and ice saturate the wood framing, setting the stage for deterioration and decay.

WEATHERPROOFING A HOUSE

Homeowners can ease their minds about possible future damage with a few simple precautions, including some that can be put into effect after a building is completed. When fortifying a house against the cold, give special attention to the overall house insulation, roof underlayment and covering, exterior wall covering and exterior trim.

Insulation

Insulation can serve the double purpose of heating and cooling a house. There are several areas in any house that should be insulated. If attic space is not meant to be used as a living area, the floor of the attic is insulated; otherwise, the attic

FIGURE E–1. Ice accumulation along roof eave.

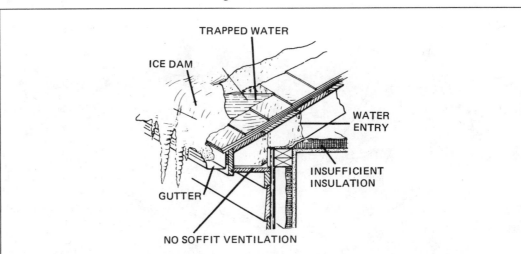

ceiling is insulated. All outside walls should be insulated, as should floors over unheated areas such as a crawl space. Insulation can be applied in the form of blankets or batts that are stapled between the studs, loose insulation that is blown into floor and wall spaces, or rigid fiberboard materials that are used structurally as sheathing or wallboard. A proper vapor barrier should be installed with any type of insulation. For example, when insulation is installed on an attic floor, there should be a vapor barrier on the floor between the insulation and the flooring.

Roof Framing

You can determine the extremes of temperature against which a house must be protected by consulting a climate zone map such as the one in Figure E–2. The extreme cold temperature and average precipitation dictate the amount of stress a roof should be expected to bear: The longer the winter season, the more snow and the greater the load the roof may have to carry. Although unexpectedly heavy snowfalls can destroy even the broadest estimate, the risk they represent does not warrant the added expense of reinforcing a roof to withstand extraordinary loads. With normal precautions you can build enough of a cushion into the load estimate to handle occasional unpredictable excesses.

Table E–1 points out the important variables in determining the amount of stress a roof can withstand—the spacing of the beams and the roof underlayment. The stress is itemized in terms of the dead load the roof always carries (the weight of the roof itself, including all finishing materials) and the live load the roof will be expected to carry (the weight of movable objects, people using the space, and snow that may accumulate on the roof). Note that the load capacity of the roof is nearly doubled by spacing roof supports 16 inches on-center, rather than 24 inches. Where heavy snow is expected all winter, beam spacing can be adjusted accordingly. In fact, the Department of Housing and Urban Development's (HUD) minimum property standards and local building codes usually stipulate that roof supports be no more than 16 inches on-center.

Roof Underlayment

As shown in Figure E–3, typical cold-weather roofing should include a plywood underlayment, roofing paper to provide a moisture barrier, and shingles or other exterior roof covering. Waterproofing is the prime consideration. Whether in the form of rain or melting snow or ice, water that enters because of loose shingles,

FIGURE E–2.   Map showing climate zones and typical extreme low temperatures in the United States.

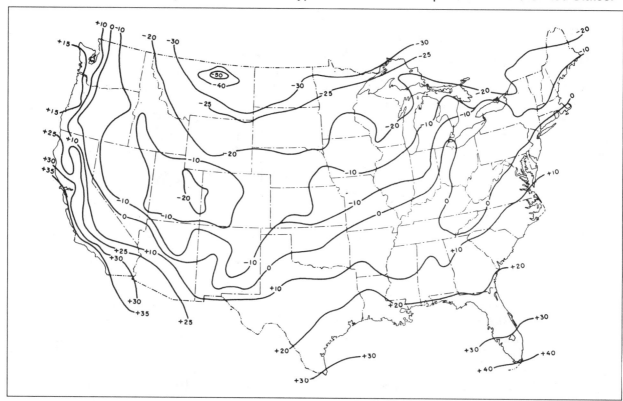

ice formation on the eaves, or simple weathering of the roof covering eventually will destroy the wood framework it saturates. The wood framework of a house may sustain considerable damage before there is any external evidence of it. You can detect water damage by simply pressing the tip of a screwdriver or penknife into attic beams at various points. If the blade enters easily, the wood is already in an advanced stage of decay and will probably have to be replaced. Such damage can proceed rapidly in warm, humid climates, so a periodic check of roof supports is useful even if there is no visible exterior damage.

Roof Covering and Siding

Unless nailed down securely, roof covering and siding will gradually loosen under the force of heavy winds. Masonry veneers should be strengthened by fastening them to the wall sheathing with metal ties.

Siding can also help insulate a house, although not as effectively as blanket and batt or blown-in insulation between the wall studs. Aluminum, vinyl or steel sidings placed over old siding or stucco walls provide some insulation—more if they are backed with insulating material such as urethane-based or styrene-based foam.

Exterior Trim

Some of the most crucial points for gauging the weatherability of a house are the corners of the siding, the joints between roof and gables, and the eave ends of the roof. Siding and roofing joints in figures E–4 and E–5 are adequately covered. Note that a waterproof barrier as well as a secure exterior covering must be provided. The eave ends of the roof are a good indicator of the care that went into the construction of the building. The shingles should extend beyond the eave line about 1½ inches, or else water will pour down the fascia, leaving dirty streaks and weakening the finish if it has been painted.

TABLE E–1.   Allowable roof loads under various conditions.

Plywood Thickness (inch)	Max. Span (inches)	Unsupported Edge-Max. Length (inches)	Allowable Roof Loads (psf) Spacing of Supports (inches center to center)										
			12	16	20	24	30	32	36	42	48	60	72
5/16	12	12	100* (130)**										
5/16, 3/8	16	16	130 (170)	55 (75)									
5/16, 3/8	20	20		85 (110)	45 (55)								
3/8, 1/2	24	24		150 (160)	75 (100)	45 (60)							
5/8	30	26			145 (165)	85 (110)	40 (55)						
1/2, 5/8	32	28				90 (105)	45 (60)	40 (50)					
3/4	36	30				125 (145)	65 (85)	55 (70)	35 (50)				
5/8, 3/4, 7/8	42	32					80 (105)	65 (90)	45 (60)	35 (40)			
3/4, 7/8	48	36						105 (115)	75 (90)	55 (55)	40 (40)		
1-1/8	72	48							175 (175)	105 (105)	80 (80)	50 (50)	30 (35)
1-1/8	72	48							145 (145)	85 (85)	65 (65)	40 (40)	30 (30)
1-1/4	72	48							160 (165)	95 (95)	75 (75)	45 (45)	25 (35)

*Allowable live load.
**Allowable total load.

FIGURE E–3.   Roof covering for typical cold weather protection.

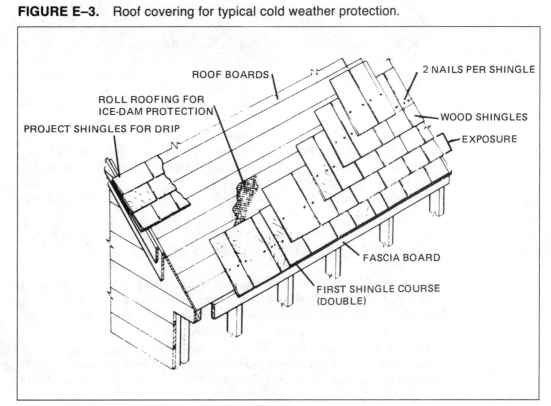

ROOF BOARDS

2 NAILS PER SHINGLE

ROLL ROOFING FOR ICE-DAM PROTECTION

PROJECT SHINGLES FOR DRIP

WOOD SHINGLES

EXPOSURE

FASCIA BOARD

FIRST SHINGLE COURSE (DOUBLE)

FIGURE E–4.   Three views of waterproofed roofing joints.

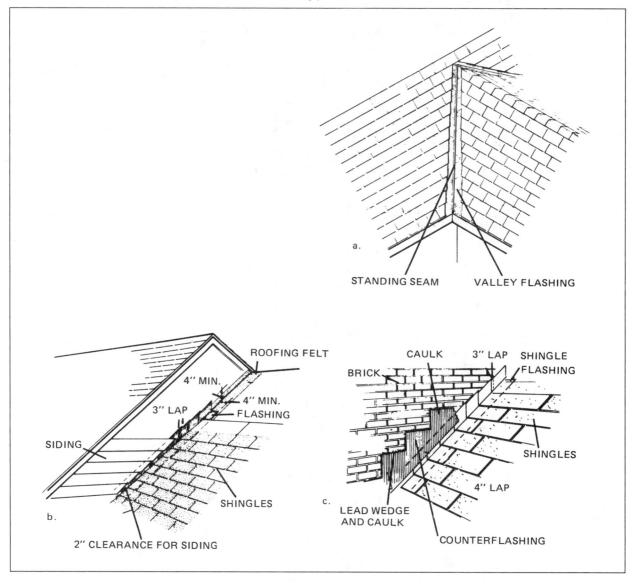

Figure E–6 illustrates two methods of protecting against ice dams that can form on the ends of eaves. One remedy is to apply sheet metal instead of shingles along the last several feet of the eaves. The shingles applied to the rest of the roof should overlap the metal. Another method is to thaw ice accumulation with a waterproof heating cable installed in a zigzag pattern along the eave.

PROTECTING A HOUSE FROM EARTHQUAKE DAMAGE

Earthquake hazards are more pronounced along the West Coast than elsewhere in the United States—Alaska has numerous earthquakes, but generally in areas that are much less densely populated than, say, California. The major faults along the Pacific Coast, such as the San Andreas, can produce reverberations all the way to the western edge of the Rocky Mountains, making parts of Utah, Montana, Wyoming and Idaho major earthquake areas as well. The Wasatch fault zone, for instance, passes through Salt Lake City and other urban centers in Utah. These

FIGURE E–5. Siding joints.

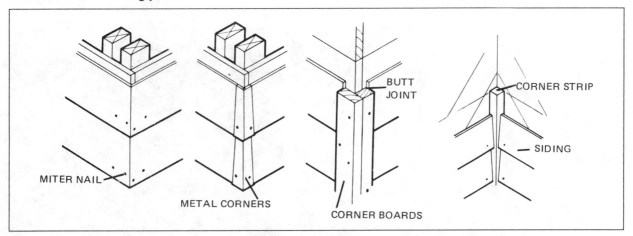

BUTT JOINT

CORNER STRIP

SIDING

MITER NAIL

METAL CORNERS

CORNER BOARDS

areas frequently are prey to the property damage and human death caused by earthquakes that measure as high as 8 points—maximum severity—on the Richter scale.

After a major earthquake, broadcasts and newspaper stories recount great devastation, since the shock usually takes an unprepared populace by surprise. There are ways to minimize the destructiveness of an earthquake, though this knowledge has not always been put into use. Even where building codes demand rigorous construction safeguards, however, thousands of older buildings do not meet the safety standards. Let's review the basic requirements for building a house that will survive an earthquake with minimal damage.

The Building Site

The first rule in protecting a house against earthquake damage is not to build it on a fault line. Even though this may seem self-evident, fault lines often are not conspicuous on visual inspection. The act of developing a piece of land may obliterate the clues that point to an active fault. Once an obvious fracture of the soil is leveled, built upon and landscaped, the fault may be unrecognizable.

Fault lines can be found on certain maps. Local libraries and bookstores will probably have maps showing fault lines; if not, they can be obtained from the state's geological survey department. Larger cities may sell these maps at state or local offices or at bookstores specializing in geographical materials. (Residents of California, in particular, have a plethora of maps to choose from.) Some of these grade large areas of land as to the likelihood that they will suffer an earthquake. This information helps to weigh the risk of owning a home in a given community. In the western states and Alaska, avoidance of proximity to a fault line may be impossible. The area that presents the least risk of earthquake damage is the best choice in this case.

An important point to remember about earthquakes is that they may include movements of the earth that are not sudden and precipitous. Active fault lines—places where the surface of the earth has split into two or more separately moving entities—may move so gradually that there is never an actual earthquake; yet any building affected by the movement will ultimately suffer some damage. These *creeping faults* can be found in every area of the country. The sides of some faults may move vertically in relation to each other; that is, one side will appear to be rising. Faults may also show lateral movement, with the two sides drifting in opposite directions, or a combination of vertical and lateral movement.

Broken gas, water and sewer lines are a threat even for homes not directly

FIGURE E–6. Ways to prevent ice accumulation along roof eaves.

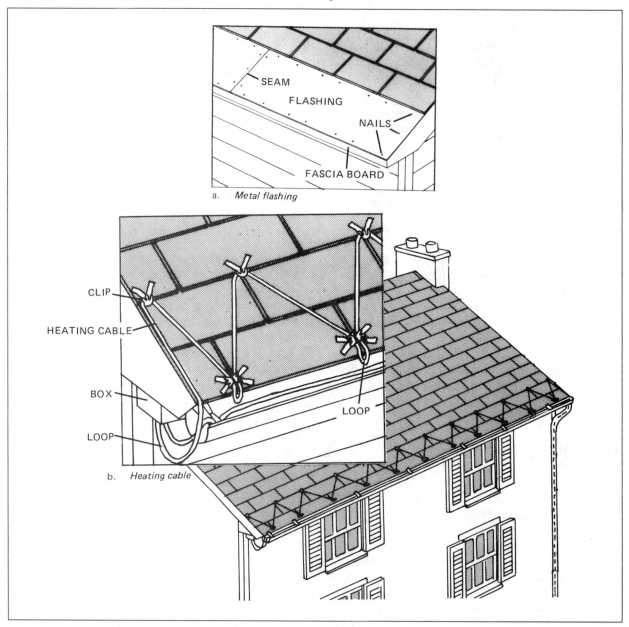

SEAM

FLASHING

NAILS

FASCIA BOARD

a.   *Metal flashing*

CLIP

HEATING CABLE

BOX

LOOP

LOOP

b.   *Heating cable*

on the fault line. Because of the extreme risk of personal injury and property damage, it is always unwise to build on a fault line or, in the case of very active faults, within a few hundred yards of the fault. Another site hazard to consider is location near a hill or mountain that might encourage a landslide in an earthquake. Likewise, a location in what could be the spillway of a dam or reservoir should be avoided in case it ruptures during an earthquake.

The risk of building in an area that will be subject to shock waves from an earthquake can be minimized by choosing a site carefully and following certain precautions. Brace and unify the individual parts of the house so that they can absorb the stress of the tremor and dissipate its effect. A particular site may not be suitable for building if the ground is composed of the soft, sandy soil most likely to shift with the lightest earthquake force. Hillsides are prone to do so, and even swimming pools have been known to slide from their original sites. The surface of seemingly flat land that was created by poorly compacted landfill will be subjected to much greater stress than one over bedrock or properly compacted landfill.

The Foundation

Ideally, the foundation of the house should have a continuous perimeter of reinforced poured concrete or concrete blocks to provide a rigid and well-anchored base for the house. A house built on well-reinforced piers, even if they are supported by bedrock, will have much more stress placed on each pier than would be placed on a comparable section of a continuous poured concrete foundation.

Figure E–7 shows three preferred methods of foundation construction. The poured concrete foundation is reinforced by wire mesh and by steel bars extending its entire length. The concrete block foundation is reinforced by steel bars extending its entire depth, anchored by poured concrete. It is important that the foundation wall be a solid unit so that it can absorb stress. If the steel bars in the concrete block foundation are not solidly anchored by poured concrete, for instance, they will vibrate with a shock wave, and the foundation blocks will separate and perhaps crack.

In a severe shock, the steel bars can be bent out of shape, and part or all of the foundation wall may collapse. For a concrete slab, both the foundation walls and the slab must be reinforced. The foundation walls or piers should have bolts imbedded in them that will anchor the frame of the house to the foundation, as shown in the examples.

The Framework

The sill of the wall frame should be bolted to the foundation; if it is not, inertia will hold the frame of the house in one place, while an earthquake moves the foundation. The result is that the house can literally slide off its foundation.

Although homes of every imaginable style have been built in earthquake-prone areas, the best precaution against vibration damage is simply to brace all framing with plywood sheathing nailed to all studs; in this way, vibrations can pass through the house. Wood or metal diagonal braces also may be used, provided they are adequately nailed to all studs they cross and anchored to both floor and ceiling. Any break in a brace (to bypass a plumbing line, for example) limits its effectiveness.

Figure E–8 shows two examples of satisfactory wall and roof bracing. Note that panel seams are staggered to minimize the stress placed on a single roof beam, which receives more stress from the end of a panel.

Outside Wall Coverings

If the proper underlayment has been used, a wide range of exterior wall coverings is acceptable. The foremost concern is that the wall covering be firmly attached, which will protect the material while increasing the stress endurance of the wall. Wood siding is well suited for a house in an earthquake-prone area, as are vertical boards placed over the seams of plywood sheathing to create a board-and-batten effect.

Older stucco houses have fared well in earthquakes because the stucco applied to chicken wire that had been nailed directly to the wood studs provided enough reinforcement to dissipate the shock stress. A stucco house built today should have the added strength of one of the types of wall bracing previously discussed, however.

Brick veneer must be fastened with metal ties to the wall sheathing or it will not be able to withstand even a minor earthquake. Unreinforced brick, stone, adobe or concrete block walls should never be used in earthquake-prone areas. Many injuries sustained in earthquakes are caused by collapsing walls or para-

FIGURE E–7.   Foundation construction techniques for earthquake-prone areas.

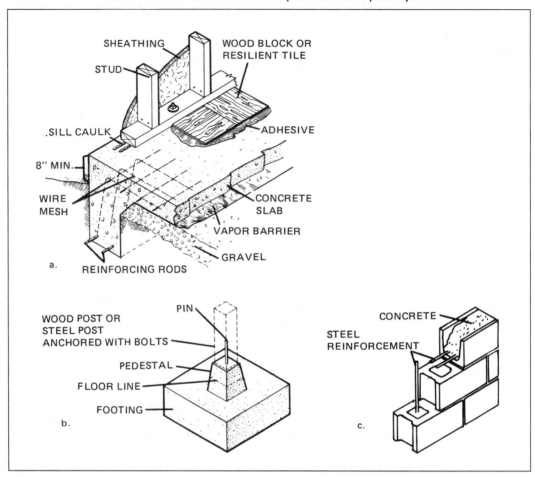

pets built of one of these materials. Chimneys built of brick or stone are equally hazardous. Unless grouted and anchored to the house by steel straps, a chimney can withstand very little stress; a shock will pound it against the house and damage both structures.

Inside Walls

Sheet rock and wood paneling will withstand the stress of earthquakes if the exterior walls have been properly braced. The interior walls should survive intact if exterior walls are braced and nailed securely to the wall studs. Otherwise, although interior paneling may add some bracing strength to the wall studs, they will not be strong enough to absorb the shock and will crack and tear off the wall. In older homes, plaster walls and ceilings should be inspected carefully for signs of imminent collapse, such as long cracks, especially around door and window frames.

Extra Precautions

An awareness of the principles involved in protecting a house against earthquake damage—bracing all components to distribute stress and prevent weak spots— makes it much easier to assess a home's potential for endurance. A newer home will probably incorporate many such features, but an older home bears careful inspection; while it may have been built well enough to have so far withstood years of stress, by now it may be so weak that the next tremors will destroy it. Objects within the house should also be braced. Metal straps fastened to the wall can be

FIGURE E–8. Wall and roof bracing.

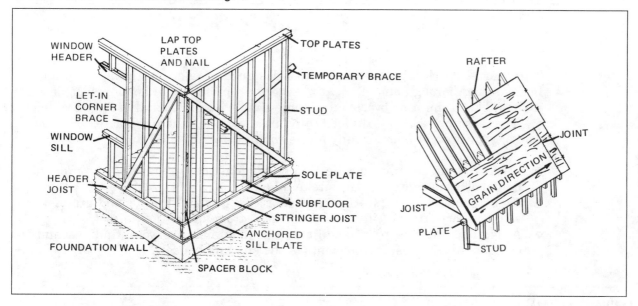

used to support water heaters. Fragile objects should be kept off high open shelves and heavy objects should be placed where they can do the least harm.

Even with physical safeguards for a building and its contents, homeowners in earthquake-prone areas should carry enough insurance to protect them against any catastrophe that might occur.

APPENDIX F: Master Inspection Checklist

This master checklist is a valuable tool designed to take you through a property in the same thorough and efficient manner as a professional home inspector. And it should keep you from overlooking some simple but potentially costly problems.

The master checklist is divided into three sections to help you assess the condition of your present house or any house you're thinking of buying:

- Forms to help ensure the collection of adequate data regarding the property's neighborhood, as well as the site and house.
- An extensive list of questions covering all aspects of the lot and grounds, as well as every crucial feature of the house—from foundation to roof.
- A detailed rating form that allows you to summarize your findings and to evaluate all the basic components of the site and house.

DATA FORMS

The best way to make sure that no details of the property and its surrounding area are overlooked is to use forms for recording the necessary information. On pages 185 through 188 are neighborhood, site and house data forms that can be used for this purpose.

At the top of the neighborhood form, record the street name or other identifiable dividing line and note the type of area adjacent to your prospective neighborhood at that boundary. A residential property adjacent to a park will usually have a higher value than a similar property adjacent to a waste disposal plant, for instance. The other categories of neighborhood data are self-explanatory. As you can see, you need to evaluate many factors before "buying a neighborhood." You'll want to be sure that it offers the right living environment for your family's lifestyle. At the same time, it's just as important to view your home as an investment whose future value will be greatly influenced by the neighborhood's evolution. Checking out a location for livability and investment potential may take some legwork, but it's worth it.

The site form can be used to record information that describes the lot. Begin with a sketch to show the property's approximate shape and street location. Important features of the site area are its size in square feet, position on the block, landscaping, utilities, improvements, soil composition and any other significant facts that add or detract from the lot.

On the house form, list construction materials used for the foundation, outside walls, roof and driveway; later on you will rate the condition of each item, as well as the general exterior and interior condition of the house. Measure each structure on the site, sketch its dimensions and compute its area in square feet.

Inside the house, note and evaluate major construction details and fixtures. Specifically, observe the interior finish, the kind of floors, the type of kitchen cabinets, the type of heating and air-conditioning systems, paneled rooms, fireplaces and all other features that affect quality. Examine the general condition of the interior for evidence of recent remodeling, cracked plaster, sagging floors and so on. Record the room dimensions and total square footage also.

CHECKLIST F–1.　Neighborhood data form.

Boundaries:

　North _____

　South _____

　East　_____

　West　_____

Adjacent to:

_____

_____

Topography: _____　☐ Urban　☐ Suburban　☐ Rural

Stage of Life Cycle of Neighborhood:　☐ Growth　☐ Equilibrium　☐ Decline

% Built Up: _____　Growth Rate:　☐ Rapid　☐ Slow　☐ Steady

Average Marketing Time: _____　Property Values:　☐ Increasing　☐ Decreasing　☐ Stable

Supply/Demand　☐ Oversupply　☐ Undersupply　☐ Balanced

Change in Present Land Use: _____

Population:　☐ Increasing　☐ Decreasing　☐ Stable　Average Family Size: _____

Average Family Income: _____　Income Level:　☐ Increasing　☐ Decreasing

Predominant Occupations: _____

Typical Properties:	% of	Age	Price Range	% Owner Occupied	% Rentals
Vacant Lots					
Single-Family Residences					
2–6-Unit Apartments					
Over 6-Unit Apartments					
Nonresidential Properties					

Tax Rate: _____　☐ Higher　☐ Lower　☐ Same as Competing Areas

Special Assessments outstanding: _____　Expected: _____

Services:　☐ Police　☐ Fire　☐ Garbage Collection　Other: _____

Distance and Direction from

　Business Area: _____

　Commercial Area: _____

　Public Elementary and High Schools: _____

　Private Elementary and High Schools: _____

　Recreational and Cultural Areas: _____

　Churches and Synagogues: _____

　Expressway Interchange: _____

　Public Transportation: _____

　　Time to Reach Business Area: _____　Commercial Area: _____

Emergency Medical Service: _____

General Traffic Conditions: _____

Proximity to Hazards (Airport, Chemical Storage, etc.): _____

Proximity to Nuisances (Smoke, Noise, etc.): _____

CHECKLIST F–2. Site data form.

Address: _____

Orientation of House: N   S   E   W

Distance to Lot Boundaries: Front _____ Sides _____ Back_____

Other Structures: _____

Best/Worst Views: _____

Dimensions: _____

Shape: _____ Square Feet: _____

Topography: _____ View: _____

Natural Hazards: _____

☐ Inside Lot   ☐ Corner Lot   Frontage: _____

Zoning: _____ Adjacent Areas: _____

Utilities: ☐ Water ☐ Gas ☐ Electricity ☐ Telephone

☐ Sanitary Sewers ☐ Storm Sewers

Improvements: ☐ Sidewalks ☐ Curbs ☐ Alley

☐ Driveway (paving: _____) Street paving: _____

Landscaping: _____

Topsoil: _____

Drainage: _____

Easements: _____

Deed Restrictions: _____

Sketch of Site:

CHECKLIST F–3. House data form.

Address: _____

House Style: traditional/contemporary

House Type: one-story/one-and-a-half story/two-story/split level/split entry/manufactured/
other _____

Age of House: _____

Room Sizes

Living room: _____

Dining room: _____

Kitchen: _____

Family room: _____

Bedrooms: 1 _____   2 _____   3 _____   4 _____   5 _____

Bathrooms: 1 _____   2 _____   3 _____

Basement: _____

Garage: _____

Structural Information

Foundation: poured concrete/concrete block/stone/brick/other _____

Wall framing: platform/balloon/plank-and-beam/other _____

Roof type: gable/hipped/gambrel/mansard/flat/other _____

Exterior

Roof covering: asphalt shingles/wood shingles/wood shakes/tile/slate/other _____

Age of roof: _____

Gutters and downspouts: aluminum/galvanized metal/wood/none

Exterior walls: wood clapboard/wood shingles/aluminum/vinyl/brick veneer/
stucco/other _____

Type of windows: double-hung/horizontal sliding/casement/fixed/
triple-track/other _____

Storm windows: yes/no

Window frames: metal/wood

Exterior doors: metal/wood/sliding glass/French/other _____

If wood: solid core/polyurethane core/hollow core

Plumbing

Water pipes: copper/galvanized metal/polybutalene plastic/other _____

Drain lines: cast iron/plastic/other _____

Water heater: gas/electric/oil

    Gallon capacity: _____

    Age: _____

Heating and Air Conditioning

Heating: central forced-air/hot water/heat pump/other _____

Air conditioning: central forced-air/heat pump/room A/C/other _____

Fuel: gas/oil/electricity

Age of equipment: _____

Electrical

Service drop: two-wire/three-wire

Service panel: fused panel/circuit-breaker panel

Wires: copper/copper-clad aluminum/aluminum

Ampere service capacity: _____

Number of circuits: _____

Insulation, Walls and Ceilings

Interior walls: wallboard/plaster/wood/wallpaper/other _____

Ceilings: wallboard/plaster/wood/tile/other _____

Insulation: batts or blanket/loose fill/rigid board/other _____

R-value: floors _____   walls _____   ceilings _____

Floor Finishes:

Kitchen: linoleum/vinyl tile/wood/carpeting/ceramic tile/other _____

Bathrooms: ceramic tile/linoleum/vinyl tile/other _____

Living room: carpeting/wood/linoleum/vinyl tile/other _____

Family room: carpeting/wood/vinyl tile/linoleum/brick/other _____

Bedrooms: carpeting/wood/vinyl tile/linoleum/other _____

Entryway: wood/vinyl tile/ceramic tile/slate/carpeting/other _____

Hallways: carpeting/wood/vinyl tile/ceramic tile/other _____

Master Inspection Checklist

The Neighborhood   Yes   No

1. Is the neighborhood *stable*, as opposed to *in decline*? _____ _____

2. Are homes well cared for? _____ _____

3. Are the lawns well kept? _____ _____

4. Are most homes in the area in the same price range? _____ _____

5. Who lives there—are their ages, incomes, number of children, interests same as yours? _____ _____

6. Is the neighborhood quiet (i.e., no irritating noise levels from automobiles, trucks, airplanes, trains, buses, etc.)? _____ _____

7. Is the neighborhood convenient to your employment? _____ _____

8. Is public transportation available? _____ _____

9. Is the neighborhood close to shopping, schools, churches, parks and recreation centers? _____ _____

10. Is the neighborhood in a low-crime area? _____ _____

11. Are property values rising? _____ _____

12. Have property taxes been steady in the past year or two? _____ _____

13. Are taxes in line with those in other areas? _____ _____

14. Is there adequate police and fire protection? _____ _____

15. Is there convenient emergency medical service? _____ _____

16. Does the area have plans for expansion and development? _____ _____

17. Does the area have any zoning restrictions? _____ _____

18. Have you checked whether any special assessments are anticipated? _____ _____

19. Are the schools of good quality? _____ _____

20. Are traffic patterns safe? _____ _____

21. Is there adequate street lighting? _____ _____

22. Do the surrounding houses conform architecturally? _____ _____

House Style and Type

23. Is the house style and type suitable for your life-style? _____ _____

24. Has the house been built by a reliable contractor? _____ _____

25. Is it covered by a warranty? _____ _____

26. Is the style consistent throughout, and the lines and detail in pleasing balance? _____ _____

	Yes	No
27. Are materials, scale and proportion consistent with the architectural style?	_____	_____
28. Does the house blend with surrounding homes?	_____	_____
29. Does the house have expansion potential?	_____	_____
30. Are the other houses in the neighborhood expensive enough so that you can recover the cost of improvements?	_____	_____
31. Does the house have good resale potential? (Ask the real estate agent. He or she has up-to-date information on what's happening in the neighborhood.)	_____	_____

The Grounds

	Yes	No
32. Does the site have all the necessary utilities?	_____	_____
33. Is the property free of any easements or deed restrictions?	_____	_____
34. Are you satisfied with the location of the site in terms of position in the block?	_____	_____
35. Is the size of the lot satisfactory?	_____	_____
36. Are the public, service and private zones of the lot well defined?	_____	_____
37. Does the house take good advantage of natural conditions (sun, breeze, view)?	_____	_____
38. Is the property well landscaped?	_____	_____
39. Is the style of the landscape compatible with the architectural style of the house?	_____	_____
40. Is the overall landscaping plan visually appealing?	_____	_____
41. Does the landscaping afford privacy?	_____	_____
42. Have the grounds been well maintained?	_____	_____
43. Does the land slope so that water drains away from the house and outdoor living areas?	_____	_____
44. Are trees and shrubs far enough away from the house? If they are too close, overhanging branches can cause serious damage to roofs, gutters and siding.	_____	_____
45. Are trees far enough away from the house, so that roots cannot penetrate cracks in the foundation or lift up the paving on driveways and walks?	_____	_____
46. Are trees healthy and at a safe distance from the house?	_____	_____
47. Will landscaping maintenance require minimal work?	_____	_____
48. If not, will extensive maintenance requirements be convenient for you?	_____	_____
49. Has proper landscaping been done to prevent soil erosion?	_____	_____
50. Does the driveway slope away from the house and garage?	_____	_____

	Yes	No
51. Is the driveway in good shape? (no severe cracks, etc.)	_____	_____
Are the walks in good shape?	_____	_____
Is the patio?	_____	_____
52. Is the driveway exit unobstructed?	_____	_____
53. Does the driveway provide a turnaround?	_____	_____
54. Are outdoor living areas screened from public view?	_____	_____
55. Are fences in good shape (no signs of deterioration—wood rot, insect damage, rust)?	_____	_____
56. Are wooden members of patios, decks or porches free of rot or insect damage?	_____	_____
57. Are walks, driveways or patios free of cracks that could cause accidents?	_____	_____

Foundation and Framing

	Yes	No
58. Is the house situated on an elevated part of the lot for good drainage?	_____	_____
59. Does water flow away from the house (not settle into the foundation)?	_____	_____
60. Are the foundation walls free of vertical cracks?	_____	_____
61. If cracks exist, are they hairline cracks? (Be sure they are not "V" cracks, as these could be part of a serious structural problem.)	_____	_____
62. From the crawl space, is the foundation free of large cracks?	_____	_____
63. Are piers in the crawl space firm and free of cracks?	_____	_____
64. Does the crawl space have adequate ventilation?	_____	_____
65. Are foundation walls straight? (Make sure there are no obvious curves or bows.)	_____	_____
66. Does the house (with a basement) have a foundation drain system; that is, gravel and pipe that lead water away from the house?	_____	_____
67. Are there properly installed vapor barriers?	_____	_____
68. Does the house smell clean (not musty)?	_____	_____
69. Are the basement walls dry?	_____	_____
70. Does the slab floor feel dry?	_____	_____
71. Are the roof, windows, and walls free of leakage warning signs?	_____	_____
72. Has there been a recent termite check by an exterminator?	_____	_____
73. Are wood beams and surfaces free of termites or wood rot?	_____	_____

	Yes	No

74. Are the floors firm? (Squeaks might be part of a serious structural problem.) _____ _____

75. Are the floors level? (Make sure they don't sag or slope.) _____ _____

76. Has the house been tested for radon gas? _____ _____

77. Is the radon level within safe standards? _____ _____

78. Are the ceilings level? (Make sure they don't sag.) _____ _____

79. Is the height of each step in the stairway the same? _____ _____

80. Is the width of each step the same size and deep enough to accommodate a large foot? _____ _____

81. Are the stairs solid when you walk on them; that is, they do not squeak or bounce when weight is applied? _____ _____

82. Is there a handrail on each stairway (particularly on steep ones)? _____ _____

Exterior Finish

Roof and Gutters

83. Look along the outer edges of the roof. Are the shingles firm (not curled or drooping)? _____ _____

84. Are all shingles, slates or tiles in good shape (none missing, cracked or broken)? _____ _____

85. Is the roof in good shape (no evidence of roof leaks)? _____ _____

86. Are flashings on the roof-mounted members in good condition? _____ _____

87. The greatest roof damage tends to occur in the valleys. Are the valleys undamaged and in good condition? _____ _____

88. Is the roof free of dark patches, indicating weak spots? _____ _____

89. Are the wood shingles or shakes free of any signs of decay or rot? _____ _____

90. Check the overhang of the roof. Is it free of any signs of wood rot? _____ _____

91. Check inside the attic for leaks. Are all rafters free of water stains and any other signs of water penetration? _____ _____

92. Does the house have proper roof ventilation? _____ _____

93. Are roof vents free of any signs of water penetration? _____ _____

94. Are there gutters and downspouts on the house? _____ _____

95. Are the soffits, gutters and downspouts made of aluminum? _____ _____

96. If not, have they been recently painted? _____ _____

97. Did you see the house in the rain? (The best time to check the roof and the gutter-downspout system.) _____ _____

98. Are all gutters free of leaks, cracks or weak spots? _____ _____

99. Are the gutters firm (not sagging)? _____ _____

	Yes	No
100. Are the downspouts attached to the gutters, and do they carry water away from the house?	_____	_____
101. Check the chimney. Are all bricks firmly in place? Is the chimney free of cracks?	_____	_____
102. Is the chimney flashing in good condition?		

Wood Siding

	Yes	No
103. Are all sections of siding firm?	_____	_____
104. Is the siding in good condition (no peeling paint or faded colors)?	_____	_____
105. Has siding been kept up so that there are no missing or decaying sections?	_____	_____
106. Is siding in good shape (no splits)?	_____	_____
107. Do all joints fit tightly together (no open gaps) to prevent water penetration?	_____	_____
108. Has the siding been nailed properly?	_____	_____
109. Is all sheathing concealed so that none shows between the boards?	_____	_____

Aluminum and Vinyl Siding

	Yes	No
110. Is the siding firm?	_____	_____
111. Do all joints fit tightly together (no open gaps) to prevent water penetration?	_____	_____
112. Is siding free of severe dents or scratches?	_____	_____
113. Is siding in good shape (no cracked or missing sections)?	_____	_____

Brick

	Yes	No
114. Is the brick in good shape (no cracked, broken or missing bricks)?	_____	_____
115. Is mortar in good shape (no signs of wear)?	_____	_____
116. Are walls straight (no bows)?		

Stucco

	Yes	No
117. Is the stucco surface free of settlement cracks, which would possibly indicate a problem in the structural wall?	_____	_____
118. Are the walls straight (no bows)?	_____	_____
119. Is the stucco firm (not pulling loose)?	_____	_____
120. Is the surface in good shape (no evidence of patches)?	_____	_____
121. Are the walls in good condition (no peeling paint or faded colors)?	_____	_____

Windows and Doors

	Yes	No
122. Do all windows fit and operate easily?	_____	_____
123. Do all doors open and close easily?	_____	_____

	Yes	No
124. Is the window glass in good shape (no cracked or broken windows)?	_____	_____
125. Are window frames in good shape (not rotted or damaged in any way)?	_____	_____
126. Are windows and doors free of water stains indicating leaks?	_____	_____
127. Are the windows weatherstripped?	_____	_____
128. Are all windows in good shape so they will not need replacing?	_____	_____
129. Are window locks in good shape (not broken)?	_____	_____
130. Are window frames in good condition (no peeling paint or faded colors)?	_____	_____
131. Are all doors in good shape (not warped; no signs of rot)?	_____	_____
132. Do the door locks operate properly?	_____	_____
133. Is the framework that surrounds the doors clean and newly painted?	_____	_____
Is the framework solid (not cracked)?	_____	_____
134. Are the exterior doors weatherstripped?	_____	_____
135. Are all doors in good condition (no peeling paint or faded colors)?	_____	_____
136. Are all storm windows and doors weathertight?	_____	_____

Garage

	Yes	No
137. Check the roof shingles. Are they in good shape (no broken, missing or deteriorating sections)?	_____	_____
138. Is the roof free of any signs of leaks?	_____	_____
139. Are the gutters and downspouts in good condition?	_____	_____
140. Do the downspouts carry water away from the garage?	_____	_____
141. Are exterior walls straight (no bulging)?	_____	_____
142. Is the foundation free of signs of defects?	_____	_____
143. Are all sections of siding firm?	_____	_____
144. Is the siding in good shape (no missing or decaying sections)?	_____	_____
145. Are the garage siding and trim in good condition (no peeling paint or faded colors)?	_____	_____
146. Is the garage floor free of any major cracks?	_____	_____
147. Is the garage floor sealed to prevent water penetration and stains?	_____	_____
148. Are all walls free of watermarks or other signs of water penetration?	_____	_____
149. Do the doors open and close properly?	_____	_____
150. Can the doors be locked?	_____	_____

	Yes	No
151. Is there an automatic door opener?	_____	_____
Does it work?	_____	_____
152. In an attached garage, inspect the door from the garage to the house. Is it fireproof?	_____	_____
153. Are the interior walls and ceiling adjacent to living spaces fireproof?	_____	_____
154. In an attached garage, is the floor of the garage lower than the house slab? (prevents toxic gases from entering the house)	_____	_____
155. Is there a piece of protective weatherstripping between the base of the door and the ground?	_____	_____
156. Is the garage wide and long enough?	_____	_____

Interior Design

Floor Plan

	Yes	No
157. Are main interior zones—living, working, sleeping—clearly separated?	_____	_____
158. Does the front door not enter directly into living room?	_____	_____
159. Is there a front hall closet?	_____	_____
160. Is there direct access from front door to kitchen, bathrooms and bedrooms without passing through other rooms?	_____	_____
161. Is the rear door convenient to the kitchen and easy to reach from street, driveway and garage?	_____	_____
162. Is a comfortable eating space for the family in or near the kitchen?	_____	_____
163. Is a separate dining area or dining room convenient to the kitchen?	_____	_____
164. Is a stairway located in a hallway or foyer instead of between levels of a room?	_____	_____
165. Are bedrooms concealed from the living room or foyer?	_____	_____
166. Are walls between bedrooms soundproof? (They should be separated by a bathroom or closet.)	_____	_____
167. Is the recreation room or family room well located?	_____	_____
168. Is the basement accessible from outside?	_____	_____
169. Are outdoor living areas accessible from the kitchen?	_____	_____
170. Are walls uninterrupted by doors and windows that could complicate furniture arrangement?	_____	_____

Kitchen

	Yes	No
171. Is base cabinet storage space sufficient?	_____	_____
172. Is wall cabinet storage sufficient?	_____	_____
173. Is counter space sufficient?	_____	_____

	Yes	No
174. Is lighting sufficient?	_____	_____
175. Is there a counter beside the refrigerator?	_____	_____
176. Is there enough window area?	_____	_____
177. Is the kitchen free of poorly placed doors that waste wall space?	_____	_____
178. Are work areas separate from heavy traffic areas?	_____	_____
179. Is there enough counter space on either side of the sink?	_____	_____
180. Is there a counter beside the range?	_____	_____
181. Are the sink, range and refrigerator close enough together?	_____	_____
182. Is the kitchen modern enough?	_____	_____
183. Are there lights over work centers?	_____	_____

Miscellaneous Things to Look For

	Yes	No
184. Does the house have at least a full bathroom on each floor?	_____	_____
185. Is there at least one bathroom for every two people?	_____	_____
186. Is there adequate closet space throughout the house?	_____	_____
187. Is the laundry area in a satisfactory location?	_____	_____
188. Does the garage have direct access to the kitchen?	_____	_____

Plumbing

	Yes	No
189. Check all exposed water pipes. Are they free of any signs of leaks, corrosion or deterioration in the water lines or their fittings?	_____	_____
190. Are all drain lines clear, with no signs of deterioration?	_____	_____
191. Are the pipes insulated?	_____	_____
192. Is the basement free of any signs of sewage backup?	_____	_____
193. Check the faucets for operation. Is there sufficient water pressure at each faucet?	_____	_____
194. Is the water clear (no rusty water coming from any faucet)?	_____	_____
195. Are faucets in good shape (no drips)?	_____	_____
196. Check all sinks in the house. Do they drain properly?	_____	_____
197. Check under the sink. Is this area free of signs of leaks or water damage?	_____	_____
198. Are countertops in good shape (no need for repair or replacement)?	_____	_____
199. Do the water pipes have shut-off valves in the basement?	_____	_____
In the kitchen?	_____	_____
In the bathrooms?	_____	_____
200. Do plumbing fixtures have proper venting?	_____	_____
201. Is there sufficient storage in the bathrooms?	_____	_____

	Yes	No
202. Are there quality fixtures?		
203. Are there sufficient electrical outlets in the bathrooms?		
204. Flush each toilet. Does each one operate properly?		
205. Does each toilet have a water shut-off valve?		
206. Do all of the toilets flush quietly? (Make sure they're not excessively noisy.)		
207. After the toilet has been flushed and filled, does it stop running?		
208. Look at the floor around the toilets. Is it free of water damage?		
209. Look carefully at the ceilings beneath the bathrooms. Are they free of water stains?		
210. Do the tubs and showers drain properly?		
211. Do the tubs and sinks hold water without seepage?		
212. Check the walls around the tubs and/or showers. Are they free of water damage?		
213. Are tiles in good shape (not cracked or missing)?		
214. Check the gallon capacity of the water heater. Does it meet your family's needs?		
215. Is the water heater in good shape? (Check its age and for signs of rust and water leaks.)		
216. If the house has a septic tank, is it free of strong odors coming from the tank area?		
217. Is the septic tank area free of standing water?		
218. Is the tank cover accessible?		
219. Does the septic system work well? (Ask the owner how often the holding tank has been pumped out over the past several years. A septic system is very costly to replace.)		
220. If there is a well, does it work well? (Ask the owner.)		

Heating and Air-Conditioning

	Yes	No
221. Does the heating and air-conditioning equipment use the least expensive fuel for the area?		
222. Does the house have energy-efficient heating and cooling equipment?		
223. Are the present utility bills acceptable for your budget?		
224. Do all rooms have air vents (or radiators)?		
225. Are the vent openings adjustable?		
226. Are the vents in the house clean and equipped with filtering devices?		

	Yes	No
227. If the house uses a hot water system, are radiators or piping free of leaks?	_____	_____
228. Is sufficient warm (or cold) air reaching all rooms through the vents (or radiators)?	_____	_____
229. Has the gas or oil furnace had an annual checkup?	_____	_____
230. Is the Freon in the central air unit free of leaks or other problems?	_____	_____
231. Do all ducts have dampers?	_____	_____
232. Look at the joints connecting individual ducts. Are they properly sealed (no open gaps through which air is leaking)?	_____	_____
233. Are the ducts (or pipes) wrapped with insulation?	_____	_____
234. Is the heating and cooling equipment relatively new? (Check to see if they will need to be replaced soon due to age.)	_____	_____
235. Does the equipment appear to be in good shape (no rust, dents, holes, etc.)?	_____	_____
236. Is the condensation line for the air conditioner clear?	_____	_____
237. Is the thermostat properly located (away from vents or ducts, etc., that may influence the temperature reading, causing the system to cycle on and off more than normal)?	_____	_____
238. Is the size of the heating and cooling unit adequate for the number of square feet in the house?	_____	_____
239. Has the owner properly maintained and serviced the chimney and fireplace?	_____	_____
240. Does the fireplace have a damper?	_____	_____
241. Is the damper tight-fitting and easy to open and close?	_____	_____
242. Does the fireplace draw well?	_____	_____
243. Are the face bricks on the fireplace solid (not coming loose from the wall)?	_____	_____
244. Are all firebricks firm?	_____	_____
245. Is grout firm (not loose or crumbling)?	_____	_____
246. Is the mantel on the fireplace level? (If not, be sure the reason is something other than a footing problem.)	_____	_____

Electrical

	Yes	No
247. Do the living areas of the house have sufficient electrical outlets?	_____	_____
248. Are all outlets in good working condition?	_____	_____
249. Are all switches and outlets properly grounded?	_____	_____
250. Are there outside electrical outlets?	_____	_____
Do they work?	_____	_____
251. Are the covers over outdoor outlets weathertight?	_____	_____

	Yes	No

252. Are all outlets three-holed? (The third hole is the grounding connection.)

253. Are all switches and outlets in good shape?

254. Do appliances have their own separate circuits?

255. Is there a main disconnect switch?

256. Pull the main disconnect switch. Does it shut off all electrical circuits? (If not, a serious defect exists in the system.)

257. Are there enough circuits to serve your needs?

258. Does the wiring meet the code?

259. Has copper or copper-clad aluminum wiring been used throughout the house instead of 100% aluminum?

260. Are all light fixtures working?

261. Are all circuit breakers working?

262. Are all fuses or circuit breakers cool to the touch? (If they are warm, a serious defect may exist in the system.)

Insulation, Interior Walls and Ceilings

263. Has an energy audit been done on the house?

If so, were the results positive?

264. Are the basement walls fully insulated?

265. Is the attic adequately insulated?

266. Are unheated areas such as garages and crawl spaces insulated?

267. Are the exterior perimeter walls insulated?

268. Does the house have good quality wall and ceiling insulation?

269. Do the insulation materials have vapor barriers?

270. Is the house free of asbestos insulation?

271. Is the house free of formaldehyde insulation?

272. Are interior walls in good shape (no major defects)?

273. Are wallboard or plaster walls free of cracks?

274. If no, are these cracks smaller than ¼ inch? (Larger ones may indicate structural failure.)

275. Are walls straight (no unsightly bows)?

276. Is all wallboard secured?

277. Are plaster walls in good shape?

278. Are the walls free of holes?

279. Are all wood panels solidly attached and in good shape?

	Yes	No
280. Are walls free of leaks? (Check for water stains.)	___	___
281. Does all wallpaper appear in good condition? (That is, it is not curled at the edges or faded.)	___	___
282. Are ceilings free of cracks?	___	___
283. If no, are these cracks smaller than ¼ inch? (Larger ones may indicate structural failure.)	___	___
284. Are all ceilings free of leaks (water stains)?	___	___
285. Are walls and ceilings in good condition (no peeling paint or faded colors)?	___	___
286. Are the plaster ceilings in good condition (no bubbles or raised portions)?	___	___
287. Are all ceiling tiles in good shape?	___	___
288. Push back suspended ceiling panels to examine hidden areas. Are they in good shape (no signs of deterioration in ceilings or walls)?	___	___

Floor Finishes and Trim

Wood Flooring

	Yes	No
289. Are the floors finished and sealed correctly?	___	___
290. Is the floor finish in good shape?	___	___
291. Are floors free of squeaks? (A squeak may simply indicate a need to be renailed, but may also be part of a more serious structural problem.)	___	___
292. Is the floor firm? (An unusual spring to the floor as you walk across it could indicate a subfloor problem.)	___	___
293. Is flooring in good shape? (Make sure there is no rotting, which usually occurs at bathrooms or door thresholds.)	___	___

Resilient Flooring

	Yes	No
294. Is the linoleum or tile smooth? (Bumps or hollows indicate the subfloor wasn't properly prepared.)	___	___
295. Is the surface of the linoleum free of cracks, tears, or noticeable marks? (If not, the only correction is total replacement of the flooring.)	___	___
296. Are individual tiles in good shape? (If not, these can be individually replaced.)	___	___

Hard Tile Flooring

	Yes	No
297. Are tiles in good shape (no cracked, loose, or missing tiles)? (Several cracked tiles could be the result of house settlement, perhaps indicating a serious structural problem.)	___	___
298. Is grout firmly in place?	___	___

	Yes	No
299. Is the flooring level? (High or low spots could pose a safety hazard.)	_____	_____
300. Is this type of flooring—particularly brick, slate, and marble—in areas that do not receive a lot of water? (These materials are slippery when wet.)	_____	_____

Wall-to-Wall Carpeting

	Yes	No
301. Are there good quality carpets in the house? (In general, the tighter the twist of the yarn, and the closer together the individual tufts in a row, the better quality the carpet is. In shags, however, density is not an important factor.)	_____	_____
302. Is there good quality padding underneath the carpets?	_____	_____
303. Are the carpets in good condition?	_____	_____
304. Are the carpets tightly stretched? (Any looseness will cause the carpet to wear much faster.)	_____	_____
305. Is the carpet free of worn or torn spots?	_____	_____
306. Are seams inconspicuous?	_____	_____
307. Is the carpet free of stains?	_____	_____
308. Are all carpets relatively clean? (Cleaning may not help excessively dirty carpeting.)	_____	_____

Trim

	Yes	No
309. Are the decorative moldings around the house in good condition?	_____	_____

Overall Rating	Good	Fair	Poor
Neighborhood	_____	_____	_____
Site	_____	_____	_____
House location	_____	_____	_____
Size of lot	_____	_____	_____
Landscaping	_____	_____	_____
Slope of land	_____	_____	_____
Walks	_____	_____	_____
Patios	_____	_____	_____
Decks	_____	_____	_____
Porches	_____	_____	_____
Fences	_____	_____	_____
House type and style meet your needs	_____	_____	_____
Expansion potential	_____	_____	_____
Resale value	_____	_____	_____

	Good	Fair	Poor
Foundation	_____	_____	_____
Drainage/site	_____	_____	_____
Framing	_____	_____	_____
Radon gas level	_____	_____	_____
Termites and other insects	_____	_____	_____
Roof covering	_____	_____	_____
Roof vents	_____	_____	_____
Gutters and downspouts	_____	_____	_____
Exterior walls	_____	_____	_____
Windows	_____	_____	_____
Exterior doors	_____	_____	_____
Chimney	_____	_____	_____
Floor plan	_____	_____	_____
Room sizes	_____	_____	_____
Kitchen	_____	_____	_____
Bathrooms	_____	_____	_____
Living room	_____	_____	_____
Dining room	_____	_____	_____
Family room	_____	_____	_____
Bedrooms	_____	_____	_____
Closets	_____	_____	_____
Storage	_____	_____	_____
Laundry area	_____	_____	_____
Basement	_____	_____	_____
Garage	_____	_____	_____
Overall plumbing system	_____	_____	_____
Drainage/plumbing	_____	_____	_____
Water pressure	_____	_____	_____
Water heater	_____	_____	_____
Septic system	_____	_____	_____
Well	_____	_____	_____
Plumbing fixtures	_____	_____	_____
Heating system	_____	_____	_____
Air-conditioning system	_____	_____	_____

	Good	Fair	Poor
Fireplace and chimney	_____	_____	_____
Wiring	_____	_____	_____
Ampere service capacity	_____	_____	_____
Number of circuits	_____	_____	_____
Number of electrical outlets per room	_____	_____	_____
Number of light switches per room	_____	_____	_____
Average dollar amount of electric bills	_____	_____	_____
Average dollar amount of gas bills	_____	_____	_____
Average dollar amount of oil bills	_____	_____	_____
Interior walls	_____	_____	_____
Ceilings	_____	_____	_____
Insulation	_____	_____	_____
Wood flooring	_____	_____	_____
Resilient flooring	_____	_____	_____
Hard tile flooring	_____	_____	_____
Wall-to-wall carpeting	_____	_____	_____
Trim	_____	_____	_____
General exterior condition	_____	_____	_____
General interior condition	_____	_____	_____

Major Problems: _____

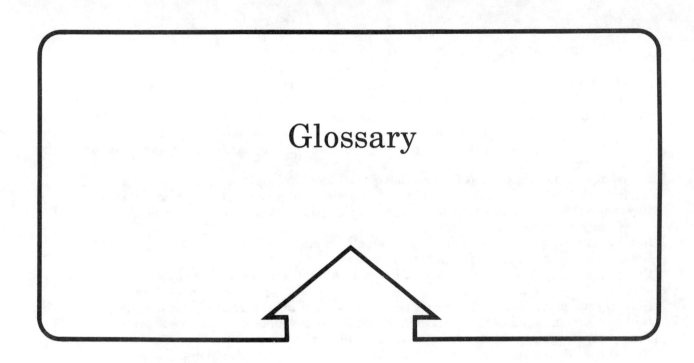

Glossary

ABT.   Association of Building Technicians.

Access.   The right to enter and leave a tract of land from a public way, sometimes by easement over land owned by another.

Acoustical material.   Sound absorbing materials, such as tile or fiberboard, which are applied to walls and/or ceilings.

Acoustical tile.   Tile, usually made of mineral, fiber or insulated metal material, having the inherent property of sound absorption.

Addition.   Any construction that adds significantly to a building's size. A second floor constructed on top of a one-level structure would be an addition.

Airway.   A space between roof insulation and roof boards for movement of air.

Anchor bolt.   A bolt that secures the sill of the house to the foundation wall.

Apron.   The flat member of the inside trim of a window placed against the wall immediately beneath the stool.

Architecture.   The art or science of building design and construction.

Asphalt tile.   A resilient floor covering (standard size is 9 inches square) laid in mastic.

Attic.   Accessible space located between the top of a ceiling and the underside of a roof. Inaccessible spaces are considered structural cavities.

Attic ventilators.   Openings in the roof or in gables to allow for air circulation.

Backfilling or backfill.   The earth or gravel used to fill in the space around a building wall after the foundation is completed.

Balloon framing.   A type of framing in which the studs extend from the top of the foundation sill to the roof. Support for the second floor is provided by a horizontal ribbon or ledge board and by joists that are nailed to the studs.

Baluster.   One of a string of small poles used to support the handrail of a stairway.

Band or **box sill.**   In pier and beam foundations, the two horizontal members that connect the pier to the floor joist. The boards are joined to create a right angle, and the joist is placed perpendicular to the upright angle. This perpendicular placement gives a foundation the necessary rigidity.

Baseboard.   A board running along the bottom of the wall parallel to the floor, which covers the gap between the floor and the wall, protects the wall from scuffs and provides a decorative accent.

Baseboard heating.   A system of perimeter heating with radiators, convectors or air outlets located in the wall. The system may be hot water, forced air or electric.

Basement.   A space of full-story height below the first floor wholly or partly below the exterior grade, which is not used primarily for living accommodations. Space, partly below grade, which is used primarily for living accommodations or commercial use is not defined by FHA as basement space.

Base shoe.   Molding used at the junction of the baseboard and the floor. Also called a *carpet strip*.

Batten.   Narrow decorative strips of wood or metal used to cover interior or exterior joints.

Bay window.   A window that forms a bay in a room, projects outward from the wall, and is supported by its own foundation.

Beam.   A structural member that transversally supports a load.

Beamed ceiling.   A ceiling with beams exposed.

Bearing plate.   A metal plate placed under a column or beam to distribute the weight of the load.

Bearing wall.   A wall that supports any vertical load in addition to its own weight.

Bed mold.   An ornamental strip laid horizontally at the juncture of the frieze and cornice soffit.

Bevel.   An angular surface across an edge of a piece of stock.

Blacktop.   Bituminous or asphalt material used in hard surface paving.

Blueprint.   (1) A working plan used on a construction job by tradespeople. (2) An architectural drafting or drawing that is transferred to chemically treated paper by exposure to strong light that turns the paper blue, thus reproducing the drawing in white.

Board and batten.   A type of vertical siding composed of wide boards and narrow battens. The boards are nailed to the sheathing with a one-half space left between them. The battens are then nailed over the spaces.

Board foot.   A measure of lumber one foot square by one inch thick; 144 cubic inches = 1 foot by 1 foot by 1 inch.

Brace.   An inclined piece of framing lumber applied to the wall or floor to stiffen a structure.

Bracing.   Framing lumber nailed at an angle to provide rigidity.

Brick veneer.   A facing of brick laid against and fastened to the sheathing of a frame wall.

Bridging.   Small wood or metal pieces placed diagonally between the floor joists. Bridgings disburse weight on the floor over adjacent joists, thus increasing the floor's load capacity.

BTU.   British thermal unit. One BTU is the amount of heat required to raise one pound of water 1 degree Fahrenheit.

Building standards.   Specific construction elements the owner or developer chooses to use throughout a building. The building standard offered an office tenant would relate to partitions, doors, ceiling tile, light fixtures, carpet, draperies and other items.

Built-up roof.   A roof composed of three to five layers of asphalt felt laminated with coal tar, pitch or asphalt, and coated with gravel. Generally used on flat or low-pitched roofs.

BX.   Electrical cable consisting of a flexible metal covering enclosing two or more wires.

Casement window.   A type of window having a sash with hinges on the side and opening outward.

Casing.   A frame, as of a window or door.

Ceiling joists.   The horizontal structural members to which the ceiling is fastened.

Cement blocks.   Blocks made primarily of cement and gravel formed into shape under pressure and used principally for construction of walls.

Cesspool.   A covered cistern of stone, brick or concrete block that functions like a septic tank. The liquid seeps out through the walls directly into the surrounding earth.

Chimney.   A stack of brick or other masonry extending above the surface of the roof that carries the smoke to the outside. The smoke is carried inside the chimney through the flue.

Chimney cap.   Ornamental stone or concrete edging around the top of the chimney stack that helps protect the masonry from the elements and improves the draught in the chimney.

Chimney flashing.   A strip of material, usually metal, placed over the junction of the chimney and the roof to make the joint watertight. Flashings are used wherever the slope is broken up by a vertical structure.

Chimney pot. A fire clay or terra-cotta pipe projecting from the top of the chimney stack. The chimney pot is decorative and increases the draught of the chimney.

Cinder fill. A layer of cinder placed between the ground and the basement floor or between the ground and the foundation walls to aid in water drainage.

Clapboard. Siding of narrow boards thicker at one edge used as exterior finish for frame houses.

Cleanout door. An exterior door located at the base of the chimney for convenient removal of the ashes that were put through the ash dump.

Collar beam. A horizontal beam connecting the rafter at the lower end. The collar beam adds rigidity and diverts the weight of snow on the roof from the exterior walls.

Collector. A device used to collect solar radiation and convert it into heat.

Column. A vertical structural member supporting horizontal members such as beams and girders.

Concrete. A combination of cement and sand, broken stone or gravel used for foundations, walks and other construction purposes.

Concrete block. Concrete compressed into the shape of a block and allowed to set until it hardens; used as a masonry unit.

Conduit. A metal pipe in which electrical wire is installed.

Cornice. (1) A horizontal projection or molding at the top of the exterior walls under the eaves that aids in water drainage. (2) Any molded projection at the top of an interior or exterior wall, in the enclosure at the roof eaves, or at the rake of the roof.

Cove molding. A molding with a concave face used as trim or as finish around interior corners.

Crawl space. A shallow space between the floor of a house and the ground.

Crown molding. Molding that is installed between the top of the wall and the ceiling.

Damper. An adjustable valve at the top of a fireplace that regulates the flow of heated gases into the chimney.

Dampproofing or **weatherproofing.** A horizontal layer of plastic, lead, asphalt or other water-resistant materials placed between the interior and exterior walls to exclude moisture.

Deciduous trees. Trees that lose their leaves annually.

Design. An architectural drawing of the plan, elevations and sections of a structure.

Dormer. A projection built out from the slope of a roof, used to house windows on the upper floor and to provide additional headroom. Common types of dormers are the gable dormer and the shed dormer.

Double corner stud or **post.** Two vertical studs joined at right angles to form the corner of the frame. The double studs are heavier than regular studs and give greater support.

Double floor. Wood construction using a subfloor and a finished floor.

Double-hung window. A type of window containing two movable sashes that slide vertically.

Double pitch. Sloping in two directions, as in a gable roof.

Double plate. Two horizontal boards on top of and connecting the studs. The plate serves as a foundation for the rafters.

Double window header. Two boards laid on edge to form the upper portion of a door or window.

Downspout. A vertical pipe made of cement, metal, clay or plastic that carries rainwater from the eaves to the ground.

Drain field. An area containing a system of underground pipes for draining septic systems or other types of liquid overflow.

Drain tile. A pipe, usually clay, placed next to the foundation footing to aid in water drainage.

Dry rot. Decay of seasoned wood caused by a fungus.

Drywall construction. Any type of interior wall construction not using plaster as finish material. Wood paneling, plywood, plasterboard, gypsum board or other types of wallboard are usually used for drywall.

Duct. A tube, pipe or channel for conveying or carrying fluids, cables, wires or tempered air. Underfloor duct systems are commonly used to provide for telephone and electrical lines.

Duplex. A house containing two separate dwelling units, side by side or one above the other.

Dutch door.   A door divided horizontally so that the top half may be opened while the lower section remains closed.

Eave.   The overhang of a sloping roof that extends beyond the walls of the house. Also called roof projection.

Exterior finish.   The outer finish of a structure including roof and wall covering, gutters and door and window frames. The term generally refers to the protective outer covering of a structure.

Exterior wall.   Any outer wall serving as a vertical enclosure of a building.

Facade.   The principal exterior face of a structure; usually the front face or front elevation of a building.

Face.   The most important side of a structure; the front or facade.

Face brick.   A better grade of brick that is used on the exterior wall of a building, frequently only on the front or principal side.

Fascia.   (1) A flat member, as on a cornice for eave. (2) The board of the cornice to which the gutter or rainwater is fastened.

Felt paper.   Paper used for sheathing on walls and roofs to serve as a barrier against heat, cold and moisture.

Fenestration.   The arrangement and design of doors and windows in a wall.

FHA.   Federal Housing Administration.

Fiberboard.   A prefabricated building material composed of wood or other plant fibers, compressed and bonded into a sheet.

Finish flooring.   The visible interior floor surface, which is usually made of a decorative hardwood such as oak. The finish flooring may be laid in strips or in a block design such as parquet.

Fire brick.   A clay brick capable of resisting high temperatures; it is used to line heating chambers and fireplaces.

Firestop.   Short boards placed horizontally between studs or joists to decrease draughts and retard fires.

Fire wall.   A wall constructed of fire-resistant materials, the purpose of which is to prevent the spread of fire within the building. The fire wall carries a standard rating that designates its ability to constrain fire in terms of hours.

Fixed window.   A window that does not open, such as a picture window.

Flashing.   Sheet metal or other impervious material used in roof and wall construction to protect a building from water seepage.

Flat roof.   A roof having a slope sufficient to provide for proper drainage.

Floor joist.   Horizontal boards laid on edge resting on the beams that provide the main support for the floor. The subflooring is nailed directly to the joists. *See Ceiling joists.*

Flue.   An enclosed passage in a chimney, duct or pipe through which smoke, hot air and gases pass upward. Flues are usually made of fire clay or terra-cotta pipe.

Footing.   A concrete support under a foundation, chimney or column that usually rests on solid ground and is wider than the structure being supported. Footings are designed to distribute the weight of the structure over the ground.

Formica.   A trade name for a plastic material that is used primarily for the top of counter areas but is also used for wall covering, as a veneer for plywood panels or as a wallboard where a fire-resistive material is desirable. Similar and competitive materials are produced under other trade names.

Foundation.   The part of a building or wall that supports the superstructure.

Foundation wall.   The masonry or concrete wall below ground level that serves as the main support for the frame structure. Foundation walls form the side walls of the basement.

Frame construction.   Construction in which the structural parts are of wood or depend on a wood frame for support.

Framing.   The rough structure of a building, including interior and exterior walls, floor, roof and ceiling.

French windows or **doors.**   A pair of glazed doors hinged at the jamb, functioning as both windows and doors.

Frieze.   A horizontal member of a cornice, set flat against a wall.

Frost line.   The depth of frost penetration in the soil. The frost line varies throughout the United States, and footings should be placed below this depth to prevent movement of the structure.

Furring strips.   Narrow strips of wood nailed or glued on walls and ceilings to form a level surface on which to fasten other materials.

Gable.   (1) The end of a building, generally triangular in shape. (2) The vertical plane which lies above the eaves and between the slopes of a ridged roof.

Gable roof.   A ridged roof, the ends of which form a gable.

Gambrel roof.   A curb roof, having a steep lower slope and a flatter one above, as seen in Dutch Colonial architecture.

Girder.   A heavy wooden or steel beam supporting the floor joists. The girder provides the main horizontal support for the floor.

Green lumber.   Freshly sawed lumber, or lumber that has had no intentional drying; unseasoned.

Grout.   A cement mixture used to fill crevices.

Gutter.   A shallow metal channel set below and along the eaves of a house to catch and carry off rainwater from the roof.

Hardwood.   Refers not to the hardness of the wood, but to a group of broad-leafed trees from which the wood is taken. Maple, oak and birch are hardwood trees. *See Softwood.*

Head casing.   The strip of molding placed above a door or window frame.

Head jamb.   A piece of finish material across the underside of the top of a door or window opening.

Hearth.   The floor of the fireplace. The front hearth, which extends out into the room, may be made of brick or decorative stone. The back hearth inside the fireplace is usually made of fire brick.

Heating system.   Any device or system for heating a building; usually a furnace or boiler used to generate hot air, hot water or steam.

Hip roof.   A pitched roof with sloping sides and ends.

Insulation.   Pieces of plasterboard, fireproofed sheeting, compressed wood-wool, fiberboard or other material placed between inner and outer surfaces, such as walls and ceilings, to protect the interior from heat loss. Insulation works by breaking up and dissipating air currents.

Jalousie.   Adjustable glass louvers in doors and windows used to regulate light and air or exclude rain.

Jamb.   A vertical surface lining the opening in the wall left for a door or window.

Joint.   The point where two surfaces join or meet.

Joist.   A heavy piece of horizontal timber, to which the boards of a floor or the lath of a ceiling are nailed. Joists are nailed edgewise to form the floor support.

Kick plate.   A metal strip placed at the lower edge of a door to protect the finish.

Lath.   Thin strips of wood, metal or gypsum fastened to rafters, ceiling joists or wall studs to act as a plaster base.

Lean-to roof.   A sloping roof supported on one side by the wall of an adjacent building.

Linear measure.   Measurement along a line.

Lintel.   A horizontal board that supports the load over an opening, such as a door or window.

Load.   Weight supported by a structural part such as a load-bearing wall.

Loft.   An attic-like space below the roof of a house or barn; any of the upper stories of a warehouse or factory.

Louver.   (1) Slats or fins over an opening, pitched so as to keep out rain or snow yet still permit ventilation. (2) A finned sunshade on a building. (3) The diffusion grill on fluorescent light fixtures. Also spelled *louvre*.

M-roof.   A roof made up of two double-pitch roofs.

Mansard roof.   A roof with two slopes or pitches on each of the four sides, with the lower slope steeper than the upper.

Mantel.   The decorative facing placed around a fireplace. Mantels are usually made of ornamental wood and topped by a shelf.

Masonry.   Anything constructed of brick, stone, tile, cement, concrete or similar materials.

Masonry wall.   A wall made of masonry materials. *See Masonry.*

Millwork.   Wooden parts of a building purchased in finished form from millwork plants and planing mills. Doors, window and door frames, trim, molding, stairways and cabinets are millwork items.

Miter.   In carpentry terminology, the ends of two pieces of board of corresponding form cut off at an angle and fitted together in an angular shape.

Molding.   A strip of decorative wood, such as that on the top of a baseboard or around windows and doors.

Monolithic.   One-piece. Monolithic concrete is poured in a continuous process so that there are no separations or joints due to different setting times.

Mosaic.   A decoration made by laying small pieces of colored glass, stone or ceramic materials in mortar or mastic to form a design.

Mud room.   A vestibule or small room used as the entrance from a play yard or alley. The mud room frequently contains a washer and dryer.

Mullion.   A thin vertical bar or divider in the frame between windows, doors or other openings.

Muntin.   The narrow vertical strip that separates two adjacent window sashes.

NAHB.   National Association of Home Builders of the United States.

NBS.   National Bureau of Standards.

Nosing.   The rounded outer face of a stair tread.

O.C. (on center).   The measurement of spacing for studs, rafters, joists and similar members in a building from the center of one member to the center of the next.

Orientation.   The situation of the house—the direction it faces.

Overhang.   The part of a roof that extends beyond the exterior wall.

Parapet.   The part of the wall of a house that rises above the roof line.

Parquet floor.   A finished floor constructed of wood blocks laid in rectangular or square patterns.

Partition.   That which subdivides space within a building—especially an interior wall.

Pier.   A column, usually of steel reinforced concrete, evenly spaced under a structure to support its weight. In a house foundation piers are formed by drilling holes in the earth to a prescribed depth and pouring concrete into them. Foundation piers that support some structures, such as bridges, may be above the ground. The term also refers to the part of a wall between windows or other openings that bear the wall weight.

Pilaster.   An upright, architectural member or vertical projection from a wall, on either one or both sides, used to strengthen the wall by adding support or preventing buckling.

Pitch.   The slope or incline of a roof from the ridge to the lower edge, expressed in inches of rise per foot of length, or by the ratio of the rise to the span.

Plank-and-beam framing.   A type of frame construction that uses heavier structural members spaced farther apart than other framing, and with the supporting posts, roof beams and roof deck left exposed to the interior as part of the decor.

Plaster finish.   The last thin layer of fine-grain plaster applied as a decorative finish over several coats of coarse plaster on the lath base. Finishing plaster usually has a high ratio of lime to sand, while coarser plasters have more sand. Plaster is pasty when applied to the wall but hardens as it dries. In newer buildings, plasterboard or gypsum is often used instead of plaster because it doesn't have to harden.

Plat.   A map representing a piece of land subdivided into lots, with streets and other details shown thereon.

Plate.   A horizontal piece that forms a base for supports. The sill or sole plate rests on the foundation and forms the base for the studs. The wall plate is laid along the top of the wall studs and forms a support base for the rafters.

Plate glass.   A high-quality glass that has been ground and polished.

Platform or **western frame.**   A type of framing in which floor joists of each story rest on the top plates of the story below (or on the foundation sill for the first story). The bearing walls and partitions rest on the subfloor of each story.

Plumb.   Vertical.

Ply.   A term to denote the number of layers or thicknesses of material, such as three-ply building or roofing paper.

Plywood.   A wood product made of three or more (but always an odd number) layers of veneer joined with an adhesive and usually laid with the grain of adjoining plies at right angles.

Prefabrication.   The manufacturing and assembling of construction materials and parts into component structural units such as floor, wall and roof panels, which are later erected or installed at the construction site.

Purlin.   A horizontal structural member used to support roof rafters or roof sheathing.

Quantity survey method.   A method for finding the reproduction cost of a building in which the costs of erecting or installing all of the component parts of a new building, including both direct and indirect costs, are added.

Quarter round.   A molding whose shape forms a quarter of a circle.

Rafter.   One of a series of sloping beams that extends from the exterior wall to a center ridge board and provides the main support for the roof.

Rails.   The horizontal members of a door, framework of a window sash or any paneled assembly.

Ranch house.   A one-story house that is low to the ground, with low-pitched gable roof or roofs. It may have a basement.

Rendering.   A term used in perspective drawing meaning to finish with ink or color to bring out the effect of the design, as in an architect's rendering of a proposed project.

Retaining wall.   Any wall erected to hold back or support a bank of earth. A retaining wall is also any wall built to resist the lateral pressure of internal loads.

Ridge board.   A heavy horizontal board set on edge at the apex of the roof to which the rafters are attached.

Riser.   The vertical face of the step that supports the tread. The riser is the part that faces you as you walk upstairs.

Roof boards.   Boards nailed to the top of the rafters, usually touching each other, to tie the roof together and form a base for the roofing material. The boards, or roof sheathing, can also be constructed of sheets of plywood.

Roofing felt.   Sheets of felt or other close-woven heavy material placed on the top of the roof boards to insulate and waterproof the roof. Like building paper, roofing felt is treated with bitumen or another tar derivative to increase its water resistance. Roofing felt is applied either with a bonding and sealing compound or with intense heat that softens the tar and causes it to adhere to the roof.

Roof sheathing.   The material, usually wood boards, plywood or wallboard, fastened to the roof rafters and onto which shingles or other roof coverings are laid.

Row house.   One of a series of individual houses having architectural unity and a common wall between each unit.

Saddle.   Two sloping surfaces meeting in a horizontal ridge, used between the back side of a chimney and a sloping roof.

Sash.   The framework that holds the glass in a window or door.

Scale.   A proportion between two sets of dimensions, such as between those of a drawing and the actual structure. The scale of a floor plan may be expressed as $\frac{1}{4}'' = 1'$. This means that one-quarter inch on the drawing is the same as one foot in the actual structure.

Sheathing.   Plywood or boards nailed to the studs and roof rafters on the exterior of a house as a foundation for the finished siding and roofing.

Shingle.   A roof or wall covering material usually made of asphalt, wood, slate or tile, applied in overlapping layers.

Shoe molding.   A thin strip of wood placed at the junction of the baseboard and the floor boards to conceal the joint. The shoe molding improves the aesthetics of the room and helps seal out draughts.

Shoring.   (1) The use of timbers to prevent the sliding of earth adjoining an excavation. (2) The timbers used as bracing against a wall for temporary support of loads during construction.

Siding.   Boards, metal or masonry sheets, nailed horizontally to the vertical studs, with or without intervening sheathing, to form the exposed surface of the outside walls of the building.

Sill.   The lowest horizontal member of the house frame, which rests on the top of the foundation walls and forms a base for the studs. The term can also refer to the lowest horizontal member in a frame for a window or door.

Slab.   A flat, horizontal reinforced concrete area, usually the interior floor of a building but also an exterior or roof area.

Sleepers.   Strips of wood laid over rough concrete floors so a finished wood floor can be applied over them.

Soffit.   Usually the underside of an overhanging cornice.

Softwood.   A general classification of lumber obtained from the group of trees having needlelike leaves. The common softwoods are cedar, fir, pine, redwood and spruce. *See Hardwood.*

Solar heating.   A system that operates by gathering the heat from the sun's rays with one or more solar collectors. Water or air is forced through a series of pipes in the solar collector to be heated by the sun. The hot air or water is then stored in a heavily insulated tank until it is needed to heat the house.

Span.   The horizontal distance between structural supports such as walls, beams, columns, girders and tresses.

Split-level house.   A house in which two or more floors are usually located directly above one another and one or more additional floors, adjacent to them, are placed at a different level.

Storm window.   An extra window usually placed on the outside of an existing window as additional protection against cold weather.

Stringer.   One of the sloping enclosed sides of a staircase that supports the treads and risers. The term can also refer to a horizontal beam that connects the uprights in a frame.

Stucco.   A cement or plaster wallcovering that is installed wet and dries into a hard surface covering.

Stud.   In wall framing, the vertical members to which horizontal pieces are attached. Studs are placed between 16 and 24 inches apart and serve as the main support for the roof and/or the second floor.

Subfloor.   Boards or plywood sheets nailed directly to the floor joists serving as a base for the finish flooring. Subflooring is usually made of rough boards, although some houses have concrete subflooring.

Sump.   A pit or reservoir used for collecting or holding water (or some other liquid) that is subsequently disposed of, usually by a pump.

Sump pump.   An automatic electric pump installed in a basement or low area to empty the sump. *See Sump.*

Superstructure.   That part of the structure above the ground or above the top of the foundation walls.

Suspended ceiling.   A ceiling system that derives its support from the overhead structural framing.

Termite shield.   A metal sheet laid into the exterior walls of a house near ground level, usually under the sill, to prevent termites from entering the house. Termite shields should be affixed to all exterior wood in the house and around pipes entering the building. Shields are generally constructed with an overhanging lip to allow for water runoff.

Tongue-and-groove.   A method of joining two pieces of board wherein one has a tongue cut into the edge and the other board has a groove cut to receive the corresponding tongue. The method is used to modify any material prepared for joining in this fashion, as tongue-and-groove lumber.

Tread.   The horizontal surface of a stair step resting on the riser. The tread is the part to step on.

Trim.   Wood or metal interior finishing pieces such as door and window casings, moldings and hardware.

Truss.   A type of roof construction employing a rigid framework of beams and members, which supports the roof load and usually achieves relatively wide spans between its supports.

U-value.   The total number of BTUs of heat transmitted in one hour per square foot of area per 1 degree Fahrenheit difference between the air on one side of a barrier and the air on the other side.

Valley.   The internal angle formed by the junction of two sloping sides of a roof.

Vapor barrier.   Material used to keep moisture from penetrating walls or floors.

Veneer.   (1) A layer of material covering a base of another substance, such as mahogany veneer overlaid on a less valuable wood. (2) A brick exterior finish over wood framing.

Vent.   A small opening to allow the passage of air through any space in a building, as for ventilation of an attic or the unexcavated area under a first-floor construction.

Vestibule.   A small entrance hall to a building or to a room.

Wainscot.   Wood lining of an interior wall. Wainscotting is also the lower part of a wall when finished differently from the wall above.

Wallboard.   A board used as the finishing covering for an interior wall or ceiling. Wallboard can be made of plastic laminated plywood, cement sheeting, plywood, molded gypsum, plasterboard, or other materials. Wallboard is applied in thin sheets over the insulation. It is often used today as a substitute for plaster walls but can also serve as a base for plaster.

Wall sheathing.   Sheets of plywood, gypsum board or other material nailed to the outside face of the wall studs to form a base for exterior siding.

Warm air system.   A heating system in which furnace-heated air moves to living space through a single register or a series of ducts, circulated by natural convection (gravity system) or by a fan or blower in the ductwork (forced system).

Waste line.   A pipe that carries waste from a bathtub, shower, lavatory or any fixture or appliance except a toilet.

Weatherstrip.   A thin strip of material, such as metal, felt or wood, used around doors and windows to keep out air, water, moisture or dust.

Window jamb trim.   A thin vertical strip of molding covering the junction of the vertical members of the window frame and the jamb.

Window sash.   A movable frame that holds the window glass. Sash windows move vertically and may be single—in which only the lower half of the window opens; or double, in which both the upper and lower portions are movable.

X-bracing.   Cross-bracing in a partition.

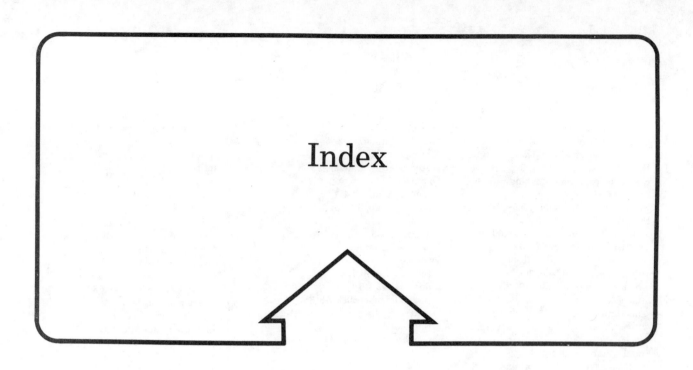

Index

Absorption cooling, 108, 109
Accoustical ceiling tile, 134, 135
Active solar heating systems, 101
Adding on or remodeling, 21–23
Air-conditioning
  central systems, 108–9
  compression and absorption cooling,
    107–8, 109
  duct insulation, 112
  and energy efficiency, 164–65, 166
  heat pumps, 109–11
  inspection checklist, 113
  room air conditioners, 109
Air-infiltration controls, 159–60,
    161–62
Air leakage test, 160
Alternating current, 117
Aluminum siding, 62–63
Aluminum soffit, gutter and down-
    spout, 61, 62–63
Amperes, 115, 116
Asbestos, 129, 134, 144
Asphalt shingles, 59
Asphalt tile flooring, 143–44
Attic fans, 166, 167
Awning windows, 67

Balloon frame, 43, 44
Basement
  inspection of, 41
  as unzoned space, 31
Base planting, 152–53
Bathrooms, 30, 83, 143
Bathtubs, 83–85
Bay windows, 68
Bedrock, 6
Bedrooms, 29–30

Bidet, 87
Blowout toilet, 85
Border planting, 153
Bottom rail, window, 66
Building codes, 3–4, 21, 46
Built-up roof, 60
BX cable, 117–18

Cap, chimney, 104, 106
Carpeting, 144–45
  inspection checklist, 148
Casement windows, 66–67
Ceiling finishes, 134–35
  inspection of, 136–39
Ceiling tile, 134
Central forced-air system, 108
Central heating systems, 97–100
Central hydronic system, air-
    conditioning, 109
Ceramic tile flooring, 142–44
Chair rail trim, 145
Check rail, windows, 66
Chimneys, 102–6
  inspection of, 107
Circuit breaker, 123–24
Circuit breaker panel, 122, 124
Circulation areas, 25
Clay soils, 5, 6
Climate and weather, and house
    orientation, 6–7
Collar beams, roof, 48
Colonial American house style, 14–15
Combination foundation, 40–41
Combustion chamber, fireplace, 106
Compression cooling, 107–8, 109
Concrete block foundation, 38–39
Concrete slab foundation, 39–40

Conduit, 119
Conventional roof framing, 48, 50
Cork walls and floors, 134–35, 142
Crown molding, 145

Damper, fireplace, 106
Decorative effects, interior wood
    paneling, 134
Deed restrictions, 4
Defective floors, 42, 45
Defective walls, 44
Defective windows and doors, 44
Detail drawings, plumbing, 82
Diagonal paneling, 134
Dining room, 29, 30
Direct current, 117
Doors, exterior, 65, 69–74
  inspection of, 71
Double-hung windows, 66, 67
Downdraft prevention, chimney, 103
Drainage system, 80
Driveways and walks, 150–51
Driveway turnaround, 151
Duct insulation, 112
Ductwork, efficiency of, 160
Dutch doors, 70

Earthquake damage, protection from,
    178–83
Easements, 4, 5
Electrical metallic tubing (EMT), 119
Electrical specifications, 120
Electrical symbols, 121
Electrical system
  electricity characteristics, 115–17
  inspection checklist, 126
  inspection of, 124–25

service to panel, 121–24
types of current and wire sizes, 117
wiring diagrams, 119–21
wiring types, 117–19
Electricity, characteristics and measurement of, 115–17
Elevations, plumbing, 81, 82
Enameled cast iron plumbingware, 89–90
Enameled steel plumbingware, 90
Energy efficiency
air-infiltration controls, 159–60, 161
ductwork efficiency, 160
equipment sizing and, 163–64
fireplace and, 162–63, 164
house orientation and, 160–61
inspection checklist, 166, 168
insulation, 162
miscellaneous means of achieving, 164–66
and water heating, 164
weatherstripping and caulking, 162
and window size, location and treatment, 161–62
Energy-efficiency ratio (EER), 163–64
English Tudor house style, 14
Equipment maintenance, and energy efficiency, 166
Equipment sizing, and energy efficiency, 163–164
Evaporative coolers, and energy efficiency, 166
Exterior finish
doors, 65, 69–74
inspection checklist, 74–78
roof coverings, 59–60
roof sheathing, 57–59
siding inspection, 64–65
wall coverings, 61–64
wall sheathing, 61
window and door inspection, 71–73
windows, 65–69
Exterior wall coverings, 61–64

Family room, 29
Fascia boards, 73
Fascias, 62
Fences, 154
Finish flooring
ceramic tile, 142–43
inspection checklist, 147–48
resilient sheet flooring, 143–44
resilient tile, 143
wood flooring, 141–42
Finish grading, 150
Finish plumbing, 83
Fireplaces, 105–7
and energy efficiency, 162–63
inspection of, 107
Fixed windows, 67, 68
Flashing, chimney, 104–5
Flat roof, 49
Flexible armored cable wiring, 117–18
Flight, stairway, 46–47
Floating slab foundation, 39–40
Floor framing, 41–42, 45

Floor plan, 31–33
plumbing, 81
Flue and flue lining, chimney, 103
Flush doors, 70
Footing, chimney, 103
Footings, 37–38
Forced heating systems, 98–100
Foundation
combination, 40–41
concrete slab, 39–40
footings, 37–38
walls, 38–39
Frame, window, 66
Framing
ceilings and roof, 48–49
floor, 41–42, 45
inspection checklist, 51–55
stairways, 45–48
wall, 43–44
windows and doors, 44
French doors, 70, 73
Fuse, 123, 124
Fused service panel, 122–23, 124

Gable roof, 49
Gambrel roof, 49
Garage, 31, 73–74
Gravel soils, 6
Gravity heating systems, 97–98
Gravity hot-water heating system, 98
Ground water, 5
Gutter inspection, 60–61

Handrail, stairway, 46, 48
Hardpan soils, 5
Head jamb, window, 66
Headroom, stairway, 48
Hearth, 105
Heating systems
chimney inspection, 107
chimneys, 102–5
forced, 98–100
gravity, 97–98
history of in America, 95–96
inspection checklist, 113–14
inspection of, 101–2
solar, 101
space, 100–101
Heat movement patterns, 96
Heat pumps, 109–11
Herringbone and horizontal paneling, 134
Hipped roof, 49
Home improvements, value of, 173
Horizontal sliding windows, 66, 67
Hot-water softeners, 88–89
House-connection pipe system, 80
House corner planting, 152
House location
inspection checklist, 10–11
land-use restrictions, 3–4
neighborhood and site inspection, 8–11
orientation on lot, 6–8
soil composition and topography, 4–6
subdivision planning, 1–3
House styles, 13–15

House types
inspection checklist, 23–24
manufactured, 20–21
one-and-a-half story, 16–18
one-story, 15–16
split-entry, 19–20
split-level, 18–19
two-story, 18
Humidity, temperature and heating system, 99

Ice accumulation, and roofs, 58–59
Inspection checklists
carpeting, 148
electrical system, 126
energy efficiency, 166, 168
exterior finish, 74–78
finish flooring, 147–48
foundation and framing, 51–55
heating and air-conditioning, 113–14
house location, 10–11
house styles and types, 23–24
insulation, walls and ceilings, 138–39
interior design, 33–36
interior trim, 148
master, 184–202
plumbing, 91–93
site finishing, 154–57
Insulation, 127–29, 174–75
duct, 112
and energy efficiency, 162
inspection of, 136, 138
Interior design
circulation areas, 25, 26
floor plan and, 31–33
inspection checklist, 33–36
living zone, 28–29
sleeping zone, 29–30
unzoned space, 30–31
work zone, 26–28
Interior trim, 145–46
inspection checklist, 148
Isometrics, plumbing, 81–82, 83

Jalousie windows, 67, 68
Kilowatts, 116–17
Kitchen, 26–28
remodeling, 27–28
Kitchen sinks, 86–87
Knob-and-tube wiring, 119, 120

Landing, stairway, 46–47
Landscaping plan, 150–54
Land-use restrictions, 3–4
Laundry facilities, 28
Laundry tubs, 87
Lavatories, 86, 87
Lawns, 154
Life-style, and energy efficiency, 166
Lighting, and energy efficiency, 165
Lights, 121
Living zone, 28–29
Longitudinal plank-and-beam roof framing, 52
L-shaped kitchen, 27

Main entrance door, 69
Main entrance planting, 152, 153
Mansard roof, 49
Manufactured house, 20–21
Masonry fireplace, parts of, 106
Mast, electrical system, 122
Mobile home, 20
Modular house, 20
Moldings and trim locations, 145
Monolithic slab foundation, 39–40
Muntins, window, 66

Narrow box cornice, 58
National Electrical Code (NEC), 115
Neighborhood, and adding on or
    remodeling, 23
Neighborhood and site inspection, 8–11
Nonmetallic sheathed cable, 118, 120
Nosing line, stairway, 46–47

Ohms, 115, 116
One-and-a-half story house, 16–18
    adding on or remodeling, 21
One-story house, 15–16
    adding on or remodeling, 21
Open and closed board roof
    sheathing, 58
Outdoor living areas, and energy
    efficiency, 166
Outdoor space, and house location, 8
Outlets, electric, 120–21

Panel doors, 70
Panelized house, 20–21
Panels, door, 69
Parallel wall kitchen, 27
Parquet floor, 142
Passive solar heating systems, 101
Patio door, 69
Pegged flooring, 142
Pier, post or column footing, 39
Pier and beam foundation, 38
Pipeless furnace, 97–98, 99
Plank-and-beam construction, 43, 45
Plank-and-beam roof framing, 52
Planting, 152–54
Plastic plumbingware, 90
Platform framing, 43, 44
Plumbing
    fixture, line and connection symbols, 84
    fixtures, 83–88
    history of, 79
    inspection checklist, 91–93
    inspection of, 90–91
    installation of, 82–83
    layout of, 81–82
    plumbing systems, 79–80
    plumbingware, 89–90
Plywood roof sheathing, 58
Poured concrete foundation wall, 39
Precut house, 21
Prefabricated chimneys, 104–5
Prefinished block wood flooring, 141–42
Prefinished strip flooring, 142
Privacy screen planting, 153–54
Private and public zones of lot, 8

Pullman kitchen, 27
Pump-forced hot-water heating system,
    99

Radon gas, 50–51, 171–72
Rails, door, 69
Rails, window, 66
Ranch plank flooring, 142
Random-width horizontal and vertical
    paneling, 134
Recessed bathtub, 84, 85
Remodeling or adding on, 21–23
    kitchen, 27–28
Resilient sheet flooring, 143–44
Resilient tile flooring, 143
Return on investment, and adding on
    or remodeling, 23
Reverse-trap toilet, 85
Ridge board, roof, 48
Rise, stairway, 45, 47
Riser, stairway, 46–47
Roll roofing, 60
Roofing felt, 58–59
Roofs
    coverings, 59–60, 176
    framing, 49–51, 52, 175
    inspection of, 60–61
    sheathing, 57–59
Room air conditioners, 109
Roughing in, plumbing, 82–83
Run, stairway, 45, 47
R-values, insulation, 127–29

Sand soils, 5, 6
Sash, window, 66
Service door, 69
Service drop, electrical system, 122
Service entrance, electrical system,
    121–22, 123
Service panel, electrical system, 122–24
Service zone of lot, 8
Shade, and energy efficiency, 160–61
Sheathing paper, 58
Shed roof, 49
Shower stall, 85
Side jambs, window, 66
Side rails, window, 66
Sill, window, 66
Silt soils, 5, 6
Single-unit heat pump, 110
Siphon-jet toilet, 85
Siphon-vortex toilet, 85
Site finishing
    driveway, walks and finish grading,
        150, 151
    inspection checklist, 154–57
    landscaping plan, 150–54
    site plan, 149–50
Skylights, 67, 68–69
Sleeping zone, 29–30
Sliding glass doors, 70, 72
Sliding windows, 66, 67
Sloped joint roof framing, 52
Smoke shelf and chamber, chimney, 106
Snack bars, 29
Soffits, 62–63

Soil composition and topography, 4–5
Soil tests, 5
Solar heating, 101
Southern exposure, advantages of, 6–7
Space heating systems, 100–101
Spanish colonial house style, 14
Special sheathed cable, 118
Split-entry house, 19–20
    adding on or remodeling, 22
Split-level house, 18–19
    adding on or remodeling, 22
Square bathtub, 84
Stainless steel plumbingware, 90
Stairways, 45–48
Steam and water circulation, two-pipe
    steam-heating system, 100
Steam-heating systems, 98, 99, 100
Stile, door, 69
Storage space, 30–31
Storm windows, 72–73
Stringer, stairway, 46–47
Stucco, 64
Subdivision planning, 1–3
Subdivision plat, 2
Swinging windows, 66–68
Switches, 119–20

Taxes and special assessments, 4
Termites, 50
Thin-wall conduit, 119
Tile or slate roofs, 60
Toilets, 85–86
Top rail, window, 66
Traditional house styles, 13–15
Transverse plank-and-beam roof
    framing, 52
Tread, stairway, 46–47
Trees, 154
Triple-track windows, 68
Trusses, roof, 48–49, 51
Two-story house, 18
    adding on, 21–22
Two-unit heat pump, 110

Uniform Plumbing Code, 80–81
Unzoned space, 30–31
Upgraded insulation guidelines, 129
Urea formaldehyde, 129
U-shaped kitchen, 27
Utilities availability, 4

Vanity lavatory, 86–87
Vapor barrier, 39, 41
V-cracks, house framing, 44
Vent piping system, 80
Vertical and horizontal paneling, 134
Vertical and horizontal siding, 62
Vertical plywood sheathing, 61
View, and house location, 7
Vinyl siding, 63
Vitreous china plumbingware, 89
Volts, 115, 116

Wainscotting, 134
Wall footing, 38

Wall framing, 43–45
Wallpaper, 135–36
Walls, 129
   gypsum wallboard, 129–31
   inspection of, 136–38
   plaster, 131–32
   wood paneling, 132–34
Wall sheathing, 61
Warm-air perimeter heating system, 100
Washdown toilet, 86
Waste-collecting system, 80
Water circulation, two-pipe gravity hot-
     water system, 99, 199
Water-cooled compressors, 109
Water heaters, 87–88
Waterproofing foundation, 39
Water-supply system, 80
Water table, 5
Watts, 116–17
Weatherproofing, 174–78
Weatherstripping and caulking, 162
Wide box cornice, 58
Width, stairway, 46–47
Windows, 65–69
   and energy efficiency, 161–62
   inspection of, 71–73
   storm, 72–73
Wire sizes, 117
Wiring diagrams, 119–21
Wiring types, 117–19
Wood flooring, 141–42
Wood-grain aluminum siding, 63
Wood rot, 50
Wood shakes and shingles, 59
Wood siding, 62
Work zone, 26–28
Year-round air conditioner, 110
Zoning, 3, 21

More Real Estate Books That Help You Get Ahead...

Mail the completed form to Real Estate Education Company 520 North Dearborn Street Chicago, Illinois 60610-4975

30-Day Money-Back Guarantee

Please send me the book(s) I have indicated. If I return any book within the 30 day period, I'll receive a refund with no further obligation.

(Books must be returned in unused, salable condition).

Payment must accompany all orders (check one)

☐ Check or money order payable to Longman

☐ Credit card charge, circle one: VISA MasterCard AMEX

Name_____

Address_____

City_____ State_____ Zip_____

Telephone No. (   )_____

Account No._____ Exp. Date_____

Signature_____

(All charge orders must be signed.)

Qty.	Order Number	Real Estate Principles/Exam Guides	Price	Total Amount
____	1. 1510-01	Modern Real Estate Practice, 11th ed	$32.95	_____
____	2. 1510-	Supplements for Modern Real Estate Practice are available for many states. Indicate desired state_____	$12.95	_____
____	3. 1510-02	Modern Real Estate Practice Study Guide, 11th ed.	$13.95	_____
____	4. 1513-01	Real Estate Fundamentals, 3rd ed.	$22.95	_____
____	5. 1970-04	Questions & Answers to Help You Pass the Real Estate Exam, 3rd ed ...	$21.95	_____
____	6. 1970-02	Guide to Passing the Real Estate Exam (ACT), 3rd ed.	$21.95	_____
____	7. 1970-01	The Real Estate Education Company Real Estate Exam Manual, 5th ed. (ETS)	$21.95	_____
____	8. 1970-06	Real Estate Exam Guide (ASI), 2nd ed.	$21.95	_____
____	9. 1970-03	How to Prepare for the Texas Real Estate Exam, 4th ed.	$19.95	_____
____	10. 1970-07	California Real Estate Exam Guide	$19.95	_____

Qty.	Order Number	Advanced Studies/Continuing Education	Price	Total Amount
____	11. 1556-10	Fundamentals of Real Estate Appraisal, 5th ed.	$38.95	_____
____	12. 1557-10	Essentials of Real Estate Finance, 5th ed.	$38.95	_____
____	13. 1559-01	Essentials of Real Estate Investment, 3rd ed.	$38.95	_____
____	14. 1551-10	Property Management, 3rd ed.	$34.95	_____
____	15. 1965-01	Real Estate Brokerage: A Success Guide, 2nd ed.	$35.95	_____
____	16. 1560-01	Real Estate Law, 2nd ed.	$38.95	_____
____	17. 1512-10	Mastering Real Estate Mathematics, 5th ed.	$25.95	_____
____	18. 1961-01	The Language of Real Estate, 3rd ed.	$28.95	_____
____	19. 1560-08	Agency Relationships in Real Estate	$25.95	_____

Qty.	Order Number	Professional Books	Price	Total Amount
____	20. 1913-01	List for Success	$18.95	_____
____	21. 1913-04	Close for Success	$18.95	_____
____	22. 1907-04	Power Real Estate Negotiation	$19.95	_____
____	23. 1927-03	Fast Start in Real Estate: A Survival Guide for New Agents	$17.95	_____
____	24. 1926-01	Classified Secrets, 2nd ed.	$29.95	_____
____	25. 1907-01	Power Real Estate Listing, 2nd ed.	$17.95	_____
____	26. 1907-02	Power Real Estate Selling, 2nd ed.	$17.95	_____
____	27. 5606-24	The Mortgage Kit	$14.95	_____
____	28. 4105-07	How to Profit from Real Estate	$19.95	_____
____	29. 4105-06	How to Sell Apartment Buildings	$19.95	_____
____	30. 4105-08	Landlord's Handbook	$21.95	_____
____	31. 1905-29	A Professional's Guide to Real Estate Finance	$34.95	_____
____	32. 1909-01	New Home Sales	$24.95	_____
____	33. 1909-03	New Home Marketing	$34.95	_____
____	34. 1922-02	Successful Leasing and Selling of Office Property, 3rd ed.	$34.95	_____
____	35. 1922-03	Successful Industrial Real Estate Brokerage, 4th ed.	$34.95	_____
____	36. 1978-02	The Recruiting Revolution in Real Estate	$34.95	_____
____	37. 1922-01	Successful Leasing and Selling of Retail Property, 3rd ed.	$34.95	_____

For Fastest Service, Call Our Toll-Free Order Hotline
1-800-621-9621 x650
(in Illinois, 1-800-654-8596 x650)

Total Book Purchase (inc. tax, if applicable)	Shipping and Handling
$ 00.00–$ 24.99	$ 4.00
$ 25.00–$ 49.99	$ 5.00
$ 50.00–$ 99.99	$ 6.00
$100.00–$249.99	$ 8.00

PRICES SUBJECT TO CHANGE WITHOUT NOTICE.

Book Total _____

Orders shipped to the following states must include applicable sales tax: AZ, CA, CO, IL, MI, MN, NY, PA, TX, VA and WI.

_____

Add postage and handling (see chart)

TOTAL _____

810077

Real Estate Education Company

520 N. Dearborn Chicago, Illinois 60610-4975

PRACTICAL MONEY-MAKERS
FROM REAL ESTATE EDUCATION COMPANY

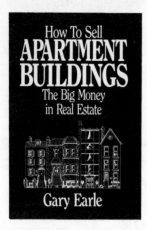

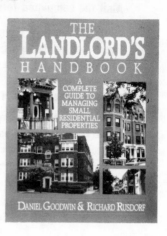

HOW TO SELL APARTMENT BUILDINGS: THE BIG MONEY IN REAL ESTATE,
by Gary Earle

This book provides you with all the details, examples, tables, and illustrations you need to identify the apartment market, understand it and profit. Read this book and you'll discover a practical, remarkably effective sales approach that can help turn your real estate license into a ticket to big commissions.

With *How To Sell Apartment Buildings,* you'll soon reap the rich rewards that go with the territory!

Contents
Sizing Up the Market • Gaining Market Knowledge • How to Price Apartment Buildings • Financing • Tax Aspects of Apartment Ownership • Cataloging Your Territory • Hot Sales Leads from Cold Calls • A Little Letter Can Go a Long Way • Meeting the Seller • Making the Offer • Negotiating the Sale • Closing the Deal • It's All Yours! • Index

6 x 9, hardcover, 200 pages
1988 copyright
Order Number 4105-06
Check box #28 on order form

POWER REAL ESTATE NEGOTIATION,
by William H. Pivar

Negotiating between buyer and seller is the hardest part of any real estate transaction. *Power Real Estate Negotiation* provides hundreds of specific, field-tested tips on negotiating transactions — and how to implement these techniques in direct interpersonal encounters. The unique interactive approach alternates between buyer's and seller's point of view, showing effective strategies and counterplays to each move of the opponent.

Includes:
• Reading the opponent's motivation
• Negotiating price and financing
• Overcoming impasses
• Closing the agreement

Contents
Negotiation Planning • Physical Aspects of Negotiation • General Negotiation Tactics • Negotiating the Price • Negotiating the Financing • Negotiating Other Issues • Impasse • Negotiating Dangers • The Agreement • Index

6 x 9, hardcover, 204 pages
1990 copyright
Order Number 1907-04
Check box #22 on order form

A PROFESSIONAL'S GUIDE TO REAL ESTATE FINANCE: TECHNIQUES FOR THE 1990's,
by Julie Garton-Good

Based on actual real estate practice, this reference provides the real estate professional with immediate answers to the most frequently asked financial questions. When clients call upon you to assist in evaluating financing options, you'll have all the answers in this new comprehensive guide.

Included are complete discussions of mortgage loan types—along with convenient checklists of the major features and pros and cons of each.

A Professional's Guide to Real Estate Finance emphasizes up-to-the-minute information, trend spotting and innovative sales strategies using financing techniques.

Contents
The Mortgage Market • Conventional Fixes-Rate Loans • Adjustable Rate Mortgages • FHA Loans • VA Loans • Special Programs • Buyer Leverage • Index

6 x 9, hardcover, 304 pages
1990 copyright
Order Number 1905-29
Check box #31 on order form

THE LANDLORD'S HANDBOOK: A COMPLETE GUIDE TO MANAGING SMALL RESIDENTIAL PROPERTIES,
by Daniel Goodwin and Richard Rusdorf, CPM

Whether you sell, manage or own small residential income properties, you'll find ideas to save time and headaches and to put money in your pocket. Two Inland Real Estate property management experts share their income-producing secrets.

Over 50 forms and checklists help you establish a smooth, profitable rental operation. Also included are tips on putting "active" self-management techniques to work to maximize tax deductions and profits.

Contents
Self-Management • Resident Relations • Marketing • Applications, Leases & Rental Agreements • Tenant Move-In • Lease Renewals • Tenant Move-Out • Rent Collection • Maintenance • Insurance • Property Taxes • Accounting • Bibliography • Appendix • Index

8-½ x 11, softcover, 236 pages
1989 copyright
Order Number 4105-08
Check box #29 on order form